Elan

# Special and Decorative Breads

\* \*

# Special and Decorative Breads

## Traditional, Regional and Special Breads
## Fancy Breads - Viennese Pastries - Croissants
## Brioches - Decorative Breads - Presentation Pieces

Alain Couet and Éric Kayser

with

Bernard, Isabelle and Valérie Ganachaud
Daniel Hervé
Léon Mégard
Yves Saunier

Under the direction of
## Jean Chazalon and Pierre Michalet

Translated by Rhona Poritzky-Lauvand and James Peterson

cicem

A copublication of
**CICEM** (Compagnie Internationale
de Consultation *Education* et *Media*)
**Paris**

and

Van Nostrand Reinhold
New York

**Paul GILLES**
*Vice President of the National
Confederation of French Bakers
(Confédération National de la Boulangerie
Française) and President of the
Commission for professional education
(Commission Formation Professionnelle).*

*In publishing this second volume of "Special and Decorative Breads", Jean CHAZALON and Pierre MICHALET have invited Eric KAYSER, Alain COUET, Bernard GANACHAUD and his daughters Valérie and Isabelle, in association with Daniel HERVÉ, Louis MEGARD and Yves SAUNIER to share their passion and love for the baking profession.*

*By working as a team, these experienced professionals share their know-how in an ever-expanding field.*

*Volume 2 of "Special and Decorative Breads" will prove to be indispensable for both the beginner and experienced professional who wish to learn new techniques or expand the range of products that they offer to their customers. This new addition to the professional baker's library includes:*

- *an expanded chapter on traditional and regional breads,*
- *an extensive chapter on Viennese and Danish pastries which includes techniques for both traditional and innovative pastries,*
- *a chapter on decorating techniques and methods as well as a long series of photos and descriptions of presentation photos including works by masters in the field. The techniques are presented in a range of difficulties to allow a professional of any level to develop an artistic sense and to offer new and varied products to his or her clientele.*

*Volume 2 contains over 1500 color photos to help the reader visualize and master the methods and techniques.*

*This second volume of "Special and Decorative Breads" is a valuable contribution to professional baking literature and will become a companion to any baker or pastry chef who wishes to continually expand his or her knowledge of the profession.*

*My congratulations to the authors and to those who have contributed to this superb volume.*

**Compagnon du Devoir Gimenez
Landais le Résolu**
*Chargé d'Études Boulangers
Compagnon du Devoir
du Tour de France*

*As an educator and as director of a commission committed to the education of baking professionals (Formation Nationale des Compagnon Boulangers du Devoir), I must express my pleasure at the appearance of the second volume of "Special and Decorative Breads". I am especially delighted by the dedication of two friends, Alain COUET and Eric KAYSER who's hard work and experience have made this volume possible.*

*These two professionals are by no means ordinary bakers as they have committed themselves to two main purposes:*
- *to help curious and enterprising bakery owners and other professionals to continually expand and learn new aspects of the baking profession,*
- *to assist beginning professionals in acquiring knowledge and know-how to become leaders in their field.*

*Professional bakers usually work out of the public eye so their careful research often goes unnoticed. The recipes and techniques which appear in volume 2 of "Special and Decorative Breads" represent the fruit of many years of tradition and patiently acquired knowledge.*

*I have no doubt that young bakers on their way to becoming serious professionals will find this volume an invaluable contribution and long-term source of information in the years to come.*

# Contents

# Introduction to the Six Chapters

## Chapter 1 - Traditional and Regional Breads

Presented in this chapter are fifteen breads from the regions of France.

These breads are extremely varied both in the type of dough used as well as the final shaping of the loaves.

## Chapter 2 - Special and International Breads

This chapter includes six breads which contain special ingredients. Also included are six breads from around Europe.

This chapter completes the special breads presented in volume 1 of "Special and Decorative Breads".

## Chapter 3 - Elaborately Shaped Breads

Twenty regional bread varieties are presented, some of which use a specially prepared dough.

Included also in this chapter are edible animals made from bread dough.

# in Special and Decorative Breads (Vol. 2)

## Chapter 4 - Viennese Yeast-Raised Pastries

*Viennese pastries are becoming more and more a critical part of a small bakery's business. This chapter includes six varieties of croissants, twenty types of brioches and a variety of Danish pastries.*

## Chapter 5 - Decorating Methods and Techniques

*This chapter illustrates and describes a wide variety of decorating techniques. Included are different types of decorating dough and how they are used, modeling of miniature animals, woven plates and platters, and an assortment of flowers and other miniature objects used for decoration.*

## Chapter 6 - Decorated Breads and Presentation Pieces

*In this area of baking, the possibilities for innovation are virtually limitless. In this chapter, experienced professionals present a selection of presentation pieces ranging from simple to sophisticated.*

# Chapter 1
# Traditional and Regional Breads

*Successful bakers continually offer an ever changing selection of breads to their clientele.*

*A selection of breads of different colors and shapes is particularly tempting.*

*This chapter illustrates and describes a selection of traditional and regional French breads which will permit almost any professional baker to diversify his or her production and provide a tempting variety of high quality breads.*

# Chapter Organization

*This chapter begins with traditional bread which is prepared using a special short kneading that gives it a flavorful, cream-colored crumb. This traditional bread is then baked in baguettes or short, thick loaves. Circle bread which combines white flour, wholewheat flour, and rye flour is also presented. Circle bread has a compact crumb and a completely different flavor than traditional bread.*

These breads are grouped into 3 categories:

*A - Breads made from white flour alone:*

• Traditional bread (short kneading, long first rising),
• Homemade-style bread (using a yeast starter or fermented dough from a previous batch),
• Rustic-style bread (prepared without rounding and shaping, with a first rising and fermented dough),
• Traditional white bread (prepared without shaping with a long first rising),
• Beaucaire bread (prepared by folding, a yeast starter, and a long first rising),
• Buttermilk bread (containing active buttermilk culture).

Each of these different styles of bread is made using a variety of techniques so that each has an individual appearance and taste.

*B - Breads made from white flour combined with rye flour*

• Peasant bread (first rising, fermented dough from a previous batch),
• Bordeaux-style bread (without shaping, first rising using fermented dough),
• Mottled bread (limited kneading, long first rising).

*C - Breads made from combinations of white flour, wholewheat flour, and rye flour*

• Old fashioned bread (first rising, fermented dough from a previous batch),
• Circle bread (first rising, fermented dough from a previous batch).

Each of these breads contains rye flour. Some also contain whole wheat flour and bise flour (light-style whole wheat flour).

All of these breads are prepared with a long first rising and with fermented dough from a previous batch.

These breads have a variety of shades ranging from pale to dark brown. Their shelf life varies depending on their size, shape, and the methods used in their fabrication.

**Traditional bread**

**Old fashioned bread**

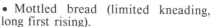

**Homemade-style bread**

**Traditional white bread**

**Bordeaux-style bread**

**Beaucaire bread**

## Criteria for judging bread quality

The quality and style of French breads depends on the traditions of the region where it is prepared. Its shape, size, the fermenting method used, the ingredients used, and the baking method all contribute to the individual style of a particular loaf.

Several criteria are used for judging and describing a bread's quality:

*The rising ratio (development)* describes the ratio between the volume and weight of the bread (density) after rising. The rising ratio varies depending on the kneading method.

*The crust* should be smooth, shiny, and golden brown. It should have a crunchy texture with no irregularities or lumps. The scoring on the crust should open and be well defined.

*The crumb* should be soft and elastic with an airy, honeycombed texture. When the dough has been kneaded at slow speed, the crumb should consist of tiny cream-colored bubbles. The texture of the crumb will be finer and a purer white when the dough is kneaded at a faster speed.

Any bread which has been properly prepared and has undergone the necessary first rising, should remain fresh for at least 12 hours after baking.

*The odor* of the freshly baked bread should be complex and appetizing with a slightly sweet edge.

The bread should also have an appealing, chewy texture.

## Classic and traditional breads

### With wheat flour only

1. Traditional bread
2. Homemade-style bread
3. Rustic-style bread
4. Traditional white bread
5. Beaucaire bread
6. Buttermilk bread

### With a mix of different flours

7. Old fashioned bread
8. Peasant bread
9. Circle bread
10. Bordeaux-Style bread
11. Mottled bread
12. Chestnut breads

## Bread's aroma

The aroma of bread develops primarily during the first rising of the dough. It is for this reason that many recipes suggest a prolonged first rising.

During the various stages of bread making, more than 200 volatile compounds (over a hundred of which have been identified) can be found in the dough. Each of these compounds, even though they are only found in trace quantities, contributes its own odor to the final collection of smells which gives a particular bread its individuality and distinction. The bulk of these compounds are produced by the action of yeast cells on natural sugars.

Many of the aromatic compounds produced during the dough's fermentation are caramelized or otherwise altered during baking. These caramelized, aromatic compounds are found primarily in the crust of the finished loaves where they contribute flavor and aroma.

## Bread and nutrition

Nutritionists are now in agreement that bread deserves a more important role in today's diet. The nutritional value of well-made bread is no longer contested. Not only is it a valuable source of carbohydrates, but it also contains important vitamins and minerals.

Experts on nutrition now recommend that from 300 to 350 g. (10.5 to 12.5 oz.) of bread, which provides from 650 to 750 calories, be consumed per day by the average man. For women, 200 to 250 g. (7 to 9 oz.), which provides from 430 to 530 calories, is considered appropriate.

Bread is considered an excellent food and an excellent source of complex carbohydrates. Complex carbohydrates are metabolized slowly whereas the simple carbohydrates provided by sugar are metabolized much more quickly.

Rustic-style bread

Peasant bread

Circle bread

Buttermilk bread

Mottled bread

Chestnut bread

# Traditional Bread (Pain Traditionnel)

**Introduction**

Traditional bread is prepared by using old fashioned techniques where bread was kneaded for a much shorter period than it is today. To compensate for the reduced kneading time used to make traditional-style breads, the dough is allowed to ferment for a much longer period than for modern types of breads. For this reason, traditional breads are sometimes referred to as " long kneaded breads ".

When preparing traditional bread:
Never use flour containing additives.
Reduce the kneading time.

Increase the length of time for the first fermentation to compensate for the diminished kneading time.

It is during the first rising that the flavor of the bread develops. The texture of the dough also changes as it ferments; it loses elasticity and develops holding power. When the kneading time is reduced, the length of the first fermentation needs to be increased proportionately so that the bread develops a full flavor and an appropriate texture.

Sometimes, fermented dough from a previous batch is combined with the new dough. This method makes it possible to shorten the time needed for the first rising.

These methods result in excellent tasting loaves with an irregular, honey combed crumb and an excellent shelf life.

**Storage**

The shelf life of traditional breads is far better than regular white bread because of the organic acids formed during the long fermentation.

**Shapes used for traditional bread**

Traditional breads can be baked in a wide variety of shapes such as baguettes, round loaves, rolls, country loaves etc.

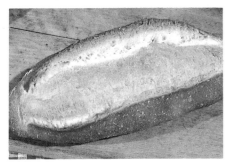

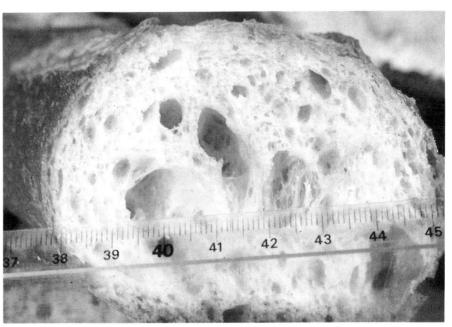

## Appearance

Traditional breads should have a deep golden crust. In general, the deeper the color of a bread's crust, the better the flavor. Obviously there is a limit beyond which the bread will burn. Most breads with pale crusts have little flavor, especially when compared with a well baked traditional loaf.

## Serving traditional bread

Traditional bread can be served at any occasion to accompany virtually any dish.

## Procedure

The work area should be between 22 and 25 °C (72 and 77 °F).

When using a kneading machine, use a base temperature of 68 °C/219 °F. Remember that the base temperature is used to calculate the temperature of the water for kneading (see Volume 1).

## Quantities

To prepare 16.86 kg. (37.15 lb.) of bread dough which will produce 67 × 250 g. (9 oz.) baguettes or 33 full sized loaves weighing 540 g. (19 oz.), the following ingredients are needed:

- 10 kg. bread flour (22 lb.)
- 6.5 l. water (6.9 qt.)
- 195 g. salt (6.9 oz.)
- 165 g. yeast (5.8 oz.)

*Note:* Depending on the fermentation time and the quality of the flour, dough from a previous batch of bread can be added in the proportion of 200 g. of dough to 1 liter of water (7 oz. dough to 34 fl. oz. water).

## Kneading

Put the flour and water into the bowl of the kneading machine and work them together for 5 minutes (frasing). Let this mixture rest for 25 minutes. Add the yeast, the salt, and the dough from a previous batch if it is being used and knead the dough for 8 minutes on slow speed.

## Checking the kneaded dough

The temperature of the finished dough should be approximately 24 °C (75 °F). The dough should be smooth and soft to the touch.

## First rising

The dough should be allowed to rise for 1/2 to 2 hours depending on how much it has expanded and on its consistency.

Press down on the dough after 30 minutes and once again after 90 minutes.

## Scaling

Divide the dough either by hand or with an automatic dough divider. Shape it into loaves. Let the loaves rest for 20 minutes.

## Shaping the loaves

Although dough can be shaped into loaves using machines designed for this purpose, hand shaping tends to drive less carbon dioxide out of the dough and usually results in a better structured crumb. Despite the advantages of hand shaping, it is rarely practical for large quantities of dough.

## Proofing

Proofing usually requires from 1 hour to 1 hour and 15 minutes depending on the temperature of the rising area or proof box. Be careful not to let the dough proof for too long.

## Preparing the oven

Preheat the oven to 230 to 250 °C (450 to 475 °F) depending on the size of the loaves. Score the surface of the loaves in the normal way.

## Baking

Inject steam into the oven before putting the loaves in the oven. Once the loaves are in the oven, additional steam can be injected at the beginning of the baking.

As soon as the loaves come out of the oven, arrange them in a basket. Avoid heaping them up on one another while they are cooling.

# TRADITIONAL BREAD

| | | | |
|---|---|---|---|
| **PREPARATION** | 10 min | 10 min | • calculate the temperatures<br>• prepare and weigh the ingredients |
| **KNEADING** | 38 min | 48 min | • combine ingredients for 5 minutes (frasing)<br>• allow mixture to rest for 25 minutes<br>• knead for 8 minutes |
| **FIRST RISING** | 2 hr | 2 hr 48 | • fold the dough after 30 minutes<br>• fold a second time after 90 minutes |
| **SCALING** | 10 min | 2 hr 58 | • weigh out the loaves |
| **RESTING** | 20 min | 3 hr 18 | |
| **SHAPING** | 15 min | 3 hr 33 | • shape the loaves into the desired shape |
| **PROOFING** | 1 hr | 4 hr 33 | • the dough is very fragile. Do not allow the dough to rise too much |
| **PREPARING FOR BAKING** | 10 min | 4 hr 43 | • inject steam into the oven before baking<br>• steam may also be injected into the oven |
| **COOLING** | 25 to 40 min | 5 hr 20 | • carefully watch over the baking keeping in mind the size of the loaves |
| **AFTER BAKING** | 10 min | 5 hr 30 | • place in a basket as soon as out of the oven |

**STORAGE :** *these loaves have an excellent shelf life as do all traditionally made breads*

# Old-fashioned Bread (Pain à l'Ancienne)

## Introduction

Old fashioned bread is similar to traditional bread. The only difference is that it contains some additional ingredients including:

10% rye flour which increases the shelf life of the bread and gives it a more complex flavor,

10% whole wheat flour which increases the fiber content of the bread and also contributes to its flavor.

Old fashioned bread has a pleasing, rustic appearance. It is usually prepared using dough taken from a previous batch of bread which enhances its flavor and increases its shelf life.

Kneading of old fashioned bread should be kept to a minimum. Excessive kneading of the dough may result in a pale color and flavorless dough.

## Storage

Old fashioned bread keeps very well. Several factors contribute to its extremely long shelf life. Among these are the addition of rye flour and a prolonged fermentation which aids in the development of organic acids.

## Shapes used for old fashioned bread

Old fashioned bread can be baked in a wide variety of shapes such as baguettes, round loaves, rolls, country loaves etc. The size of the loaves can vary from 250 g. (9 oz.) to 1 kg. (35 oz.).

## Appearance

Old fashioned bread usually has a thick, brown crust. This is desirable because it contributes to the character of

an old fashioned loaf. The formation of this crust is encouraged by using a small amount of steam during baking and by baking at a relatively low temperature.

Old fashioned bread loaves should be only lightly floured before baking. If the loaves are coated with too thick a layer of flour, the flour can prevent the coloration of the crust which will in turn adversely affect the flavor of the bread.

### Serving old fashioned bread

Old fashioned bread is excellent when served with pâtés and other pork products as well as fish and raw seafood. Many people find it a welcome alternative to rye bread which is often served with these foods.

### Procedure

The work area should be between 22 and 25 °C (72 and 77 °F).

When using a kneading machine, use a base temperature of 62 °F/208 °F. The base temperature is used to calculate the temperature of the water when it is added to the dough. Add the temperature of the work area to the temperature of the flour and subtract this figure from the base temperature given above. The result gives the temperature which should be used for the water.

### Quantities

To prepare 16.8 kg (37.1 lb.) of old fashioned bread dough which will produce 67 × 250 g. (9 oz.) baguettes, 33 full sized loaves weighing 500 g. (17.5 oz.), or 17 × 1 kg. (35 oz.) loaves, the following ingredients are needed:

8.5 kg. bread flour (18.7 lb.)
850 g. rye flour (30 oz.)
850 g. whole wheat flour (30 oz.)
6.3 l. water (6.6 qt.) - 195 g. salt (6.9 oz.)
165 g. yeast (5.8 oz.)
2 kg (70 oz.) fermented dough

### Kneading

Put the rye flour, the whole wheat flour, the white flour, and the water into the bowl of the kneading machine and work them together for 5 minutes (frasing). Let this mixture rest for 25 minutes. This resting period makes it possible to somewhat reduce the kneading time.

Add the yeast, the salt, and the dough from a previous batch if it is being used. Knead the dough for 8 minutes at medium speed.

### Checking the kneaded dough

The temperature of the finished dough should be approximately 24 °C (75 °F). The dough should be smooth and soft to the touch.

### First rising

The dough should be allowed to rise for approximately 45 minutes depending on its consistency, and the temperature and humidity of the rising area or proof box.

### Scaling

Divide the dough into sections either by hand or with an automatic dough divider depending on the number of loaves being baked.

Shape the sections into balls for thick loaves. Fold the sections over themselves for baguettes.

Let the sections of dough rest for 20 minutes after this preliminary shaping.

### Shaping the loaves

It is always preferable to shape loaves by hand, but in large bakeries this is often impractical.

If a fine crust is wanted, the loaves can be baked directly on the oven floor with the fold on the bottom. Baking in canvas bread holders or on a well-floured flat surface with the fold on top will result in loaves with thicker crusts.

### Proofing

Proofing usually requires from 1 hour to 1 hour and 15 minutes depending on the consistency of the dough and the temperature of the rising area or proof box. Be careful not to let the dough proof for too long.

### Preparation for baking

Preheat the oven to 225 °C (450 °F) for large loaves and to 240 °C (475 °F) for baguettes.

Use a drum sieve to sprinkle the surface of the loaves with flour just before they go into the oven.

Score the loaves with a crisscross, polka cut.

### Baking

Inject steam into the oven before baking. Do not inject additional steam once the loaves are in the oven.

Keep close watch on the color of the loaves during baking. The crust colors quickly because of the rye flour.

Count on approximately 30 minutes baking time for a 500 g. (17.5 oz.) loaf and 20 minutes for a baguette weighing 250 g. (9 oz.).

As soon as the loaves come out of the oven, arrange them in a basket. Avoid heaping them up on one another while they are cooling.

## OLD FASHIONED BREAD

| | | | |
|---|---|---|---|
| PREPARATION | 10 min | 10 min | • calculate the temperatures<br>• prepare and weigh the ingredients |
| KNEADING | 38 min | 48 min | • combine ingredients for 5 minutes (frasing)<br>• allow mixture to rest for 25 minutes<br>• knead for 8 minutes |
| FIRST RISING | 45 min | 1 hr 33 | • the time needed depends on the consistency |
| SCALING | 15 min | 1 hr 48 | • weigh out the loaves |
| RESTING | 20 min | 2 hr 8 | • the dough can be folded over itself 20 minutes to give the bread more structure |
| SHAPING | 15 min | 2 hr 23 | • shape the loaves into the desired shape |
| PROOFING | 1 hr 15 | 3 hr 38 | • Do not allow the dough to rise too much |
| BEFORE BAKING | 10 min | 3 hr 48 | • inject steam into the oven before baking |
| BAKING | 20 to 45 min | 4 hr 30 | • carefully watch over the baking keeping in mind the size of the loaves<br>• be aware that these loaves brown quickly |
| COOLING | 5 min | 4 hr 35 | • place in a basket as soon as out of the oven |

**STORAGE** : *these loaves have an excellent shelf life*

# Homemade-style Bread (Le Pain de Ménage)

## Introduction

This homemade style bread was known in the fourteenth century as " pain coquille " but the current French name, "pain de ménage " came into usage around the middle of the seventeenth century.

The bread originated in the middle east where centuries ago street vendors used to compete with bakeries by crying " pain de ménage " or in English, " homemade bread ".

By the nineteenth century, the bread was popular in France and can be seen on postcards printed during the first world war. It has an appealing crumb with a coarsely honeycombed crumb and a shiny, golden crust. In fact bakers often sprinkle water on the loaves at the end of baking to give added sheen.

In France, homemade style bread was originally made with a spontaneously leavened sourdough starter. New batches of dough were then inoculated with dough taken from a previous batch and a small amount of yeast (5 to 7 g. per liter of water 1 to 1 1/2 teaspoons per 35 fl. oz.).

Today, homemade style bread can be made using a spontaneously leavened sourdough starter or dough taken from a previous batch. The most important factor, however, is to make sure that the dough rises adequately during the first fermentation.

## Storage

Because homemade style bread is made with a sourdough starter or from dough taken from a previous batch, it keeps well for several days. The slow fermentation used for homemade style bread and the size of the loaves also contribute to its long shelf life.

## Shapes used for homemade style bread

Homemade style bread is almost always baked in large round or thick elongated loaves weighing from 700 g. (24.5 oz.) to 2 kg. (70 oz.).

## Appearance

Homemade style bread should have an appetizing, thick, brown crust. It should have a crumb with irregular holes and a creamy color due to the short kneading time used.

## Serving homemade style bread

Because of its full, tangy flavor, homemade style bread can be served with pork products such as pâtés and sausages as well as cold meats and desserts.

## Procedure

The work area should be between 22 and 25 ºC (72 and 77 ºF).

When using a kneading machine, use a base temperature of 68 ºC/219 ºF. The dough should then be kneaded in two stages: 4 minutes at slow speed and 10 minutes at medium speed (see below).

## Ingredients

To prepare 10.81 kg. (23.83 lb.) of dough which can be used to prepare 12 sections of 900 g. (31.5 oz.) each, use the following ingredients:

### *Using dough from a previous batch*
5 kg. flour (11 lb.) - 100 g. salt (3.5 oz.)
60 g. yeast (2.1 oz.) - 3 l. water (3.2 qt.)
2.5 kg. dough from a previous batch (5.5 lb.)

### *Using a sourdough starter*
5 kg. flour (11 lb.)
100 g. salt (3.5 oz.)
35 g. yeast (1.2 oz.)
3 l. water (3.2 qts.)
2.1 kg. sourdough starter (73.5 oz.)

## Kneading

Put the flour, the salt, and the yeast which has been first diluted with the

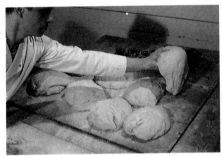

water, in the bowl of the kneading machine. Work the mixture together for approximately 4 minutes at slow speed until the dough has a medium-firm consistency. Continue the kneading for 10 minutes at medium speed. After the first 5 minutes of kneading at medium speed, add the dough from a previous batch or the sourdough starter.

### Checking the kneaded dough

The temperature of the finished dough should be approximately 24 °C (75 °F).

The dough should be quite firm. Be sure and cover the dough after kneading to prevent the formation of a skin.

### First rising

The dough should be allowed to rise for 1 hour if dough from a previous batch is used and for 2 hours if a sourdough starter is used.

Fermentation times will of course vary depending on the temperature and humidity of the work area as well as the temperature of the dough after kneading.

### Scaling

Weigh the dough by hand being care-

ful to avoid using too much flour.
Shape each section into balls and let rest for 25 minutes.

### Shaping the loaves

Shape the loaves by hand. Once the loaves have been shaped, they should be placed on either long or round canvas bread holders or directly on a floured baking surface. The loaves should be baked with the seal on the bottom for a normal crust and with the seal on top for a thick crust.

### Proofing

The loaves should be proofed for 1 1/2 to 2 hours when using dough from a previous batch and for 3 1/2 hours when using a sourdough starter. The rising area or proof box should be from 26 to 27 °C (79 to 80 °F). Be careful to avoid excess proofing.

### Preparation for baking

Preheat the oven to approximately 225 °C (450 °F). The temperature can be raised or lowered slightly depending on the size of the loaves. The temperature should be lowered as soon as the loaves begin to brown.

Score the loaves using a crisscross pattern for round loaves and a diagonal pattern for long loaves.

### Baking

Inject steam into the oven before baking the loaves.

Loaves weighing 900 g. (31.5 oz.) should be baked from 40 to 45 minutes. Watch the loaves carefully and adjust the temperature as necessary.

As soon as the loaves come out of the oven, place them in baskets or on cooling racks.

## HOMEMADE-STYLE BREAD (using dough from a previous batch)

| PREPARATION | 15 min | 15 min | • calculate the temperatures<br>• prepare and weigh the ingredients |
|---|---|---|---|
| KNEADING | 14 min | 29 min | • 4 minutes (frasing) on slow speed<br>• knead for 10 minutes more at medium speed<br>• add dough after 5 minutes of kneading |
| FIRST RISING (*) | 1 hr 30 | 1 hr 59 | • punch down the dough midway<br>• let rise for 45 minutes when using dough<br>• 1 hr 15 minutes with sourdough starter |
| SCALING | 5 min | 2 hr 4 | • shape round sections for weighing |
| RESTING | 25 min | 2 hr 29 | |
| SHAPING | 6 min | 2 hr 35 | • shape the loaves into the desired shape |
| PROOFING | 2 hr 30 | 5 hr 5 | • the proof box should be at 26 °C (79 °F)<br>• do not let the leaves rise excessively |
| PREPARING FOR BAKING | 5 min | 5 hr 10 | • inject steam into the oven before baking<br>• carefully regulate the oven temperature |
| BAKING | 45 min | 5 hr 55 | • carefully watch over the baking keeping in mind the size of the loaves |
| COOLING | 5 min | 6 hr | • place the loaves in a basket |

STORAGE : these loaves have an excellent shelf life
* If sourdough starter is being used, an extra hour should be added to the rising time.

19

# Rustic-style Bread (Pain Rustique)

## Introduction

The preparation of rustic-style bread is straightforward and simple in appearance but requires experience and care so that the character of the bread is not compromised.

Rustic-style bread differs from most breads in that the sections of dough are not shaped into loaves once they are weighed. They are simply left as they are – in rectangular sections. The fact that the dough is not shaped into loaves is beneficial to the bread and improves the texture and color of the crumb as well as the bread's flavor. Because rustic-style bread is not shaped, a step is eliminated and time is saved.

Several traditional and country-style bread making techniques have been put together to develop a recipe for a rustic style bread that can be prepared in a modern bakery with modern equipment and ingredients.

Monsieur Calvel, who developed the recipe given below has incorporated the

techniques for making the traditional flat bread from Lodève as well as bread from Beaucaire, and old-fashioned round rye bread.

### Storage

Rustic-style bread has an excellent shelf life especially when prepared using dough from a previous batch. Allowing the dough to rise in a single, large batch as well as baking it in relatively large loaves both contribute to its long shelf life.

### Shapes used for rustic-style bread

In larger bakeries, rustic-style bread dough is divided into sections by machine. Usually the rectangular sections are then stretched slightly into elongated loaves.

### Appearance

Rustic-style bread should have a medium brown crust and should be lightly coated with flour. When correctly prepared, rustic-style bread should rise well, and should have a crumb with large holes and a creamy color.

### Serving rustic-style bread

Rustic-style bread is extremely versatile and can be served with practically any foods.

### Procedure

The work area should be between 22 and 25 °C (72 and 77 °F).

When using an electric mixer with a paddle blade, calculate the water temperature using a base temperature of 208 °F/62 °C.

When using a kneading machine, use a base temperature of 204 °F/60 °C.

When preparing rustic-style bread it is recommended to allow the dough to rest after an initial blending of the ingredients (frasing) and to continue the kneading approximately 20 minutes later. This resting allows the baker to reduce the kneading time by 20% and improves the bread's flavor by keeping the flour pigments intact.

### Ingredients

To prepare 10 kg. (22 lb.) of dough which will produce 20 500 g. (17 oz.) loaves or 40 250 g. (9 oz.) loaves, the following ingredients are needed:
5 kg. bread flour (11 lb.)
3.3 l. water (56 fl. oz.)
100 g. salt (3.5 oz.)
80 g. yeast (3 oz.)
1.52 kg. dough from a previous batch – 4 to 24 hours fermentation (53.5 oz.)

### Kneading

Combine the flour and water in an electric mixer or kneading machine. Work at slow speed for 4 minutes (frasing).

Stop the mixer or kneading machine and allow the dough to rest for 20 minutes. Knead the dough at medium speed for 8 minutes if using a kneading machine or for 5 minutes if using the electric mixer. Add the yeast, the salt, and

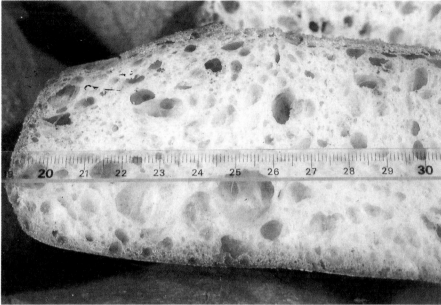

the dough from a previous batch halfway during kneading.

### Checking the kneaded dough

The temperature of the finished dough should be approximately 24 °C (75 °F). The dough should be smooth and soft to the touch.

Be sure and cover the dough after kneading to prevent the formation of a skin.

### Proofing

Allow the dough to rise for 50 minutes in a single mass. Punch it down and transfer it to appropriately sized tubs and allow it to rise 20 minutes more. It is then ready for sectioning.

### Shaping the loaves

The dough can be divided into sections either by machine or with a pastry cutter.

Pull on the sections slightly to give them a rectangular shape.

### Proofing

Proofing usually requires from 1 hour to 1 hour and 15 minutes depending on the temperature of the rising area or proof box.

Cover the loaves to prevent a skin from forming.

Be careful to not let the dough proof for too long.

### Preparation for baking

Preheat the oven to from 240 to 250 °C (475 to 500 °F) depending on the size of the loaves. Score the loaves using diagonal or crisscross patterns.

### Baking

Inject steam into the oven before putting in the loaves.

Usually the loaves require 30 to 35 minutes of baking for 500 g. (17 oz.) loaves and 20 minutes for 250 g. (9 oz. loaves). As soon as the loaves come out of the oven, arrange them in a basket. Avoid heaping them on one another while they are cooling.

## RUSTIC-STYLE BREAD

| | | | |
|---|---|---|---|
| **PREPARATION** | **15** min | **15** min | • calculate the temperatures<br>• prepare and weigh the ingredients |
| **KNEADING AND FIRST RESTING** | **30** min | **45** min | • combine ingredients (frasing)<br>• allow dough to rest<br>• continue kneading at medium speed |
| **FIRST RISING** | **1** hr **20** | **2** hr **5** | • punch down the dough after 50 minutes<br>• let rest in appropriate size tubs |
| **SHAPING** (dividing) | **5** min | **2** hr **10** | |
| **PROOFING** | **1** hr | **3** hr **10** | • avoid drafts in the rising area<br>• do not let the leaves rise excessively |
| **PREPARING FOR BAKING** | **5** min | **3** hr **15** | • inject steam into the oven before baking<br>• carefully regulate the oven temperature |
| **BAKING** | **20** to **35** min | **3** hr **45** | • carefully watch over the baking keeping in mind the size of the loaves |
| **COOLING** | **5** min | **3** hr **50** | • place the loaves in a basket as soon as they come out of the oven to avoid condensation |

**STORAGE :** *these loaves have a very good shelf life*

# Peasant Bread (Pain Paysan)

## Introduction

Peasant bread is similar to both country bread and rye/wheat bread (pain méteil). Traditionally it is shaped into thick loaves which are then scored in a leaf-like pattern. It should have a light coating of flour.

Peasant bread is straightforward to prepare and requires no special techniques. Most bakers prefer to use a sponge starter (poolish) or dough taken from a previous batch to encourage the development of acetic acid so important to the bread's flavor and shelf life. Years ago, bakers often prepared this bread using half milk and half water instead of water alone.

## Storage

Peasant bread has an excellent shelf life due to the use of sponge starter, sourdough starter, or dough taken from a previous batch.

## Shapes used for peasant bread

Traditionally, peasant bread was baked in large round loaves but today's bakers usually prepare it in thick, elongated loaves to satisfy the demands of customers for a more convenient shape. Some bakers, however, are returning to baking the loaves in the traditional round shapes and then slicing the loaves on electric bread slicers for the convenience of customers.

## Appearance

Peasant bread has a relatively thick crust due to a long slow baking and from the habit of some bakers of decreasing the oven temperature at various stages during baking. The crust can be made more crumbly and easier to chew by adding butter or other fats as well as milk to the bread dough.

## Serving peasant bread

Peasant bread can be served with sauced dishes, cold meats, pork products, cheeses, etc.

## Ingredients

To prepare 7 kg. (15.4 lb.) of bread dough which will produce 14 loaves weighing 500 g. (17 oz.) each, the following ingredients are needed:

2.1 kg. dough from a previous batch which has fermented for 4 hours minimum (74 oz.)

1.5 kg. white flour (53 oz.)

1.5 kg. light pumpernickel rye flour (53 oz.)

60 g. salt (2.1 oz.)

40 g. yeast (1.4 oz.)

1.8 l. water (61 fl. oz.)

## Procedure

The work area should be between 22 and 25 °C (72 and 77 °F).

When using an electric mixer with a paddle blade, calculate the water temperature using a base temperature of 60 °C/204 °F.

When using a kneading machine, use a base temperature of 62 °C/208 °F.

## Kneading

Combine the rye flour, the wheat flour, the salt, and the yeast combined with the water in either the bowl of the mixer or the kneading machine.

Add the dough from a previous batch three minutes before the end of kneading to avoid damaging its gluten structure by kneading it a second time.

Kneading times:
- using an electric mixer: 4 minutes at slow speed for the initial mixing of the ingredients (frasing) and 5 minutes more at medium speed;
- using a kneading machine: 4 minutes at slow speed for the initial mixing followed by 8 minutes at medium speed.

## Checking the kneaded dough

The temperature of the finished dough should be approximately 24 °C (75 °F).

Be sure and cover the dough during the first rising to prevent the formation of a skin.

## First rising

Depending on the consistency and temperature of the kneaded dough, the first rising should be relatively prolonged. For long thick loaves, count on approximately 50 minutes.

## Scaling

Dough for peasant bread can be divided either by hand or by machine.

Round the dough into sections being careful not to use too much flour. Let them rest for about 10 minutes.

## Shaping the loaves

It is best to shape the dough by hand both for round and long loaves. Hand shaping encourages the development of a natural, honeycombed crumb.

After the loaves are shaped, arrange them with the seal on the bottom. Sprinkle the loaves lightly with flour using a sieve and score the tops. The loaves can be decorated like leaves by scoring on each side or using a sausage cut going from side to side over the loaves. Scoring the loaves before proofing will cause the design to expand and stand out more dramatically after baking.

## Proofing

Proof the loaves for approximately 1 hour and 30 minutes.

## Preparation for baking

Preheat the oven to 240 °C (475 °F). Turn the oven down to 220 °C (450 °C) during baking to eliminate excess moisture from the interior of the loaves.

## Baking

Steam should be injected into the oven before baking. Be sure and eliminate the steam from the oven near the end of baking to help the loaves dry out slightly.

For 500 g. (17 oz.) loaves, count on approximately 30 minutes for baking.

| PEASANT BREAD | | | |
|---|---|---|---|
| PREPARATION | 15 min | 15 min | • calculate the temperatures<br>• prepare and weigh the ingredients |
| KNEADING | 9 min | 24 min | • combine ingredients on slow speed for 4 min<br>• knead for 5 minutes on medium speed |
| FIRST RISING | 50 min | 1 hr 14 | • cover to prevent a skin from forming |
| SCALING | 5 min | 1 hr 19 | • gently round off sections; avoid excess flour |
| RESTING | 10 min | 1 hr 29 | |
| SHAPING | 8 min | 1 hr 37 | • make thick, long loaves or round loaves<br>• score before proofing |
| PROOFING | 1 hr 30 | 3 hr 07 | • avoid drafts in the rising area<br>• do not let the loaves rise excessively |
| PREPARING FOR BAKING | 5 min | 3 hr 12 | • inject steam into the oven before baking |
| BAKING | 30 min | 3 hr 42 | • decrease oven temperature during baking |
| COOLING | 5 min | 3 hr 47 | • place the loaves in a basket as soon as they come out of the oven to avoid condensation |

STORAGE : these loaves have a very good shelf life

# Circle Bread (Pain à Rainures)

### Introduction

This bread is named after the characteristic grooved appearance made on its surface with a circular cooling rack.

Circle bread originated in Germany and is based on an excellent mixture of different flours including whole wheat, light pumpernickel rye flour, and bise flour (a light type of whole wheat flour used in France – in America, a mixture of 12.5 parts whole wheat flour combined with 87.5 parts bread flour is sometimes substituted.) The whole wheat flour used in the dough supplies vitamins, minerals, fatty acids and proteins.

The bise flour gives the bread a slightly sweet flavor with a light taste of hazelnuts. Rye flour contributes acidity to the bread dough which gives the bread an agreeable tang and improves its shelf life.

Vegetable oil is also added to the bread dough which softens the texture of the crust and crumb.

Circle bread is easy to recognize because it is round and relatively flat with notches in the sides giving the impression that the loaves are made up of sections.

### Storage

Because of circle bread's excellent shelf life, it can be sold 2 to 3 days after it is baked and can be eaten up to 4 days after baking. Its excellent shelf life is due to the different flours used in making the dough as well as the addition of fermented dough from a previous batch. Circle bread is best eaten the day after it is baked.

### Shapes used for circle bread

Circle bread is shaped into round loaves which are flattened after an initial resting period.

The rounds of dough should be notched around the sides with a pastry cutter to give the finished bread a sectioned appearance. Place a round cooling rack over the loaves and sprinkle them with white flour.

### Appearance

Circle bread should be lightly floured and have a medium thick crust with circular grooves which give it an appetizing appearance.

### Serving circle bread

Because of its richness, circle bread can be served with sauced meats as well as pork products and raw shellfish platters.

### Procedure

The work area should be between 22 and 25 °C (72 and 77 °F).

When kneading the dough in an electric mixer with a paddle blade, the base temperature should be 64 °C/211 °F. Knead the dough for 3 minutes at slow speed, then for 5 minutes more at medium speed. When using a kneading

machine, use a base temperature of 208 °F/62 °C. Knead the dough for 4 minutes at slow speed and for 8 minutes more at medium speed.

## Ingredients

To prepare 11.8 kg. (26 lb.) of bread dough which will produce 16 740 g. (26 oz.) loaves, the following ingredients should be used:

2 kg. bise flour or substitute (see above) (70.5 oz.)
2 kg. whole wheat flour (70.5 oz.)
1.9 kg. light pumpernickel rye flour (67 oz.)
4 l. water (134.4 fl. oz.)
240 ml. vegetable oil (8 fl. oz.)
140 g. salt (5 oz.)
120 g. yeast (4 oz.)
1.4 kg. fermented dough (49 oz.)

## Kneading

Dissolve the yeast in the water and

put it into the mixing bowl or kneading machine with all the other ingredients except the fermented dough. The fermented dough should be added 3 minutes before the end of kneading to ensure that it is not overworked.

### Checking the kneaded dough

The temperature of the finished dough should be approximately 25 °C (77 °F) at the end of kneading. The dough should be smooth and relatively soft to the touch.

Be sure and cover the dough after kneading to prevent the formation of a skin.

### First rising

The dough should be allowed to rise for approximately one hour. Punch it down 30 minutes into the rising.

### Scaling

Divide the dough into 740 g. (26 oz.) sections. Gently shape them into balls and let rest.

### Shaping the loaves

Shape the sections into round loaves. Let them rest for 5 to 10 minutes before flattening them with a rolling pin.

### Proofing

Proof the loaves from 1 hour and 15 minutes to 1 hour and 30 minutes in a proof box.

When the loaves have finished proofing, set a round cooling rack over the top of the loaves and sprinkle them with flour using a sieve.

Make notches in the sides of the loaves with a pastry cutter.

### Baking

Preheat the oven to 230 °C (450 °F). Inject steam into the oven before putting in the loaves. The steam should be blown out 15 minutes into the baking.

740 g. loaves (26 oz.) require approximately 45 minutes of baking.

These loaves should be well baked with a crisp outer crust.

## CIRCLE BREAD

| | | | |
|---|---|---|---|
| PREPARATION | 15 min | 15 min | • calculate the temperatures<br>• prepare and weigh the ingredients |
| KNEADING | 10 min | 25 min | • combine ingredients on slow speed for 4 min<br>• knead for 6 minutes on medium speed |
| FIRST RISING | 1 hr | 1 hr 25 | • punch down the dough after 30 minutes |
| SCALING | 5 min | 1 hr 30 | • gently round off sections |
| RESTING | 10 min | 1 hr 40 | |
| SHAPING | 15 min | 1 hr 55 | • shape into round loaves then flatten |
| PROOFING | 1 hr 15 | 3 hr 10 | • watch the proofing closely<br>• do not let the loaves over rise<br>• flour the loaves using the cooling rack<br>• make notches in the loaves |
| BEFORE BAKING | 3 min | 3 hr 13 | • blow out steam 15 minutes into baking |
| BAKING | 45 min | 3 hr 58 | • loaves should be well done or crumb will be pasty and soft |
| COOLING | 3 min | 4 hr 01 | • place the loaves in a basket as soon as they come out of the oven to avoid condensation |

STORAGE : *these loaves have an excellent shelf life*

# Traditional White Bread (Pain de Froment)

## Introduction

As its name suggests, traditional white bread is made from high quality, unbleached white flour which gives it an appealing, nut-like flavor.

The time needed for preparing traditional white bread depends on several factors such as the consistency of the dough, the length of the first rising, and the amount of yeast added to the dough.

## Storage

Because traditional white bread dough often contains fermented dough from a previous batch and is made into relatively large loaves. It has an excellent shelf life. Large loaves can be eaten up to 3 days after baking and 500 g. (17 oz.) loaves can be served 2 days after baking. Smaller loaves can be served the day after baking.

## Shapes used for traditional white bread

Traditional white bread is cut into sections which are then twisted into spirals. They can be prepared in a wide variety of sizes and sold by weight.

## Appearance

Traditional white bread has a medium brown crust. The thickness of the crust depends on the length of time the bread has been proofed and whether the loaves have been baked in an extremely hot oven for the entire baking period or if the oven temperature has been decreased during baking.

Certain doughs will result in loaves with relatively thick crusts.

Traditional white bread, however, because it is composed entirely of unbleached, white wheat flour can be baked so the loaves have thinner crusts.

### Serving traditional white bread

Traditional white bread can be served with cold meats, fish, mild-flavored cheeses and pork products such as salami and pâté. It can also be sliced and served as toast.

### Procedure

The work area should be between 22 and 25 °C (72 and 77 °F).

When using either a kneading machine or an electric mixer with a paddle blade, use a base temperature of 60 °C/ 204 °F. When using the electric mixer, knead the dough for 4 minutes at slow speed then continue kneading for 4 minutes more at medium speed. When using a kneading machine, knead the dough for 4 minutes at slow speed and 8 minutes more at medium speed.

The quality of the dough is improved and the kneading time can be reduced 20% by allowing the dough to rest for 20 minutes after the first stage of kneading (frasing).

### Resting

Combine the water and flour at slow speed. Let the dough rest for 20 minutes and continue kneading at medium speed.

### Ingredients

To prepare 5 kg. (11 lb.) of bread dough which will produce 20 250 g. loaves or 10 500 g. loaves, the following ingredients are needed:
2.5 kg. bread flour (5.5 lb.)
50 g. salt (1.7 oz.)
50 g. yeast (1.7 oz.)
1.6 l. water (54 fl. oz.)
800 g. fermented dough (28 oz.)

### Kneading

Place the flour, the salt, and the yeast which has been previously combined with the water in the bowl of the mixer or kneading machine.

Keep a close eye on the consistency of the dough at the beginning of kneading. If it becomes necessary to add water or flour to adjust the consistency, the first stage of the kneading (frasing; at slow speed) should be lengthened slightly.

Halfway through the kneading, add the fermented dough.

Continue kneading the dough until it is well mixed and smooth.

### Checking the kneaded dough

The temperature of the finished dough should be approximately 25 °C (77 °F). The dough should be smooth and soft to the touch.

Cover the dough after kneading to prevent the formation of a skin.

### First rising

The dough should be allowed to rise for 2 to 2 1/2 hours – traditional white bread is less susceptible to over rising than other types of dough. Punch down the dough 1 hour into the rising.

### Scaling

Traditional white bread can be sold either in standard size loaves or it can be baked in a variety of shapes and sizes and sold by the pound. Scaling can be done in one of 2 ways:
a) Divide the bread by hand without weighing it.
b) Divide the dough into sections using an automatic dough divider. Do not try to shape the sections before they have rested for 5 to 10 minutes.

### Shaping the loaves

Twist the loaves and place them either on a flat surface for baking or in curved, canvas holders.

### Proofing

Proofing usually requires 1-1/2 hours depending on the temperature of the rising area or proof box.

Put the loaves in the proof box immediately after shaping to prevent the formation of a skin.

### Baking

Preheat and inject steam into the oven before inserting the loaves. Lower the oven temperature by 10 °C (20 °F) as soon as the loaves begin to brown.

For 250 g. (9 oz.) loaves, approximately 15 minutes are required for baking. Count on 25 minutes for 500 g. (17 oz.) loaves. As soon as the loaves come out of the oven, arrange them in a basket. Avoid heaping them up on one another while they are cooling.

## TRADITIONAL WHITE BREAD

| | | | |
|---|---|---|---|
| **PREPARATION** | **15** min | **15** min | • calculate the temperatures<br>• prepare and weigh the ingredients |
| **KNEADING** | **8** min | **23** min | • combine ingredients on slow speed; continue kneading on medium speed |
| **FIRST RISING** | **2** hr | **2** hr **23** | • protect the dough from air to prevent a skin from forming |
| **SCALING** | **5** min | **2** hr **28** | • do not try to shape the sections |
| **RESTING** | **10** min | **2** hr **38** | |
| **SHAPING** | **5** min | **2** hr **43** | • twist the loaves |
| **PROOFING** | **1** hr **30** | **4** hr **13** | • protect the dough from drafts<br>• do not allow the dough to over rise (because the dough is fragile, it can fall in the oven) |
| **PREPARING FOR BAKING** | **5** min | **4** hr **18** | • inject steam into the oven before baking<br>• start baking in very hot oven |
| **BAKING** | **15** to **25** min | **4** hr **40** | • lower the oven temperature 10 °C (20 °F) as soon as bread begins to brown<br>• watch baking closely |
| **COOLING** | **5** min | **4** hr **45** | • place in a basket to avoid condensation |

**STORAGE**: traditional white bread has an excellent shelf life

# Bordeaux-style Bread
# (Pain Rustique Bordelais)

## Introduction

Bordeaux-style bread is derived from the rustic bread recipe given on page 20 Bordeaux-style bread is characterized by the addition of rye flour. Rye flour improves the shelf life of breads but at the same time, if too much is used, can cause the crumb to be too fragile because of its low gluten content.

To compensate for rye flour's low gluten content, a quantity of yeast starter or fermented dough which has been al-lowed to rise for a longer than normal period (the excessive rising activates gluten-related proteins) is usually added to the dough.

Bordeaux-style bread has a relatively dense crumb because of the rye flour it contains and rises less than rustic breads made exclusively with wheat flour. At the same time, Bordeaux-style bread has a characteristic tangy flavor missing in rustic bread made exclusively with wheat flour.

## Storage

Bordeaux-style bread has an excellent shelf life because it contains rye flour and undergoes a prolonged first rising.

## Shapes used for Bordeaux-style bread

Bordeaux-style bread is divided into square or rectangular sections after a prolonged first rising. After the bread is cut into sections it undergoes no further shaping. The fact that it is not shaped

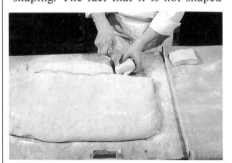

contributes to its excellent flavor and texture.

Bordeaux-style bread can be sectioned into exact predetermined weights using an automatic dough divider. It can also be weighed by hand which makes it necessary to sell it by the pound.

### Appearance

Bordeaux-style bread should have a lightly floured, brown crust. It should have a relatively light textured, honeycombed crumb with a pale gray color.

### Serving Bordeaux-style bread

Bordeaux-style bread is especially good when served with raw shellfish including oysters and pork products such as salami and pâtés.

### Procedure

The work area should be between 22 and 25 °C (72 and 77 °F).

When using an electric mixer with a paddle blade, use a base temperature of 59 °C/202 °F. Knead the dough for 4 minutes at slow speed (frasing) and 7 minutes more at medium speed.

When using a kneading machine, use a base temperature of 61 °C/206 °F. Knead the dough for 4 minutes at slow speed and 10 minutes more at medium speed.

### Ingredients

To prepare 7.7 kg. (17 lb.) of bread dough which will produce 14 550 g. (19.4) loaves or 28 275 g. (9.5 oz.) loaves, the following ingredients are needed:

3 kg. white flour (6.6 lb.)
1 kg. light pumpernickel rye flour (35 oz.)
80 g. salt (2.8 oz.)
60 g. yeast (2.1 oz.)
2.6 l. water (88 fl. oz.)
960 g. fermented dough (34 oz.)

The fermented dough should be added 3 minutes before the end of kneading either in the electric mixer or kneading machine. It is best to cut fermented dough into several pieces before adding it to a fresh dough to help it work in quickly. The fermented dough should have fermented for at least 6 hours at 22 °C/72 °F or for 15 hours at 7 °C/45 °F before being added to the dough.

### Kneading

Put the white flour, the rye flour, the salt, and the yeast which has first been dissolved in the water, in the bowl of the electric mixer or kneading machine. Check the consistency of the dough after the preliminary combining of the ingredients (frasing).

### Checking the kneaded dough

The temperature of the dough should be between 24 and 25 °C (75 and 77 °F) at the end of kneading. The dough should be smooth and soft to the touch.

Cover the dough after kneading to prevent the formation of a skin on its surface.

### First rising

The dough should be allowed to rise approximately 1 hour. The exact time needed for the first rising depends on the temperature of the dough and the temperature and humidity of the rising area.

After 40 minutes, punch down the dough. The dough can be punched down either before or after it is weighed and sectioned into loaves.

### Scaling

Scale the dough by hand or with an automatic dough divider. Place the sections on a lightly floured surface for baking. Once the loaves have been divided, leave them as they are. Do not try to shape them.

### Proofing

Proof the loaves in a proof box at 25 °C/77 °F.

Avoid letting the loaves over rise in the proof box or they will not rise in the oven and may even fall.

### Preparation for baking

Preheat the oven to between 240 and 250 °C (475 and 500 °F).

Score the loaves with either crisscross or diagonal patterns.

Lightly dust the loaves with flour using a sieve.

### Baking

Inject steam into the oven before and during baking.

Count on 30 minutes of baking for 550 g. (19.5 oz.) loaves and 18 minutes for 275 g. (9.5 oz.) loaves. Carefully watch the loaves during baking.

As soon as the loaves come out of the oven, arrange them in a basket. Avoid heaping them up on one another while they are cooling.

## BORDEAUX-STYLE BREAD

| | | | |
|---|---|---|---|
| PREPARATION | 15 min | 15 min | • calculate the temperatures<br>• prepare and weigh the ingredients |
| KNEADING | 11 min | 26 min | • slow speed for 4 minutes (frasing)<br>• continue kneading 7 min (medium speed)<br>• add fermented dough 3 min before the end |
| FIRST RISING | 40 min | 1 hr 06 | • let the dough rise as a single mass |
| SCALING | 5 min | 1 hr 11 | • punch down dough if using an automatic dough divider |
| RESTING | 20 min | 1 hr 31 | • cover to prevent the formation of a skin |
| DIVIDING | 9 min | 1 hr 40 | • divide the loaves by hand or machine |
| PROOFING | 1 hr | 2 hr 40 | • proof in proof box<br>• do not allow the dough to over rise |
| PREPARING FOR BAKING | 5 min | 2 hr 45 | • inject steam into the oven before baking<br>• adjust the oven temperature as needed |
| BAKING | 22 to 35 min | 3 hr 15 | • bake bread in a hot oven<br>• turn down the oven temperature halfway |
| COOLING | 5 min | 3 hr 20 | • place in a basket to avoid condensation |

STORAGE : Bordeaux-style bread can be sold 2 days after baking and eaten for up to 3 days after

# Beaucaire Bread (Pain de Beaucaire)

Before the turn of the century, Beaucaire bread was a staple bread in the lower Rhone valley, in southern France. Originally it was made using a spontaneously leavened, natural starter, but the recipe has been since adapted to more modern methods.

Even though Beaucaire bread has a characteristic appearance, recipes vary depending on the region where it is made.

**Procedure**

Beaucaire bread is prepared using sections of dough which are given a series of folds or " turns ". These are then cut into rectangles.

To obtain 16.45 kg. (36.3 lb.) of dough which will produce 27 loaves weighing 600 g. (21 oz.) each or 53 loaves weighing 310 g. (11 oz.), the following ingredients are needed:

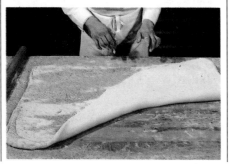

### Yeast starter
250 g. yeast (9 oz.)
3.4 kg. flour (7.5 lb.)
2 l. water (67.5 fl. oz.)
### Finished dough
6.6 kg. flour (14.5 lb.)
220 g. salt (7.5 oz.)
4 l. water (135 fl. oz.)
### Preparation
See page 13.
### Kneading
Put the yeast starter along with the water used in the finished dough in the bowl of the electric mixer or kneading machine. Add the flour and begin kneading.

Kneading machine: 4 minutes on slow speed (frasing) and 10 minutes on medium speed.

Electric mixer: 4 minutes on slow speed (frasing) and 6 minutes on

medium speed.

The salt should be stirred into the dough at the end of kneading.

Let the dough rise for 45 minutes. Flatten the dough and work it into a rectangular shape.

a) Fold the dough sideways; one half into the center, the other half folded over the first fold.

b) Roll out one end of the rectangle of dough and fold it lengthwise into the center. Fold the other end completely over the first fold. Flatten the edges of the rectangles with the fist. Let the sections of dough rest for several minutes.

c) Roll out the rectangle.

d) Lightly moisten one half (lengthwise) of the rectangle with water. Lightly dust the moistened end with bread flour.

e) Flip the dough over onto a floured work surface and stretch it to the desired size with the hands or with a rolling pin.

### Proofing
1 hour to 1 hour 30 minutes.

### Cutting the dough
Cut the edges of the dough with a pastry cutter. (There is a special, large pastry cutter used for Beaucaire bread which measures 31 by 20 cm./12 x 8 in.) Cut the dough into sections. The size of the sections depends of course on the desired size of the loaves. One typical size measures 3 by 3.5 cm./1/2 by 1 in. and weighs 250 g. (9 oz.).

Place the cut out sectons of dough on the oven conveyor or peel. Split the ends of each of the loaves with a small pastry cutter and score the surface of the loaves from end to end. Although the scoring is optional, it not only adds a decorative touch but helps the loaves open more during baking.

### Baking
Inject steam into the oven before baking. The oven should be preheated to approximately 230 °C (450 °F). As soon as the loaves come out of the oven, arrange them in baskets or on cooling racks.

## BEAUCAIRE BREAD

| | | | |
|---|---|---|---|
| **PREPARING THE YEAST STARTER** | **5** min | **5** min | • calculate the temperatures<br>• prepare and weigh the ingredients |
| **KNEADING THE YEAST STARTER** | **8** min | **13** min | • always use slow speed |
| **FIRST RISING OF THE YEAST STARTER** | **1** hr **30** to **2** hr | **1** hr **43** | • the time required for fermenting the yeast starter depends on the temperature |
| **PREPARING THE FINISHED DOUGH** | **15** min | **1** hr **55** | • calculate the temperatures<br>• prepare, weigh and measure the raw ingredients |
| **KNEADING** | **14** min | **2** hr **09** | • knead 4 minutes on slow speed (frasing)<br>• knead for 10 minutes on medium speed<br>• the dough should be medium firm |
| **FIRST RISING** | **45** min | **2** hr **54** | • rising time depends on strength and temperature of the dough and on temperature and humidity of the work area |
| **TURNING THE DOUGH** | **30** min | **3** hr **24** | • fold the dough over itself in two directions<br>• let rest for 10 minutes, roll with a rolling pin and fold again |
| **PROOFING** | **1** hr to **1** hr **30** | **4** hr **30** | • cover the dough to prevent a skin from forming |
| **CUTTING THE DOUGH** | **10** min | **4** hr **40** | • cut the edges of the rectangle of dough<br>• cut the loaves to the desired size<br>• make cuts in the sides of the loaves |
| **PREPARING FOR BAKING** | **10** min | **4** hr **50** | • score the loaves (optional)<br>• adjust the oven temperature as needed |
| **BAKING** | **20** to **40** min | **5** hr **20** | • adjust the oven temperature depending on the size of the loaves |
| **COOLING** | **5** min | **5** hr **25** | • cool in baskets or on cooling racks. |

STORAGE : Beaucaire bread has a very good shelf life

# Buttermilk Bread (Pain au Babeurre)

## Introduction

Buttermilk bread is especially popular in Germany where it is prepared using a variety of techniques and recipes. Buttermilk is released during the churning of butter and contains either the natural bacteria contained in unpasteurized cream or is inoculated with a laboratory culture when pasteurized cream is used.

When buttermilk is used in bread making, it contributes lactose fermenting bacteria which contribute to the bread's flavor. It also helps improve shelf life by contributing natural acids. Buttermilk is also of nutritional value because of its high mineral content. Some bakers replace buttermilk with fresh cheese but the result is often unsatisfactory.

## Storage

The slow first rising and the addition of buttermilk both contribute to a long shelf life.

## Shapes used for buttermilk bread

Buttermilk bread is usually shaped into thick, elongated loaves but can also be presented in horseshoe shaped loaves. Normally the loaves weigh from 200 g. (7 oz.) to 500 g. (17 oz.).

## Appearance

Buttermilk bread should have a thin, brown, appetizing crust. Some bakers lightly flour the loaves before baking.

Buttermilk bread rises less and more slowly than other types because of the buttermilk or fresh cheese that it contains. Buttermilk bread is especially good when served with raw vegetables.

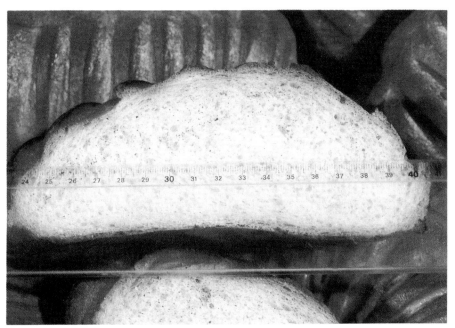

## Procedure

The work area should be between 22 and 25 °C (72 and 77 °F).

When using an electric mixer with a paddle blade, use a base temperature of 58 °C/200 °F. Knead the dough at slow speed for 4 minutes (frasing) and for 6 minutes more at medium speed.

When using a kneading machine, use a base temperature of 60 °C/204 °F. Knead the dough for 4 minutes at slow speed and for 10 minutes more at medium speed.

## Ingredients

### Using buttermilk

3.9 kg. flour (8.6 lb.)
1.1 l. water (37 fl. oz.)
1.1 l. buttermilk (37 fl. oz.)
130 g. yeast (4.5 oz.)
75 g. salt (2.6 oz.)
70 g. malt (2.5 oz.)
625 g. fermented dough (22 oz.)

### Using fresh cheese

3.6 kg. white flour (7.9 lb.)
1 l. water (34 fl. oz.)
400 ml. milk (14 fl. oz.)
800 g. stiff, fresh cheese (28 oz.)
50 g. malt (1.8 oz.)
1 kg. fermented dough (35 oz.)
80 g. yeast (2.8 oz.)
70 g. salt (2.5 oz.)

## Kneading

Place the flour, salt, buttermilk or fresh cheese, the malt, the milk, and the yeast first dissolved in the water in the electric mixer or kneading machine.

Combine the ingredients (frasing) as described above. Keep close watch on the consistency of the dough. Add the fermented dough to the fresh batch 4 minutes before the end of kneading.

## Checking the kneaded dough

The dough should be 25 °C (77 °F) when it is finished kneading. It should be smooth and soft to the touch.

Be sure and cover the dough after kneading to prevent a skin forming on its surface.

## First rising

The dough should be allowed to rise for approximately 35 minutes depend-

ing on the temperature of the dough and the temperature and humidity of the rising area.

## Scaling

Section and weigh the dough by hand. Shape the sections of dough into balls and let them rest for 15 minutes.

## Shaping the loaves

The dough should be shaped by hand. When preparing horseshoe shaped loaves, first shape the dough into long loaves leaving the center thicker than the ends. The long loaves should then be bent into a horseshoe shape and baked with the seam facing down. The loaves can be baked either on sheets of parchment paper or directly on the baking surface.

## Proofing

Allow the loaves to rise for approximately 1 hour and 15 minutes depending on the temperature and humidity of

the work area. The loaves should be proofed either in a proof box or moist rising area. Keep checking the loaves during proofing to prevent them from over rising.

## Preparation for baking

The oven temperature should be between 220 and 230 °C (425 and 450 °F). for 500 g. (17 oz.) loaves and between 230 and 240 °C (450 and 475 °F) for 250 g. (9 oz.) loaves.

Score the loaves just before baking.

## Baking

Steam should be injected into the oven before and during the first part of baking. Loaves weighing 500 g. (17.5 oz.) should be baked for approximately 25 minutes, 250 g. (9 oz.) loaves for 15 minutes. As soon as the loaves come out of the oven, arrange them in a basket. Avoid heaping them up on one another while they are cooling.

## BUTTERMILK BREAD

| | | | |
|---|---|---|---|
| **PREPARATION** | 15 min | 15 min | • calculate the temperatures<br>• prepare and weigh the ingredients |
| **KNEADING** | 10 min | 25 min | • combine ingredients 4 minutes (frasing)<br>• continue for 6 min on medium speed |
| **FIRST RISING** | 35 min | 1 hr | • rising time will depend on temperature |
| **SCALING** | 5 min | 1 hr 05 | • shape into rounds and let rest |
| **RESTING** | 15 min | 1 hr 20 | |
| **SHAPING** | 7 min | 1 hr 27 | • shape as desired |
| **PROOFING** | 1 hr | 2 hr 27 | • proof in proof box or moist rising area<br>• do not allow the dough to over rise |
| **PREPARING FOR BAKING** | 5 min | 2 hr 32 | • inject steam into the oven before baking<br>• adjust the oven temperature as needed |
| **BAKING** | 15 to 25 min | 2 hr 55 | • turn down the oven temperature near the end of baking to avoid too much browning |
| **COOLING** | 5 min | 3 hr | • place in a basket to avoid condensation |

**STORAGE :** Buttermilk bread can be sold up to 2 days after baking

# Mottled Bread (Pain Marin Tigré)

**Introduction**

Because of the increased popularity of old-style, regional, and unusual breads, French bakers have adapted breads from Holland, Germany, and Eastern Europe to French baking techniques. Mottled bread which has long been prepared in Holland and Northern Germany is just beginning to be appreciated in France and in the United States. It is prepared in a wide variety of shapes including round and long loaves as well as being sometimes baked in decorative molds.

The mottled surface of this bread is due to a special technique where a light bread dough is brushed on the top of the loaves before baking. This technique which is described here for one type of bread is also adaptable to other bread recipes.

The light dough which is brushed on the surface of the loaves is similar in consistency to a sponge starter. It is applied to the loaves using one of two methods:

1. It is brushed on the loaves as soon as they are shaped and allowed to proof along with the loaves.

2. It is prepared after the loaves have been shaped and allowed to rise in a warm place. It is then brushed on the proofed loaves just before baking.

The mottled bread recipe given below includes rye flour which contributes to the flavor and shelf life of the bread as well as butter which gives the bread a finer crumb and also lengthens its shelf life.

## Storage

Mottled bread has an excellent shelf life and can be sold up to 2 days after it is baked. It can be served for up to 3 days after baking. The rye flour and butter contained in mottled bread as well as the relatively prolonged rising time which causes the development of organic acids, all contribute to mottled bread's excellent shelf life.

## Shapes used for mottled bread

Mottled bread is usually baked in thick, elongated loaves (batards).

## Appearance

As its name suggests, mottled bread should have dark, brown patches over a light brown crust.

Mottled bread is relatively dense after baking and rises less than some other types of bread because of the relatively short kneading time used.

## Serving mottled bread

Mottled bread goes well with cheese–especially when served with a raclette–as well as pork products such as salami and pâté.

## Procedure

The temperature of the work area should be between 22 and 25 °C (72 and 77 °F).

When using an electric mixer with a paddle blade, use a base temperature of 60 °C/204 °F. Knead the dough for 4 minutes at slow speed (frasing) and for 4 minutes more at medium speed.

When using a kneading machine, use a base temperature of 62 °C/208 °F. Knead the dough for 5 minutes at slow speed (frasing) and for 6 minutes more at medium speed.

## Ingredients

To prepare 7 kg. (15.4 lb.) of dough which will produce 14 500 g. (17 oz.) loaves or 20 350 g. (12.5 oz.) loaves, the following ingredients are needed:
- 3.8 kg. bread flour (8.4 lb.)
- 380 g. light pumpernickel rye flour (13.5 oz.)
- 2.47 l. water (83.5 fl. oz.)
- 190 g. butter (6.5 oz.)
- 75 g. salt (2.5 oz.)
- 75 g. yeast (2.8 oz.)

*Semi-liquid dough for surface*
Combine:
- 100 g. rice flour (3.5 oz.)
- 10 g. yeast (2 tsp.)
- 10 g. sugar (2 tsp.)
- 10 ml. oil (2 tsp.)
- 5 g. salt (1 tsp.)
- 90 ml. water (3.2 fl. oz.)
- 1 pinch flour

## Kneading

Place the yeast which has first been dissolved in the water, in the bowl of the mixer or kneading machine.

Knead the dough for 4 minutes at slow speed (frasing) and for 4 minutes more if using a mixer or 6 minutes more if using a kneading machine.

## Checking the kneaded dough

The temperature of the finished dough should be approximately 24 °C

(75 °F). The dough should be soft and smooth to the touch.

Be sure and cover the dough after kneading to prevent a skin from forming.

## First rising

Let the dough rise from 50 to 60 minutes depending on the temperature of the dough and the temperature and humidity of the rising area. Make sure the dough is protected from drafts during rising.

## Scaling

Section and weigh the dough by hand. Be careful to avoid using an excess of flour. Gently round the sections of dough and let them rest for 10 to 15 minutes before shaping.

## Shaping the loaves

Shape the dough by hand into thick, elongated loaves.

Once the loaves have been shaped, brush their surface with the semi-liquid dough.

Because the semi-liquid dough has fermented before the loaves are baked, it will have a cracked surface.

## Proofing

Proofing usually requires from 1 hour and 15 minutes to 1 hour and 30 minutes depending on the temperature of the proof box or proofing area. Be careful not to let the dough over rise.

## Baking

Preheat the oven to approximately 230 °C (450 °F). Inject steam into the oven before baking.

Bake 250 g. (9 oz.) loaves for approximately 25 minutes. Count on 30 to 35 minutes for 500 g. (17 oz.) loaves.

Carefully watch the loaves to prevent excess browning during baking. As soon as the loaves come out of the oven, arrange them in a basket. Avoid heaping them up on one another while they cool.

## MOTTLED BREAD

| PREPARATION | 15 min | 15 min | • calculate the temperatures<br>• prepare and weigh the ingredients |
|---|---|---|---|
| KNEADING | 8 min | 23 min | • slow speed for 4 minutes (frasing)<br>• continue for 4 min on medium speed |
| FIRST RISING | 55 min | 1 hr 18 | • punch down the dough after 30 minutes of rising |
| SCALING | 5 min | 1 hr 23 | • gently round the sections and let rest |
| RESTING | 15 min | 1 hr 38 | |
| SHAPING | 10 min | 1 hr 48 | • brush with semi-liquid dough after shaping |
| PROOFING | 1 hr 20 | 3 hr 08 | • proof in proof box or steam chamber<br>• do not allow the dough to over rise |
| PREPARING FOR BAKING | 5 min | 3 hr 13 | • inject steam into the oven before baking<br>• adjust the oven temperature as needed |
| BAKING | 25 to 40 min | 3 hr 50 | • remember that baking time varies 40 min depending on size of the loaves |
| COOLING | 5 min | 3 hr 55 | • place in a basket to avoid condensation |

STORAGE: *Very good*

# Chestnut Breads (Pains à la Châtaigne)

*Chestnut bread recipes often come from the Ardèche, a mountainous region in southeastern France famous for its chestnuts.*

*The traditional breads of the Ardèche often include chestnut flour which is used in a wide variety of local breads.*

*In recent years, largely due to the work of Yves Saunier who has done much to* *popularize and update the traditional breads of the Ardèche region, chestnut flour is again being used in bakeries eager to expand the breads available to their clientele.*

**Tips for marketing chestnut breads**

To help familiarize your customers with these breads, loaves decorated with chestnut leaves and husks are a highly visible means of sparking interest in chestnut breads. Don't hesitate to let customers taste samples of chestnut bread.

If bread is called for in catered functions, be sure and include some chestnut bread to encourage further interest.

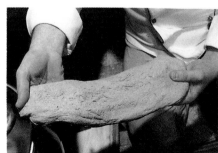

# 1. Chestnut bread using a yeast starter

## Ingredients

180 g. yeast starter (6.5 oz.)
300 g. high gluten flour (10.5 oz.)
160 g. chestnut flour (5.5 oz.)
12 g. salt (2 1/2 tsp.)

25 g. yeast (1 oz.)
280 ml. water (9 fl. oz.)

Base temperature: 68 °C/219 °F.
Temperature of dough after kneading: 25 °C/77 °F.

## Procedure

*Kneading:* 2 minutes on slow speed followed by 15 minutes on medium speed.

*First rising:* 40 minutes.

*Proofing:* 1 hour 30 minutes.

*Baking:* 30 minutes at 240 °C/275 °F.

## Tips

Chestnut bread should be weighed into 300 g. (10.5 oz.) loaves and placed directly on the baking surface. Be sure and score the length of the loaf before baking.

Avoid using too hot an oven for baking.

## Serving chestnut bread

Chestnut bread goes particularly well with goat's cheese and salads containing walnuts or walnut oil. Because of the full, characteristic flavor of chestnut bread, it should be served with assertively flavored foods.

# Butter-enriched chestnut bread

**Serving butter-enriched chestnut bread**
Because of the butter it contains, butter-enriched chestnut bread has a soft crumb which makes it excellent for toast. It is also excellent when served with smoked salmon or foie gras.

# Honey chestnut bread

**Serving honey chestnut bread**
Honey chestnut bread is excellent toasted and buttered and served at breakfast. It is especially liked by children who appreciate its mildly sweet taste.

**Storage**
Honey chestnut bread can be stored for 2 to 3 days if protected from air.

# Chestnut brioche

**Serving chestnut brioche**
Because of the richness of chestnut brioche, it can be eaten alone in the same way as a croissant or regular brioche.

It is also excellent when toasted and served with smoked salmon or fish butters.

Chestnut brioche makes a nice addition to a cold buffet.

## Procedure

*Kneading:* 2 minutes at slow speed followed by 15 minutes at medium speed.

*First rising:* 45 minutes.

*Proofing:* 1 hour 30 minutes.

*Baking:* 35 minutes at 230 °C/450 °F.

## Ingredients

350 g. high gluten flour (12.5 oz.)
150 g. chestnut flour (5.5 oz.)
50 g. butter (1.8 oz.)
12 g. salt (1 1/2 tsp.)
30 g. yeast (1 oz.)
220 ml water (8 fl. oz.)

## Tips

Divide the dough into relatively small sections of 100 g. (3.5 oz.). Roll the sections into small loaves about 15 cm. (6 in.) long. Cut them from side to side using a sausage cut and brush twice with egg wash before baking.

To prevent the loaves from sagging during baking, they can be baked in bread molds or in canvas which will hold their shape.

If different types of breads are being prepared, each should be cut in a distinctive way so they can be told apart.

## Procedure

*Kneading:* 2 minutes at slow speed followed by 15 minutes at medium speed.

*First rising:* 35 minutes.

*Proofing:* 1 hour 30 minutes.

*Baking:* 35 minutes at 230 °C/450 °F. Make a crisscross, polka cut in the loaves after shaping.

## Ingredients

180 g. chestnut flour (6.5 oz.)
300 g. high gluten flour (10.5 oz.)
200 g. yeast starter with 4 hours of fermentation (7 oz.)
14 g. salt (3 tsp.)
25 g. yeast (1 oz.)
290 ml. water (10 fl. oz.)
50 g. honey (1.8 oz.)

Base temperature: 219 °F/68 °C.
Temperature of kneaded dough: 26 °C/79 °F.

## Tips

Do not over knead the dough so it is too smooth.

Do not let the sections of dough overproof.

Never use more than 30% chestnut flour in relation to the rest of the flour.

Bake small loaves (100 g./3.5 oz.).

Brush twice with egg wash before baking.

## Procedure

*Kneading:* 2 minutes at slow speed followed by 15 minutes at medium speed.

*First rising:* 1 hour 20 minutes.

*Proofing:* 1 hour.

*Baking:* 35 minutes at 230 °C/450 °F.

## Ingredients

150 g. chestnut flour (5.5 oz.)
350 g. high gluten flour (12.5 oz.)
1 egg (50 g./1.8 oz.)
12 g. salt (1 1/2 tsp.)
25 g. sugar (1 oz.)
25 g. yeast (1 oz.)
200 ml. water (7 fl. oz.)
40 g. powdered milk (1.4 oz.)
100 g. butter (3.5 oz.)
150 g. peeled chestnuts (5.5 oz.)

Base temperature: 75 °C/231 °F.
Temperature of the dough after kneading: 27 °C/81 °F.

## Tips

Divide the dough into 100 g. (3.5 oz.) loaves. Insert 3 chestnut halves in the middle of each loaf while they are being shaped.

Brush each loaf twice with egg wash.

These loaves should be baked a short time before they have proofed completely.

Make cuts in the loaves before baking. Do not cut too deeply into the loaves or the chestnut halves may slip out during baking.

Make sure that the loaves are thoroughly baked. This ensures that the chestnut halves enclosed in the loaves will be completely dry and not susceptible to molds or mildew.

# Chapter 2

# Special and International Breads

## A variety of new possibilities

The breads presented in this chapter, many of which are new and unusual, will allow bakers to offer a wider range of products to their clientele.

There is growing interest in European breads in both France and the United States. As Europeans and Americans travel more, there is a greater willingness to appreciate the breads of other countries.

The breads presented here all have a characteristic shape and an appetizing appearance. Some contain durham flour and have a pale yellow crumb.

Most special and international breads have an excellent shelf life.

The preparation of these breads is straightforward and shouldn't present any particular difficulties. Their appetizing appearance and flavor makes them hard to resist.

# Chapter Organization

## Review

*A wide range of special breads has already been presented in the first volume of Special and Decorative Breads. A list of these breads is given below:*

Apricot, apple, and prune breads
Seaweed bread
Brown bread
Brié bread
Four-grain bread
Chorizo bread
Cumin bread
Carrot bread
Herb bread
Carrot-herb bread
Whole-wheat bread with dried fruits
Wheat-germ bread
High-gluten bread
Low-gluten bread
Gruau bread
Italian bread
Corn bread
Méteil bread (Wheat/rye bread)
Pullman bread
Normandy cider bread
Hazelnut, walnut, and almond breads
Onion and bacon bread
Olive bread
Barley bread
Provençale fougasse
Sesame-seed bread
Soy bread
Bran bread
Surprise breads
Viennese breads

### This chapter comprises two families of breads:

#### 1. Special breads

These breads usually contain additional ingredients which give them a distinctive flavor and character. Except when preparing potato bread, the special ingredients are added near the end of kneading.

Not only do each of these breads have their own flavor but they have distinctive shapes and appearances.

Except for flat breads, these loaves have an excellent shelf life.

#### 2. International breads

**Arab-style bread** (prepared with whole-wheat flour and oil).

Oil is added to this bread at the beginning of kneading to soften the dough. Arab-style bread has an excellent shelf life with a soft crumb and a thin crust.

**Italian-style hand bread**
(white flour + oil)

Oil is used in this bread so the dough becomes more malleable and is easily worked into the characteristic hand shape.

**Jewish- and Tunisian-style breads**

These breads are prepared with semolina flour. They have an agreeable flavor and a characteristic yellow crumb. They are relatively fragile.

## 1. Special breads (with added ingredients)

Poppy seed bread

Lemon bread

Prosciutto bread

Potato bread

Paprika bread

Cheese bread

## The baker's important role

The techniques and work methods that the professional baker uses for bread making are almost as varied as the wide assortment of breads found in a well stocked bakery.

A successful bakery must have a large assortment of high-quality breads in order to satisfy a sophisticated clientele and have their repeat business. A bakery window filled with breads of all different shapes and colors will help draw the attention of passersby. Each of the many methods that a baker uses has its own advantages and difficulties which must be integrated into the work schedule.

The ideas and directions given in this book are only starting points for the professional baker. The success of the breads presented here will ultimately depend on the baker's experienced eye and judgement. The final decisions about preparing the dough, shaping the loaves, and the final baking will depend on the baker's judgement and experience.

## Professional baking terms

*Resting (détente):* Resting period for kneaded dough before it is shaped into loaves.

*Rising tolerance (tolérance au pointage):* The amount of variation in rising time that a dough can undergo without being adversely affected.

*Turn (tourne):* Manually or mechanically turning the dough to give it the desired shape.

*Proofing tolerance (tolérance à l'enfournement):* The amount of variation in proofing time that a dough can undergo without being adversely affected.

*Texture in the mouth (mâche):* The feeling or texture of the bread when it is chewed.

*Straight-dough method (travail direct):* When bread dough is prepared using the straight-dough method, commercial yeast is added directly to the dough. The time required for the first rising then depends on the amount of yeast which is used.

*Yeast fermentation (fermentation panaire à la levure):* Refers to fermentation using commercial yeast.

*Indirect method (travail indirect):* Bread dough prepared using the indirect method contains a sponge starter, a yeast starter, or fermented dough taken from a previous batch.

*Incorporate butter (beurrer):* Adding butter to the dough used for making croissants.

*Rising molds (bannetons):* Traditionally made out of wicker, rising molds come in a variety of shapes (crown, round, long, etc.) and are usually covered with canvas and used to hold the shaped loaves during proofing.

*Crusting (croûter):* Refers to the formation of a skin on improperly covered raw dough.

*Egg wash (dorure):* A mixture of beaten eggs and sometimes milk or water used for glazing certain types of dough.

# 2. International breads

**Tunisian-style bread**

**Jewish-style bread**

**Arab-style bread**

**Bavarian-style bread**

**Three seasons bread**

**Italian-style hand bread**

# Poppy Seed Bread (Pain Graines de Pavot)

### Introduction

The characteristic blue coating of poppy seed bread makes these breads especially appealing in a bake shop window. Poppy seed bread is best prepared using a sponge starter. The poppy seeds are incorporated into the dough during kneading.

Poppy seed bread does not present the baker with any unusual difficulties.

### Storage

Poppy seed bread prepared with sponge starter has an excellent shelf life. It can also be prepared using a yeast starter or with a mixed starter using dough from a previous batch.

### Shapes used for poppy seed bread

Poppy seed bread is usually prepared in short, thick loaves with a braid running down the middle. The poppy seeds are then used to decorate the sides of the loaves. It can also be shaped into round loaves with the poppy seeds worked into the dough or used to decorate the tops of the loaves.

### Appearance

Poppy seed bread should have a brown crust with a light blue hue caused by the poppy seeds. Because the poppy seeds add weight to the dough, miniature poppy seed loaves rise less than other bread varieties. Poppy seed bread has a very attractive crumb.

### Serving poppy seed bread

Poppy seed bread can be served alone as a snack or used to accompany salads or meats.

### Procedure

The work area should be between 22 and 25 °C (72 and 77 °F).

When using an electric mixer with a paddle blade, use a base temperature of 58 °C/200 °F. Knead the dough for 4 minutes at slow speed (frasing) followed by 8 minutes at medium speed.

When using a kneading machine, use a base temperature of 60 °C/ 204 °F. Knead the dough for 4 minutes at slow speed (frasing) and for 10 minutes more at medium speed.

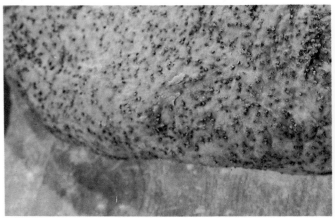

## Ingredients

To prepare 3 kg. (6.6 lb.) of dough which will produce 50 miniature round loaves weighing 60 g. (2.1 oz.) or 10 short thick loaves weighing 300 g. (10.5 oz.) each, the following ingredients are needed:

1.025 kg. sponge starter (36 oz.)
1.1 kg. white bread flour (39 oz.)
500 ml. water (17 fl. oz.)
70 g. butter (2.5 oz.)
35 g. salt (1.2 oz.)
10 g. yeast (2 tsp.)
30 g. powdered milk (1.1 oz.)
230 g. poppy seeds (8 oz.)

## Preparing the sponge starter

Use a base temperature of 68 °C/ 215 °F.

Combine 15 g./1 tbsp. of yeast with the water and then add the flour. Combine the ingredients with a whisk or with the hands.

The sponge requires approximately 4 minutes to prepare.

Cover the sponge and let it rise from 1 1/2 to 2 hours in a 22 to 25 °C (72 to 77 °F) rising area.

## Kneading

Combine the water called for in the recipe with the yeast. Pour this mixture over the sponge and then add the flour, the salt, the powdered milk, and the butter.

Check the consistency of the dough after the initial kneading (frasing). It should have a soft texture.

Incorporate the poppy seeds into the dough one minute before the end of kneading.

## Checking the kneaded dough

The temperature of the dough should be 24 °C (75 °F) at the completion of the kneading.

Protect the dough from drafts in the rising area. During this stage it can be covered with plastic wrap or a cloth.

## First rising

Allow the dough to rise for 50 minutes to 1 hour depending on its consistency.

Punch down the dough or give it a turn 30 minutes into the rising.

Cover the dough.

## Scaling

Divide the dough by hand into 60 g. (2.1 oz.) sections.

Round the sections and let rest for 9 minutes.

## Shaping the loaves

Round the loaves a second time.

Moisten the surface of the loaves and roll the tops in the poppy seeds.

Place the loaves on sheet pans covered with parchment paper or on canvas cloths with the seams on the bottom.

## Proofing

Proof the loaves for 50 minutes to 1 hour depending on the temperature of the proofing area.

The loaves should double in volume but avoid overproofing because the poppy seeds make the finished loaves particularly fragile.

## Preparing for baking

Preheat the oven to 250 °C (475 °F). The loaves can be scored at this point or lightly poked with the tip of a knife.

## Baking

Be careful not to overcook the loaves. They require approximately 15 minutes for baking.

Arrange the breads in wicker baskets or on cooling racks as soon as they come out of the oven.

## POPPY SEED BREAD

| | | | |
|---|---|---|---|
| PREPARING THE SPONGE | 5 min | 5 min | • prepare and weigh the raw ingredients<br>• dissolve the yeast in the water called for in the recipe<br>• cover the sponge |
| KNEADING | 5 min | 10 min | • knead the mixture by hand or electric mixer |
| FERMENTATION | 1 hr 30 to 2 hr | 2 hr 10 | • make sure the dough is well covered<br>• the dough can be refrigerated |
| PREPARING AND KNEADING THE FINISHED DOUGH | 15 min | 2 hr 25 | • calculate the temperatures<br>• prepare, weigh, and measure ingredients<br>• check the consistency of the dough and its final temperature: 24 °C (75 °F) |
| FIRST RISING | 55 min to 1 hr | 3 hr 25 | • punch down the dough after 30 minutes<br>• the time needed for rising depends on the consistency of the dough<br>• protect the dough from drafts during rising |
| SCALING | 5 min | 3 hr 30 | • round the sections of dough |
| RESTING | 10 min | 3 hr 40 | |
| SHAPING | 10 min | 3 hr 50 | • round the sections a second time<br>• the sections of dough can be rolled in poppy seeds |
| PROOFING | 50 min to 1 hr | 4 hr 50 | • the rising time depends on the temperature of the work area |
| PREPARING FOR BAKING | 5 min | 4 hr 55 | • bake the loaves in a hot oven<br>• inject steam into the oven |
| BAKING | 15 min | 5 hr 10 | • carefully watch the coloring of the loaves |
| COOLING | 5 min | 5 hr 15 | • arrange the bread in wicker baskets |

STORAGE : *Poppy seed bread has a good shelf life.*

# Prosciutto Bread (Pain au Jambon)

## Introduction

Because butter is used in the dough, Prosciutto bread has a smooth, fine textured crumb.

Prosciutto bread is straightforward to prepare. It is made like most other breads except that cubes of prosciutto or ham are added to the dough at the end of kneading.

Although prosciutto bread can be baked in almost any shape loaf, it is presented here as a split loaf which can be easily cut in two lengthwise.

## Storage

When prosciutto bread is baked in split loaves as shown here, it tends to dry out relatively quickly. Its shelf life can be greatly improved by using fermented dough and by a prolonged first rising.

## Shapes used for prosciutto bread

Almost any shape can be used for making prosciutto bread. In general, it is baked in either 250 g. (9 oz.) or 500 g. (17 oz.) loaves.

## Appearance

Prosciutto bread should have a relatively thin, brown crust with a fine and appetizing crumb. The appearance of the crumb is enhanced by the cubes of prosciutto.

## Serving prosciutto bread

Prosciutto bread is nourishing and makes an excellent snack. It can be served alone or with a salad.

## Procedure

The work area should be between 22 and 25 °C (72 and 77 °F).

When using an electric mixer with a paddle blade, use a base temperature of 59 °C/202 °F. Knead the dough for 4 minutes at slow speed (frasing) followed by 6 minutes at medium speed.

When using a kneading machine, use a base temperature of 61 °C/206 °F. Knead the dough for 4 minutes at slow speed (frasing) and for 9 minutes more at medium speed.

## Ingredients

To prepare 4.2 kg. (9.2 lb.) of bread dough which will produce 14 loaves of 300 g. (10.5 oz.) each, the following ingredients are needed:

2 kg. bread flour (70.5 oz.)
40 g. salt (1.4 oz.) - 40 g. yeast (1.4 oz.)
400 g. fermented dough (14 oz.) (fermented for a minimum of 4 hours at 20 °C/68 °F).
120 g. butter (4 oz.)
400 g. prosciutto or ham (14 oz.)

### Kneading

Combine the flour, the salt, the butter, and the yeast which has been first dissolved in the water, in the bowl of the electric mixer or kneading machine. Check the consistency of the dough after the first stage of kneading (frasing).

Add the previously fermented dough to the fresh dough 3 minutes before the end of kneading.

Add the ham to the dough 1 minute before the end of kneading.

### Checking the kneaded dough

At the end of kneading, the temperature of the dough should be 24 °C/75 °F.

The dough should have a medium firm consistency.

Be careful to cover the dough after kneading to prevent the formation of a skin.

### First rising

The dough should be allowed to rise for approximately 50 minutes.

If the dough is somewhat soft, it is advisable to punch down the dough (either by hand or in a machine) 25 minutes into the first rising. This reinforces the gluten structure of the dough.

As is true with all breads, the time needed for the first rising will vary depending on the temperature of the dough and the humidity and temperature of the work area.

### Scaling

Weigh the dough into sections.

If the dough has a medium firm consistency, gently round the sections.

Let the dough rest for approximately 15 minutes depending on its consistency.

### Shaping the loaves

Shape the dough into thick, elongated loaves. The length of the loaves can vary depending on the weight of dough used for each section.

Lightly sift flour over the tops of the loaves. Rye or rice flour work best for this.

Press down on the loaves with a rolling pin to create a well running length-

wise down the middle. Fold each side in toward the center of the loaf. Turn the loaves upside down onto sheet pans or canvas cloths for proofing.

### Proofing

Proofing usually requires approximately 1 hour. It is best to proof the loaves in a proof box or moist rising area.

If the dough is relatively stiff, it should be allowed slightly more time for proofing than loaves shaped from a softer dough. Softer dough will rise more in the oven, thus compensating for the shortened proofing time.

### Preparing for baking

For baking small loaves, it is best to use a hot oven to prevent them from drying out.

Preheat the oven to from 240 to 250 °C (450 to 475 °F).

Flip the loaves right side up on to the baking surface just before they go into the oven.

### Baking

Inject steam into the oven before putting in the loaves. Once the loaves are in the oven, additional steam can be injected in the oven at the beginning of baking.

For small loaves weighing 250 g. (9 oz.) each, bake for 18 to 20 minutes. For larger loaves weighing 500 g. (17 oz.) count on 25 to 28 minutes.

As soon as the loaves come out of the oven, arrange them in a basket. Avoid heaping them up on one another while they are cooling.

## PROSCIUTTO BREAD

| | | | |
|---|---|---|---|
| PREPARATION | 15 min | 15 min | • calculate the temperatures<br>• prepare and weigh the ingredients<br>• cut the ham in cubes |
| KNEADING | 10 min | 25 min | • combine ingredients 4 minutes (slow speed)<br>• finish at medium speed for 6 minutes<br>• add the fermented dough and the cubes of ham near the end of kneading |
| FIRST RISING | 50 min | 1 hr 25 | • depends on the consistency of the dough<br>• cover to prevent a skin from forming |
| SCALING | 5 min | 1 hr 30 | • round or gently shape the sections depending on the consistency of the dough |
| RESTING | 15 min | 1 hr 35 | • keep the dough away from drafts |
| SHAPING | 10 min | 1 hr 45 | • work into the desired shape |
| PROOFING | 1 hr to<br>1 hr 20 | 2 hr 45 | • use a proof box |
| PREPARING FOR BAKING | 5 min | 2 hr 50 | • inject steam before and during baking<br>• use a very hot oven for small loaves |
| BAKING | 18 to 28 min | 3 hr 10 | • be careful to not let the loaves dry out |
| COOLING | 5 min | 3 hr 15 | • allow the loaves to cool in baskets or on cooling racks. Do not stack them during cooling |

STORAGE : *Prosciutto bread has a limited shelf life when it is baked in split loaves*

# Paprika Bread (Pain au Paprika)

### Introduction

Most bread is served along with other foods; it is used as an accompaniment to a meal but should never dominate the flavor of any of the dishes. The character of a particular bread depends on a variety of factors such as its origin, the methods used in its preparation and the type of equipment used (e.g. wood- or gas-fired ovens).

Breads should be chosen according to what types of food they are being served with. Relatively bland foods such as cold meats require light, delicately flavored breads while spicy foods are best served with fuller-flavored breads.

Paprika bread has a dense crumb and holds well without drying out. It is easy to prepare.

### Storage

Like most breads, the shelf life of paprika bread benefits from a long first rising. Small loaves and rolls, however, have a shorter shelf life than large loaves. For this reason, some bakers prefer to bake rolls for sale in the morning and larger loaves for sale later in the day.

### Shapes used for paprika bread

Paprika bread dough can be baked in any size or shape but it is recommended that it be shaped in a distinctive way so it is not easily confused with other types.

Usually the size of the loaves varies from 300 to 500 g. (10.5 and 17.5 oz.).

### Appearance

Paprika bread has an appealing reddish crust and an appetizing, rust-colored crumb.

The loaves shown here are easily broken in half and shared.

### Serving paprika bread

Paprika bread is best served with grilled meats.

### Procedure

The work area should be between 22 and 25 °C (72 and 77 °F).

When using an electric mixer with a paddle blade, use a base temperature of 60 °C/204 °F. Knead the dough for 4 minutes at slow speed (frasing) followed by 5 minutes at medium speed.

When using a kneading machine, use a base temperature of 62 °C/ 208 °F. Knead the dough for 4 minutes at slow speed (frasing) and for 7 minutes more at medium speed.

## Ingredients

To prepare 3.3 kg. (7.3 lb.) of dough which will produce 11 loaves weighing 300 g. (10.5 oz.) or 6 loaves weighing 550 g. 19.5 oz.) each, the following ingredients are needed:

2 kg. bread flour (70.5 oz.)
40 g. salt (1.4 oz.)
40 g. yeast (1.4 oz.)
1.2 L. water (40.5 fl. oz.)
20 g. paprika (4 tsp.)

## Kneading

Combine the flour, the salt, and the yeast which has been dissolved in the water, in the bowl of the electric mixer or kneading machine.

Although the paprika can be added at any time during kneading, most bakers add it 1 minute before the end of kneading.

Check the consistency of the dough after kneading.

## Checking the kneaded dough

The temperature of the dough should be 24 to 25 °C (75 to 77 °F) at the completion of the kneading.

The dough should be have a relatively soft texture.

Cover the dough to prevent a skin from forming.

## First rising

Allow the dough to rise for 1 to 1 1/4 hours depending on the temperature and humidity of the rising area.

Punch down the dough or give it a turn 30 minutes into the kneading in order to eliminate carbon dioxide and reactivate the fermentation.

## Scaling

Divide the dough into sections by hand. Avoid using too much flour. Round the loaves and let them rest for 15 minutes.

## Shaping the loaves

Round the loaves a second time and let them rest for 10 minutes. Dust the tops of the loaves with rye or rice flour.

Split each section of dough in two with a rolling pin. Turn the loaves upside down on canvas cloths for proofing.

## Proofing

Allow approximately 1 hour and 10 minutes for proofing depending on the temperature of the proof box or steam chamber.

Avoid excess proofing.

## Baking

Preheat the oven to approximately 240 °C (475 °F) depending on the size of the loaves.

Inject steam into the oven before and during the first stage of baking to give the loaves a golden brown crust and an appealing sheen.

Smaller loaves weighing 300 g. (10.5 oz.) should be baked for 20 to 25 minutes, larger loaves slightly longer – 30 to 35 minutes. Check the loaves during baking to prevent the crust from becoming too dark. Place the loaves in wicker baskets or on cooling racks as soon as they come out of the oven.

| PAPRIKA BREAD | | | |
|---|---|---|---|
| **PREPARATION** | **15** min | **15** min | • calculate the temperatures<br>• prepare and weigh the raw ingredients |
| **KNEADING** | **9** min | **24** min | • knead for 4 minutes on slow speed<br>• continue for 5 minutes on medium speed<br>• add the paprika at the end of kneading |
| **FIRST RISING** | **1** hr | **1** hr **25** | • punch down the dough after 30 minutes |
| **SCALING** | **5** min | **1** hr **30** | • round the sections and let them rest |
| **RESTING** | **15** min | **1** hr **45** | |
| **SHAPING** | **7** min | **1** hr **52** | • work the sections into desired shape |
| **PROOFING** | **1** hr **10** | **3** hr **02** | • proof the loaves in a proof box<br>• watch the proofing; avoid overproofing |
| **PREPARING FOR BAKING** | **5** min | **3** hr **07** | • inject steam into the oven<br>• bake in a hot oven |
| **BAKING** | **20** min | **3** hr **30** | • carefully watch the coloring of the loaves<br>• lower the oven temperature near the end |
| **COOLING** | **5** min | **3** hr **35** | • arrange the breads in wicker baskets or on cooling racks |

**STORAGE** : Large loaves keep well but smaller loaves and rolls have a limited shelf life.

# Lemon Bread (Pain au Citron)

## Introduction

Lemon bread is made by adding lemon zests to bread dough. The combination works particularly well with rye bread, méteil bread (wheat/rye bread), peasant bread, and pullman bread.

Lemon bread is a relatively recent innovation. It is most popular around the holiday season when it is served with oysters and raw shellfish.

These loaves have a pleasing lemon scent which is noticeable as soon as the bread is sliced.

Here the loaves are presented in the shape of lemons which makes it easy to distinguish them from other types in the bakery.

Lemon bread can be prepared in the same way as other types without relying on special techniques.

The basic dough for lemon bread is prepared with a combination of wheat and rye flours. The lemon shape of the loaves also improves their shelf life. In the recipe given below, dough from a previous batch is incorporated into the lemon bread dough; this improves its shelf life.

Lemon bread can be sold up to 3 days after baking and can be served up to 4 days after baking.

### Appearance and shapes of lemon bread

Lemon bread can be baked in round loaves, thick loaves, or in the lemon shape shown above.

The weight of lemon loaves varies from 200 to 500 g. (7 to 17.5 oz.) or more.

Lemon bread has an appealing brown crust and a dense crumb. The crust is quite thick especially when rye flour is used.

### Serving lemon bread

Lemon bread is excellent when served with oysters, raw shellfish, and pork products such as pâtés, terrines, salami, etc.

## Procedure

The work area should be between 22 and 25 °C (72 and 77 °F).

When using an electric mixer with a paddle blade, use a base temperature of 64 °C/211 °F. Knead the dough for 4 minutes at slow speed (frasing) followed by 5 minutes at medium speed.

When using a kneading machine, use a base temperature of 68 °C/ 215 °F. Knead the dough for 4 minutes at slow speed (frasing) and for 7 minutes more at medium speed.

## Ingredients

To prepare 4 kg. (8.8 lb.) of dough which will produce 16 loaves weighing 250 g. (9 oz.) each or 10 loaves weighing 400 g. (14 oz.) each, the following ingredients are needed:

1.050 kg. rye flour (37 oz.)
600 g. white wheat flour (21 oz.)
750 g. fermented dough from a previous batch (6 hours minimum fermentation at 23 °C/73 °F).
40 g. salt (1.4 oz.)
40 g. yeast (1.4 oz.)
1.460 L. water (49.5 fl. oz.)
10 lemon zests
20 g. gluten (optional) (4 tsp.)

This recipe is based on a combination of wheat and rye flour (méteil bread). When preparing lemon flavored rye bread or pullman bread, prepare the dough in the regular way and incorpo-

rate the zests of 5 lemons per kilogram (2.2 lb.) of flour.

## Kneading

Place the rye flour, wheat flour, salt, and the yeast which has first been dissolved in the water called for in the recipe, in the bowl of the electric mixer or kneading machine.

Add the previously fermented bread dough 3 minutes before the end of kneading.

Add the lemon zests 1 minute before the end of kneading.

During kneading, check the consistency of the dough. When rye flour is used in bread dough, it is especially important that the dough not be kneaded for too long.

These breads are improved by using a well-fermented dough from a previous batch as shown here or a sourdough starter.

The temperature of the dough at the end of kneading should be 2 to 3 degrees Celsius (4 to 6 degrees Fahrenheit) higher than most types of bread dough.

## Checking the kneaded dough

The temperature of the dough after kneading should be from 26 to 27 °C (79 to 81 °F).

The dough should have a medium firm consistency.

Cover the dough to prevent a skin from forming.

## First rising

Let the dough rise for approximately 45 minutes depending on the consistency of the dough, the length of time it was kneaded, and the type of starter which was used.

## Shaping the loaves

Shape the dough into short, thick loaves with pointed ends. For a lemon shape, lightly round the sections of dough into ovals and work the ends so they come to a point.

Lemon bread loaves can also be decorated by sifting white flour over the tops and carefully scoring the loaves lengthwise.

## Proofing

Proof the loaves for approximately 1 hour depending on the temperature of the proof box or steam chamber.

Avoid excess proofing.

## Preparing for baking

Preheat the oven to 230 °C (450 °F). Inject steam into the oven before putting in the loaves.

## Baking

After several minutes of baking, eliminate the steam from the oven.

Bake 250 g. (9 oz.) loaves for 23 to 26 minutes and 500 g. (17.5 oz.) loaves for 30 to 35 minutes.

Be sure the loaves are thoroughly baked.

Arrange the loaves in wicker baskets or on cooling racks as soon as they come out of the oven.

# LEMON BREAD

| PREPARATION | 15 min | 15 min | • calculate the temperatures<br>• prepare and weigh the raw ingredients<br>• prepare the lemon zests |
|---|---|---|---|
| KNEADING | 9 min | 24 min | • knead for 4 minutes on slow speed<br>• continue for 5 minutes on medium speed<br>• add the fermented dough 3 minutes before the end of kneading<br>• add the lemon zests 1 minute before the end of kneading |
| FIRST RISING | 45 min | 1 hr 09 | • protect the dough from drafts |
| SCALING | 5 min | 1 hr 14 | • round the sections and let them rest |
| RESTING | 10 to 15 min | 1 hr 24 | |
| SHAPING | 7 min | 1 hr 31 | • work the sections into the desired shape |
| PROOFING | 1 hr | 2 hr 31 | • proof in a proof box or steam chamber<br>• do not overproof; dough is fragile |
| BEFORE BAKING | 5 min | 2 hr 36 | • saturate the oven with steam before baking |
| BAKING | 23 to 35 min | 3 hr | • make sure the loaves are thoroughly baked<br>• eliminate the steam from the oven halfway |
| COOLING | 5 min | 3 hr 05 | • arrange the breads in wicker baskets |

STORAGE : Lemon bread has a very good shelf life.

# Potato Bread (Pain à la Pomme de Terre)

### Introduction

The potato was first cultivated in South America in what are now Chili and Peru.

It was first popularized in France at the beginning of the 19th century by Parmentier. Since then it occasionally replaces some of the flour used for making bread. The primary advantage of substituting a certain amount of potato for flour is that it greatly improves the shelf life of the loaves.

It is possible to replace between 25 and 30% of the flour in a recipe with potato. If more potato is used, the bread dough looses its elasticity, becomes heavy, and will tear during proofing.

Potato bread has many of the same characteristics as dark grain breads which share its long shelf life. Despite its long shelf life, potato bread is best eaten within 24 hours of baking.

Potato bread is usually prepared with freshly mashed potatoes but it can also be prepared with potato starch or potato flakes.

Potato bread has an excellent flavor and a shiny, appetizing appearance.

### Storage

Potato bread has an excellent shelf life because potatoes and previously fermented dough are used in its preparation.

### Shapes used for potato bread

Potato bread is usually baked in thick long loaves, and round loaves. Occasionally it is also shaped into large country loaves. The size of the loaves usually varies from 250 g. (9 oz.) to 800 g. (28 oz.).

### Appearance

Loaves of potato bread should have a shiny, golden crust. The thickness of the crust varies depending on whether the oven temperature was decreased during baking and whether or not steam was used. In any case, the crust should have a pleasant, crunchy texture.

## Serving potato bread

Potato bread is excellent when served with cold red meats or fish.

## Procedure

The work area should be between 22 and 25 °C (72 and 77 °F).

When using an electric mixer with a paddle blade, use a base temperature of 58°/200 °F. Knead the dough for 4 minutes at slow speed (frasing) followed by 5 minutes at medium speed.

When using a kneading machine, use a base temperature of 208 °F/62 °C. Knead the dough for 4 minutes at slow speed (frasing) and for 8 minutes more at medium speed.

## Ingredients

To prepare 8 kg. (17.6 lb.) of dough which will produce 16, 500 g. (17 oz.) loaves or 32, 250 g. (9 oz.) loaves, the following ingredients are needed:
2 kg. white flour (70.5 oz.)
1.8 kg. light whole-wheat flour or 1 part standard whole-wheat flour to 7 parts bread flour (63.5 oz.)
880 g. mashed potatoes (31 oz.)
80 g. salt (2.8 oz.)
100 g. yeast (3.5 oz.)
2.24 l. water (76 fl. oz.)
50 g. powdered milk (1.8 oz.)

## Kneading

Combine the white flour, the bise flour (bise flour is a light whole-wheat flour which can be replaced by the mixture given above under " ingredients "), the salt, the powdered milk, the mashed potatoes or potato starch, and the yeast which has been first dissolved in the water, in the bowl of the electric mixer or kneading machine.

Check the consistency of the dough after the first stage of kneading (frasing); it should be relatively stiff.

Add the previously fermented dough to the fresh dough 3 minutes before the end of kneading.

## Checking the kneaded dough

At the end of kneading, the temperature of the dough should be 24 °C/75 °F.

Be careful to cover the dough after kneading to prevent the formation of a skin.

## First rising

The dough should be allowed to rise for 40 to 50 minutes depending on the temperature of the dough and the humidity and temperature of the rising area.

## Scaling

Section and weigh the dough by hand.

Gently shape the dough into round sections and let them rest for about 15 minutes before the final shaping.

## Shaping the loaves

Shape the sections of dough by hand.

Once the loaves have been formed, they can be partially rolled in rye flour so the tops of the loaves are floured.

## Proofing

Proofing usually requires from 50 to 70 minutes. The proofing should be carried out in a proof box or moist rising area.

Because potato bread dough is fragile, be especially careful to not let the dough proof for too long.

## Preparing for baking

Preheat the oven to approximately 240 °C (475 °F). The exact temperature should be adjusted depending on the size of the loaves.

Lower the temperature to 230 °C (450 °F) half way through the baking.

Make sausage or crisscross cuts in the loaves before baking.

## Baking

Inject steam into the oven before baking. Once the loaves are in the oven, additional steam should be injected in the oven near the beginning of baking.

Count on 20 to 25 minutes of baking for 250 g. (9 oz.) loaves and 30 to 35 minutes for large loaves of 500 g. (17 oz.).

As soon as the loaves come out of the oven, arrange them in a basket. Avoid heaping them up on one another while they are cooling.

## POTATO BREAD

| | | | |
|---|---|---|---|
| PREPARATION | 15 min | 15 min | • calculate the temperatures<br>• prepare and weigh the ingredients |
| KNEADING | 12 min | 27 min | • combine ingredients 4 minutes (slow speed)<br>• finish at medium speed for 8 minutes<br>• add the fermented dough near the end of kneading |
| FIRST RISING | 45 min | 1 hr 12 | • cover to prevent a skin from forming |
| SCALING | 5 min | 1 hr 17 | • gently round the sections of dough |
| RESTING | 15 min | 1 hr 32 | |
| SHAPING | 7 min | 1 hr 39 | • work into the desired shape |
| PROOFING | 1 hr | 2 hr 39 | • use a proof box<br>• do not let the loaves rise too much |
| PREPARING FOR BAKING | 5 min | 2 hr 44 | • inject steam before and during baking<br>• adjust the oven temperature as needed |
| BAKING | 20 to 35 min | 3 hr 15 | • make adjustements for the size and coloring of the loaves<br>• blow the steam out of the oven near the end |
| COOLING | 5 min | 3 hr 20 | • allow the loaves to cool in baskets or on cooling racks. |

STORAGE : Potato bread can be sold up to 2 days after baking.
It may be eaten up to 3 or 4 days after baking

# Cheese Bread (Pain au Fromage)

## Introduction

When selecting bread to be served with a meal, many of the same criteria used for selecting wines can be applied. Bread should be carefully chosen so that it goes well with the foods being served. When serving breads over the course of an elaborate meal, delicately flavored breads with a pale or white crumb should be served first. As the meal progresses, fuller flavored and darker breads can be served. The only exception to this rule is that white bread can be served with the cheese (in France, cheese is served after the main course). The cheese bread contains cubes of gruyère cheese worked into a white bread base. The bread is then rolled out into flat loaves with a rolling pin so that it resembles a fougasse provençale.

## Storage

Because cheese bread is rolled out into rectangles, it contains relatively little crumb. It should be eaten the same day it is baked. If kept for too long, it becomes brittle and dry and has almost the consistency of a thick cracker.

## Shapes used for cheese bread

Cheese bread dough can be baked in almost any shape including thick elongated loaves and traditional shapes. The shape presented here, however, is similar to a traditional fougasse.

## Serving cheese bread

Cheese bread is excellent when served with salads, fresh pasta, and rice but it can also be served alone as a snack.

## Procedure

The work area should be between 22 and 25 °C (72 and 77 °F).

When using an electric mixer, use a base temperature of 60 °C/204 °F. Knead the dough for 4 minutes at slow speed (frasing) followed by 5 minutes at medium speed.

When using a kneading machine, use a base temperature of 62 °C/208 °F. Knead the dough for 4 minutes at slow speed (frasing) and for 7 minutes more at medium speed.

## Ingredients

To prepare 2 kg. (4.4 lb.) of dough which will produce 13 fougasse style cheese breads weighing 150 g. (5.5 oz.) each or 5 larger fougasse style breads weighing 400 g. (14 oz.) each, the following ingredients are needed:

1 kg. bread flour (35 oz.)
100 ml. vegetable oil (3.5 fl. oz.)

20 g. salt (4 tsp.) - 20 g. yeast (4 tsp.)
110 g. fermented dough (4 oz.)
500 ml. water (17 fl. oz.)
250 g. diced gruyère cheese (9 oz.)

## Kneading

Combine the flour, the salt, the vegetable oil, and the yeast which has been first dissolved in the water, in the bowl of the electric mixer or kneading machine. Check the consistency of the dough after the fist stage of kneading (frasing); it should be relatively stiff.

Add the previously fermented dough to the fresh dough 4 minutes before the end of kneading. Add the diced cheese 1 minute before the end of kneading.

## Checking the kneaded dough

At the end of kneading, the temperature of the dough should be 25 °C/77 °F.

Be careful to cover the dough after kneading to prevent the formation of a skin.

## First rising

The dough should be allowed to rise for 30 minutes depending on the temperature of the dough and the humidity and temperature of the rising area. Be sure to keep the dough away from drafts or sudden changes in temperature.

## Scaling

Cut the dough into equal size sections. Fold them over themselves and let them rest for 15 minutes so they will be easier to roll out.

## Shaping the loaves

Roll the dough into rectangular sheets using a rolling pin. For 150 g. (5.5 oz.) loaves, the rectangles of dough should measure 16 cm (6.5 in.) long by 10 cm. (4 in.) wide by 7 mm. (1/4 in.) thick.

The rectangles can then be further shaped into traditional fougasse shapes (see volume 1). Place the rolled out dough on baking sheets lined with parchment paper. The paper is necessary to prevent the cheese in the breads from sticking to the oven floor.

## Proofing

Proofing usually requires approximately 1 hour. The proofing should be carried out in an area free from drafts such as a proof box or moist rising area.

Avoid proofing the cheese bread for too long.

## Preparing for baking

The fougasses should be baked in a hot oven. Preheat the oven to between 240 and 250 °C (450 and 475 °F) depending on the size and thickness of the breads.

When cheese bread is baked in the traditional fougasse shape, it should be well cooked but never dried out.

## Baking

Inject steam into the oven before baking. Once the loaves are in the oven, additional steam should be injected during the first half of the baking.

Flat, fougasse style cheese breads should be baked for 13 minutes for 150 g. (5.5 oz.) loaves and for approximately 18 minutes for 400 g. (14 oz.) loaves.

## CHEESE BREAD

| PREPARATION | 15 min | 15 min | • calculate the temperatures<br>• prepare and weigh the ingredients<br>• cut the gruyere cheese into dice |
|---|---|---|---|
| KNEADING | 9 min | 24 min | • combine ingredients 4 minutes (slow speed)<br>• finish at medium speed for 5 minutes<br>• add the fermented dough and the cubes of cheese near the end of kneading |
| FIRST RISING | 30 min | 54 min | • cover to prevent a skin from forming |
| SCALING | 7 min | 1 hr 01 | • weigh and gently shape the sections |
| RESTING | 15 min | 1 hr 16 | |
| SHAPING | 10 min | 1 hr 26 | • roll out with a rolling pin and place on sheets of parchment paper |
| PROOFING | 1 hr | 2 hr 26 | • do not let the loaves rise too much |
| PREPARING | 5 min | 2 hr 31 | • use a very hot oven |
| BAKING | 13 to 18 min | 2 hr 45 | • do not bake too long or dough will dry out |
| COOLING | 5 min | 2 hr 50 | • cool in baskets or on cooling racks |

STORAGE : Cheese bread should be eaten the same day it is baked

# Tunisian-style Bread (Pain Tunisian)

## Introduction

Tunisian bread is simple and straightforward to prepare. It is made with semolina flour traditionally made from North African durum wheat and is usually shaped into round, cake-like loaves. The loaves are rolled out flat and then brushed with egg wash to help them color. They are then usually baked in a moderate oven.

Tunisian bread contains vegetable oil and powdered milk. The vegetable oil gives a soft texture to the crumb while the powdered milk enriches the dough, improves its flavor and helps the loaves color in the oven. White bread flour, which comprises 50% of the flour used in the recipe helps the bread rise.

Tunisian bread has an appetizing, rustic appearance.

## Storage

The ingredients used and the shape of Tunisian bread both contribute to a long shelf life.

## Shapes used for Tunisian bread

Tunisian bread is usually shaped into flat, round, cake-like loaves. The loaves usually weigh from 300 g. (10.5 oz.) to 500 g. (17.5 oz.).

## Appearance

Tunisian bread has a light brown crust. The crust is thin and delicate due to the vegetable oil in the dough.

Tunisian bread should not be allowed to rise too much at any stage; the loaves should be flat with a dense, tight crumb.

## Serving Tunisian bread

Its agreeable flavor makes Tunisian bread well suited to accompany a wide variety of dishes. It can also be eaten alone as a snack.

## Procedure

The work area should be between 22 and 25 °C (72 and 77 °F).

When using an electric mixer, use a base temperature of 60 °C/204 °F. Knead the dough for 4 minutes at slow speed (frasing) followed by 5 minutes at medium speed.

When using a kneading machine, use a base temperature of 208 °F/62 °C. Knead the dough for 4 minutes at slow speed (frasing) and for 7 minutes more at medium speed.

## Ingredients

To prepare 4.9 kg. (10.8 lb.) of dough which will produce 14 loaves weighing 350 g. (12.5 oz.) each, the following ingredients are needed:

1.5 kg. white bread flour (53 oz.)
1.5 kg. semolina flour (53 oz.)
60 g. salt (2.1 oz.)
90 g. yeast (3.2 oz.)
60 g. powdered milk (2.1 oz.)
750 ml. vegetable oil (25.5 fl. oz.)
940 ml. water (32 fl. oz.)

## Kneading

Combine the bread flour, the semolina flour, the salt, the powdered milk, the vegetable oil, and the yeast which has been first dissolved in the water, in the bowl of the electric mixer or kneading machine.

Check the consistency of the dough after the first stage of kneading (frasing); it should be relatively stiff.

Cover the dough after needing to prevent a skin from forming on its surface.

## First rising

The dough should be allowed to rise for 30 minutes depending on the temperature of the dough and the humidity and temperature of the rising area. Be sure to keep the dough away from drafts or sudden changes in temperature.

## Scaling

Weigh the dough into sections by hand. Be careful not to use much flour when working with the dough.

Round the sections of dough and let them rest for 15 minutes before the final shaping.

## Shaping the loaves

Flatten each of the rounded sections of dough into disks with a rolling pin. Place the disks either directly on the baking surface or on sheets of parchment paper.

## Proofing

Proofing usually requires approximately 1 hour. The proofing should be carried out in an area free from drafts such as a proof box or moist rising area.

## Preparing for baking

Preheat the oven to approximately 250 °C (475 °F).

Brush the surface of the loaves with egg wash to help them color during baking.

Poke the surface of the loaves with a skewer to make sure they rise evenly.

## Baking

Inject steam into the oven before putting in the loaves. Additional steam should also be injected into the oven at the beginning of baking.

Watch the loaves closely during baking. If the surface of the loaves puffs up unevenly, poke the swelled up section with a skewer.

Count on 15 to 18 minutes of baking for 300 g. (10.5 oz.) loaves.

As soon as the flat loaves come out of the oven, place them in wicker baskets or on racks to cool.

## TUNISIAN-STYLE BREAD

| | | | |
|---|---|---|---|
| **PREPARATION** | **15** min | **15** min | • calculate the temperatures<br>• prepare and weigh the ingredients |
| **KNEADING** | **9** min | **24** min | • combine ingredients 4 minutes (slow speed)<br>• finish at medium speed for 5 minutes |
| **FIRST RISING** | **30** min | **54** min | • cover to prevent a skin from forming |
| **SCALING** | **5** min | **59** min | • weigh and gently shape the sections of dough |
| **RESTING** | **15** min | **1** hr **14** | |
| **SHAPING** | **7** min | **1** hr **21** | • roll out into disk shaped loaves |
| **PROOFING** | **1** hr | **2** hr **21** | • keep the dough away from drafts |
| **PREPARING FOR BAKING** | **5** min | **2** hr **26** | • poke the loaves with a skewer<br>• brush the loaves with egg wash<br>• bake in a hot oven |
| **BAKING** | **13** to **18** min | **2** hr **40** | • do not let the loaves get too brown<br>• do not bake for too long |
| **COOLING** | **5** min | **2** hr **46** | • cool in baskets or on cooling racks. |

**STORAGE :** *Tunisian-Style bread has a fairly good shelf life*

# Arab-style Bread (Pain Arabe)

## Introduction

Traditional Arab-style bread (also called Pita bread) is still baked in the Middle East where an extremely hot oven (500 °C/925 °F) is used. The dough is rolled out into 4 mm. (1/8-in.) disks and baked for only 1 minute. The disks of dough swell quickly, leaving the inside of the loaves hollow. The insides of the breads are then filled with vegetables, meat, or cheese.

In Europe and the United States, few bakeries are equipped with ovens which provide the necessary high temperatures. For this reason, when Arab-style bread is prepared in these countries, it is baked in small round loaves which have been enriched with butter.

Allow the butter-enriched dough to rest for several minutes then cut it into different sized sections. Roll the sections together with a rolling pin or a dough sheeter.

Once the dough has been rolled out into strips, thin them on one side. Make cuts along 1/3 of the length of the strips keeping them 1 cm. (1/2 in.) apart.

Lastly, roll the strips of dough around themselves.

The dough should now have a rosette shape. The seeds are added just before baking.

Here the loaves are shown as rolls which have been enriched with butter.

## Storage

The shelf life of Arab-style breads is good especially considering the size of the loaves.

## Shape and appearance of the loaves

The dough is usually baked in small round loaves weighing 80 to 125 g. (2.5 to 4.5 oz.) each. Larger loaves are also baked in round shapes.

Arab-style bread should have a fine crust with a pale brown sheen; it should be smooth and appetizing.

Smaller loaves have a relatively dense crumb with a fine texture.

## Procedure

The work area should be between 22 and 25 °C (72 and 77 °F).

When using an electric mixer with a paddle blade, use a base temperature of 60 °C/204 °F. Knead the dough for 4 minutes at slow speed (frasing) followed by 6 minutes at medium speed.

When using a kneading machine, use a base temperature of 62 °C/ 208 °F. Knead the dough for 4 minutes at slow speed (frasing) and for 10 minutes more at medium speed.

## Ingredients

To prepare 5.6 kg. (12.5 lb.) of dough which will produce 70 loaves weighing 80 g. (2.8 oz.) each or 45 loaves weighing 125 g. (4.5 oz.) each, the following ingredients are needed:

1.5 kg. whole wheat flour (53 oz.)
1.5 kg. bise flour (53 oz.) (see note)
660 g. fermented dough from a previous batch (23 oz.) (fermented for at least 4 hours at 20 °C/68 °L)
1.65 l. water (58 fl. oz.)
60 g. salt (2.1 oz.)
100 g. yeast (3.5 oz.)
130 g. butter (4.5 oz.)

*Note:*   Bise flour is a variety of light, whole wheat flour which is marketed in France. In the United States, a mixture of half white bread flour and half whole wheat flour can be substituted.

## Kneading

Place the whole wheat flour, the bise flour, the salt, the butter, and the yeast which has been dissolved in the water, in the bowl for the mixer or kneading machine.

When the kneading is almost completed, add the fermented dough. If the fermented dough is added earlier, it may become over-oxygenated (remember it has been kneaded once before).

Check the consistency of the dough after the first stage of kneading (frasing).

## Checking the kneaded dough

The temperature of the dough should be from 24 to 25 °C (75 to 77 °F) at the end of kneading.

Protect the dough from drafts and make sure it is covered to prevent the formation of a skin.

## First rising

Let the dough rise for 25 to 30 minutes depending on the temperature and humidity of the work area.

## Scaling

Divide the dough into sections having the desired weight.

Round the loaves and let them rest for 9 minutes.

## Shaping the loaves

Round the loaves a second time.
Place the loaves on canvas cloths or on sheet pans.

## Proofing

Proof the loaves in a proof box or steam chamber for 1 to 1 1/4 hours depending on the temperature of the work area.

## Preparing for baking

Preheat the oven to 260 °C (500 °F).
Score the loaves with a single cross or crisscross pattern.

## Baking

Inject steam into the oven before and during the first stage of baking.

Bake for 14 to 16 minutes for 80 g. (2.5 oz.) loaves and for 16 to 18 minutes for 125 g. (4.5 oz.) loaves. Be careful to not overcook the loaves.

As soon as the loaves come out of the oven, arrange them in wicker baskets or on cooling racks.

# ARAB-STYLE BREAD

| PREPARATION | 15 min | 15 min | • calculate the temperatures<br>• prepare and weigh the raw ingredients |
|---|---|---|---|
| KNEADING | 10 min | 25 min | • knead for 4 minutes on slow speed<br>• continue for 6 minutes on medium speed<br>• add the fermented dough at the end of kneading |
| FIRST RISING | 25 to 30 min | 50 min | • the rising time will depend on the consistency of the dough |
| SCALING | 5 min | 55 min | • round and let rest for 10 minutes |
| RESTING | 10 to 15 min | 1 hr 05 | • make sure the dough is covered and protected from air |
| SHAPING | 5 min | 1 hr 10 | • round the sections of dough into disks |
| PROOFING | 1 hr to 1 hr 15 | 2 hr 10 | • proof the loaves in a proof box or steam chamber |
| PREPARING FOR BAKING | 5 min | 2 hr 15 | • inject steam into the oven<br>• the loaves can be coated with poppy seeds or sesame seeds before baking |
| BAKING | 14 to 18 min | 2 hr 30 | • bake the loaves in a hot oven |
| COOLING | 5 min | 2 hr 35 | • arrange the breads in wicker baskets |

STORAGE : *Arab-style bread has a limited shelf life because of the small size of the loaves*

# Three Seasons Bread (Pain des 3 Saisons)

## Introduction

Country breads are often based on a combination of rye flour and whole wheat flour or wheat flour to which some rye flour has been added. The amount of rye flour used depends on the region and the style of bread being prepared. Three seasons bread is based on Viennese bread dough to which dried fruits and nuts have been added. The resulting bread has a delicate crumb, a soft texture, and an appealing brown crust. It also has a good shelf life. The creamy colored crumb is particularly attractive when offset by the dried fruits and nuts.

## Storage

Three seasons bread can be sold up to 2 days after it is baked and eaten for up to 3 days after. Fermented dough or sponge starter incorporated into the dough will shorten the rising time needed and also improve the flavor, appearance, and shelf life of the breads.

## Shapes and appearance

Three seasons bread can be shaped into short, thick loaves or in round loaves.

Three seasons bread has a fine, crunchy crust with a light, golden brown sheen. The crumb is slightly sweet and has an airy " melt-in-the-mouth " texture.

## Serving three seasons bread

Three seasons bread can be spread with butter and served at lunch or used to accompany salads. It also makes an excellent afternoon snack, especially when served with chocolates.

Three seasons bread is rich enough so that it can be eaten anytime of the day as a snack.

## Procedure

When using an electric mixer with a paddle blade, use a base temperature of 60 ºC/204 ºF. Knead the dough for 4 minutes at slow speed (frasing) followed by 6 minutes at medium speed.

When using a kneading machine, use a base temperature of 60 ºC/204 ºF. Knead the dough for 4 minutes at slow speed (frasing) and for 9 minutes more at medium speed.

## Ingredients

To prepare 2.5 kg. (5.5 lb.) of dough

which will produce 5 loaves weighing 500 g. (17.5 oz.) each or 25 miniature loaves weighing 100 g. (3.5 oz.) each, the following ingredients are needed:
1 kg. high gluten bread flour (35 oz.)
20 g. salt (4 tsp.) - 150 g. butter (5.5 oz.)
40 g. yeast (1.4 oz.) - 50 g. sugar (1.7 oz.)
40 g. powdered milk (1.4 oz.)
300 g. fermented dough from a previous batch (10.5 oz.)
600 ml. water (20.5 fl. oz.)
100 g. hazelnuts (3.5 oz.)
100 g. walnuts (3.5 oz.)
100 g. raisins (3.5 oz.)

## Kneading

Place the flour, the salt, the sugar, the butter, the powdered milk, and the yeast which has been dissolved in the water, in the bowl of the mixer or kneading machine. Halfway through the kneading, add the fermented dough.

Add the dried fruits and nuts 30 seconds before turning off the mixer or kneading machine.

The temperature of the dough should be 25 °C (77 °F) at the end of kneading. Protect the dough from drafts and make sure it is covered to prevent the formation of a skin.

## First rising

Allow the dough to rise for approximately 40 minutes depending on the temperature and humidity of the work area. The dough can be punched down halfway through the fermentation to improve rising.

## Scaling and shaping the loaves

Divide and weigh the dough into different sized sections depending on the tastes of the customers.

Round the loaves and let them rest for about 15 minutes.

Shape the loaves by hand into the desired shapes. Place the larger sections of dough on canvas cloths. Smaller loaves can be placed on special sheet pans used for Viennese breads.

## Proofing

Proof the loaves for approximately 1 hour depending on the temperature and the holding power of the dough (this is a function of the method used). Bake the loaves on sheet pans or canvas cloths.

## Preparing for baking

Preheat the oven to 250 °C (475 °F) for miniature loaves or to 240 °C (450 °F) for large loaves which should be well browned but not overcooked.

Poke holes into the loaves or score them using a sausage cut.

## Baking

Inject steam into the oven before and during the first stage of baking.

Bake 500 g. (17.5 oz.) loaves for 20 to 25 minutes and 100 g. (3.5 oz.) loaves for 10 to 15 minutes.

Keep close watch on the loaves during baking. They should have a golden brown crust and a moist crumb.

These breads are especially fragile so they should be left on racks until they have completely cooled.

# THREE SEASONS BREAD

| PREPARATION | 15 min | 15 min | • calculate the temperatures<br>• prepare and weigh the raw ingredients |
|---|---|---|---|
| KNEADING | 12 min | 27 min | • knead on slow and then medium speed<br>• keep checking the consistency of the dough |
| FIRST RISING | 40 min | 1 hr 07 | • the dough can be punched down halfway |
| SCALING | 5 min | 1 hr 12 | • weigh and round the sections |
| RESTING | 15 min | 1 hr 27 | • cover the sections |
| SHAPING | 8 min | 1 hr 35 | • gently work the sections of dough |
| PROOFING | 1 hr | 2 hr 35 | • proofing time will depend on the temperature<br>• protect the loaves from air during proofing |
| PREPARING FOR BAKING | 5 min | 2 hr 40 | • inject steam into the oven<br>• carefully regulate the oven temperature<br>• score the loaves |
| BAKING | 15 to 25 min | 3 hr 05 | • baking time depends on the size of the loaves<br>• do not let the loaves bake too long and dry out |
| COOLING | 5 min | 3 hr 10 | • arrange the breads in wicker baskets as soon as they come out of the oven |

STORAGE : *Three seasons bread can be sold up to 2 days after baking. It can be served up to 3 days after baking.*

# Jewish-style Bread (Pain Juif)

## Introduction

This appealing bread is characterized by its spiral, corkscrew shape.

Jewish-style bread has an excellent flavor which is enhanced with the addition of herbs before baking. It has a creamy colored crumb, the result of a shortened kneading time which preserves the carotin contained in the flour.

Vegetable oil is added to Jewish-style bread to soften the dough and make it more elastic. Eggs are also used to enrich the dough, give the crumb a finer, softer texture, and to provide lecithin which improves the physical and nutritive properties of the dough. The addition of the eggs and vegetable oil also increases the volume of the finished loaves.

## Storage

Jewish-style bread has a relatively good shelf life.

## Shapes used for Jewish-style bread

Jewish-style bread is usually shaped into round loaves or twisted, spiral loaves. Usually it is sprinkled with Provençal herbs just before it is baked which enhance both its flavor and appearance.

## Appearance

Jewish-style bread has a very characteristic appearance. It has a tight textured, pale yellow crumb, and an appealing brown crust.

## Serving Jewish-style bread

Jewish-style bread, because it is sprinkled with Provençal herbs, goes well with grilled meats and fish. When prepared without herbs it can be served in the same way as ordinary French bread.

## Procedure

The work area should be between 22 and 25 °C (72 and 77 °F).

When using an electric mixer with a paddle blade, use a base temperature of 60 °C/204 °F. Knead the dough for 4 minutes at slow speed (frasing) followed by 4 minutes at medium speed.

When using a kneading machine, use a base temperature of 62 °C/208 °F. Knead the dough for 4 minutes at slow speed (frasing) and for 6 minutes more at medium speed.

### Ingredients

To prepare 6.8 kg. (15 lb.) of dough which will produce 16, 400 g. (14 oz.) loaves, the following ingredients are needed:

4 kg. semolina flour (8.8 lb.)
80 g. salt (2.8 oz.)
120 g. yeast (4 oz.)
120 ml. vegetable oil (4 fl. oz.)
8 eggs
2 l. (app.) water (67 fl. oz.)

### Kneading

Combine the semolina flour, the salt, the vegetable oil, the eggs, and the yeast which has been first dissolved in the water, in the bowl of the electric mixer or kneading machine.

The oil can also be added at the second stage of kneading–when the mixer or kneading machine is turned to medium speed.

Check the consistency of the dough after the first stage of kneading (frasing).

### Checking the kneaded dough

The temperature of the kneaded dough should be approximately 26° (79 °F).

The dough should have a medium-firm consistency.

Cover the kneaded dough to prevent a skin from forming on its surface.

### Resting the dough

The kneaded dough should be allowed to rest for 10 to 15 minutes depending on the consistency and strength of the dough.

### First rising

The dough should be allowed to rise for 10 to 15 minutes depending on the temperature of the dough and the humidity and temperature of the rising area. Be sure to keep the dough away from drafts or sudden changes in temperature.

### Scaling

Section and weigh the dough by hand. Fold the sections over themselves if twisted loaves are being prepared or gently mound them for round loaves.

Let the shaped sections rest for 10 minutes.

### Shaping

These loaves should be shaped by hand.

Gently round the sections of dough. Wait for 10 minutes and then press on them to flatten.

For "corkscrew" loaves, work the sections of dough into lengths using the same method as for baguettes but leaving the center somewhat thicker than the ends. Take the two ends of the lengths of dough and twist them in opposite directions.

Place the loaves on sheets of parchment paper or directly on the baking surface.

### Proofing

Allow the loaves to proof for approximately 1 hour in a proof box or moist rising area.

Watch the loaves closely during proofing. They should not be allowed to over rise.

### Preparing for baking

Preheat the oven to approximately 240 °C (475 °F).

Brush the loaves with egg wash and sprinkle them with provençal herbs (herbes de Provençe).

### Baking

Inject steam into the oven before baking. Once the loaves are in the oven, additional steam can be injected into the oven during the beginning of baking.

Count on approximately 20 minutes for 400 g. (14 oz.) "corkscrew" loaves and from 25 to 30 minutes for 400 g. (14 oz.) round loaves.

Carefully watch the baking to prevent the loaves from drying out.

As soon as the loaves come out of the oven, arrange them in a basket or on a cooling rack.

## JEWISH-STYLE BREAD

| PREPARATION | 15 min | 15 min | • calculate the temperatures<br>• prepare and weigh the ingredients |
|---|---|---|---|
| KNEADING | 8 min | 23 min | • combine ingredients 4 minutes (slow speed)<br>• finish at medium speed for 4 minutes |
| FIRST RISING | 10 to 15 min | 38 min | • this short rising is to allow the dough to rest |
| SCALING | 5 min | 43 min | • fold the sections of dough over themselves |
| RESTING | 10 min | 53 min | |
| SHAPING | 7 min | 1 hr | • shape into round or "corkscrew" loaves |
| PROOFING | 1 hr | 2 hr | • proof the loaves in a proof box |
| BEFORE BAKING | 5 min | 2 hr 05 | • inject steam before and during baking |
| BAKING | 20 min | 2 hr 25 | • do not let the loaves dry out |
| COOLING | 5 min | 2 hr 30 | • cool in baskets or on cooling racks |

STORAGE : *Jewish-Style bread has a good shelf life*

# Bavarian-style Bread (Pain de Bavière)

## Introduction

As the name indicates, Bavarian-style bread originated in Germany. The ingredients used in its preparation vary depending on the region, but rye flour and white bread flour are always included. Bise flour, a light style whole-wheat flour is also sometimes used. Bavarian-style bread is usually made using previously fermented dough or a yeast starter. Either of these encourages the development of lactic and acetic acid which improve the bread's flavor and shelf life.

Because Bavarian-style bread contains a fairly high percentage of rye flour, it is necessary to use a starter or fermented dough which has had at least 8 hours to ferment and mature. In this way, the acid level is high enough to guarantee successful fermentation and baking. Bavarian-style bread has an appetizing appearance, an excellent tangy flavor, and is highly nutritious.

Bavarian-style bread has an excellent shelf life due both to the use of fermented dough or starter and to the rye flour it contains.

## Shapes used for Bavarian-style bread

Bavarian-style bread is usually baked in round loaves with leaf designs cut into their surfaces. The size stet of the loaves varies from 500 g. (17.5 oz.) to 1 kg. (35 oz.).

The loaves have a relatively thick, brown crust.

The loaves are well rounded, rise to medium height during baking, and have a relatively tight structured crumb.

## Serving Bavarian-style bread

Bavarian-style bread is excellent with oysters, raw seafood platters, and pork products such as pâté, salami, and ham.

## Procedure

The work area should be between 22 and 25 °C (72 and 77 °F).

When using an electric mixer with a paddle blade, use a base temperature of 62 °C/208 °F. Knead the dough for 4 minutes at slow speed (frasing) followed by 4 minutes at medium speed.

When using a kneading machine, use a base temperature of 64 °C/211 °F. Knead the dough for 4 minutes at slow speed (frasing) and for 7 minutes more at medium speed.

## Ingredients

To prepare 9.3 kg. (20.5 lb.) of dough which will produce 17 loaves weighing 550 g. (19.5 oz.) or 10 loaves weighing 935 g. (33 oz.) each, the following ingredients are needed:

1 kg. white bread flour (35 oz.)
1 kg. bise flour (light style whole-wheat flour–a mixture of 1 part whole-wheat flour to 7 parts white bread flour can be substituted.)
1 kg. light pumpernickel rye flour (35 oz.)
100 g. salt (3.5 oz.)
150 g. yeast (5.5 oz.)
1 kg. fermented dough (35 oz.)
3.1 l. water (105 fl. oz.)
30 g. gluten (optional) (1 oz.)
30 ml. wine vinegar (optional) (1 fl. oz.)

### Kneading

Combine the different flours, the salt, the gluten, the vinegar, and the yeast which has been first dissolved in the water, in the bowl of the electric mixer or kneading machine.

Check the consistency of the dough after the first stage of kneading (frasing).

Add the fermented dough 2 to 3 minutes before the end of kneading.

### Checking the kneaded dough

The temperature of the kneaded dough should be approximately 26° (79 °F).

The dough should have a medium stiff consistency.

Cover the kneaded dough to prevent a skin from forming on its surface.

### First rising

The dough should be allowed to rise for 40 minutes depending on the temperature of the dough and the humidity and temperature of the rising area.

### Scaling

Section and weigh the dough by hand.

Gently round the sections of dough and let them rest for 15 minutes.

### Shaping the loaves

Bavarian-style bread dough can be worked into virtually any shape but round loaves are the most common.

Place the loaves either directly on the baking surface or in canvas cloths. Make sure the seam is on the bottom of the loaves.

### Proofing

The loaves should be allowed to proof for between 1 hour and 1 hour and 15 minutes. It is best to carry out the proofing in a proof box or moist rising area to help prevent a skin from forming on the loaves.

Be careful to not let the loaves over rise.

### Preparing for baking

Preheat the oven to approximately 230 °C (450 °F). The temperature should be adjusted according to the size of the loaves. Make decorative cuts in the surface of the breads by making two oblique rows of lines.

### Baking

Inject steam into the oven before and during the first stage of baking.

Count on approximately 35 minutes for 500 g (17.5 oz.) loaves and 50 to 55 minutes for 1 kg. (35 oz.) loaves.

Let the loaves dry out slightly at the end of the baking.

## BAVARIAN-STYLE BREAD

| PREPARATION | 15 min | 15 min | • calculate the temperatures<br>• prepare and weigh the ingredients |
|---|---|---|---|
| KNEADING | 11 min | 26 min | • combine ingredients 4 minutes (slow speed)<br>• finish at medium speed for 7 minutes<br>• add the fermented dough 4 minutes before the end of kneading |
| FIRST RISING | 40 min | 1 hr 06 | • the dough can be punched down after 20 minutes if it seems too soft |
| SCALING | 5 min | 1 hr 11 | • round the sections of dough and allow to rest |
| RESTING | 15 min | 1 hr 26 | |
| SHAPING | 9 min | 1 hr 35 | • work into the desired shape |
| PROOFING | 1 hr | 2 hr 35 | • protect the loaves from drafts<br>• do not let the loaves rise too much |
| PREPARING FOR BAKING | 5 min | 2 hr 40 | • inject steam before and during baking<br>• adjust the oven temperature as needed |
| BAKING | 35 to 55 min | 3 hr 15 | • the loaves should be well cooked even slightly dry |
| COOLING | 5 min | 3 hr 20 | • cool in baskets or on cooling racks |

STORAGE : Bavarian-Style bread can be sold up to 2 or 3 days after baking
It may be eaten up to 3 or 4 days after baking

# Italian-style Hand Bread (Main Italienne)

## Introduction

Although Italian in origin, these fanciful breads are typically baked in southern France.

## Type of bread dough used

Standard bread dough or country bread dough.

Olive oil can be added to the bread (about 10%) to give it a more regional character.

Oil added to the bread dough gives it a softer dough and a finer crumb. Oil also lengthens the shelf life of these breads.

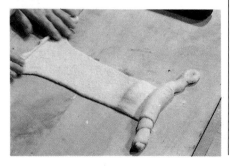

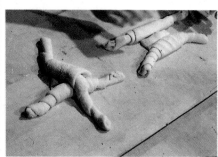

## Shaping the hands

Roll the dough into a thin sheet about 70 by 15 cm. (28 by 6 in.) with a rolling pin or dough sheeter.

Tightly roll each end of the sheet until the two rolls meet in the center.

Flatten the center of the two attached rolls with a rolling pin (the rolling pin should be perpendicular to the rolls of dough).

Fold the top half of the dough over the bottom half so that the top rolls of dough fit between the bottom rolls thus forming a hand with four fingers.

*Note:* The heavier and thicker the rolls of dough, the more it is necessary to roll the fingers to lengthen them so that the hands are well-proportioned.

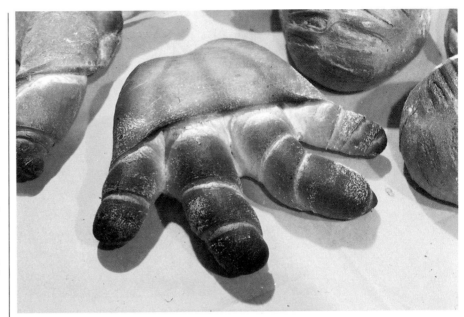

## Baking

Place the sheets of parchment paper with the hands on the oven conveyor or directly on the peel if they have been proofed on canvas cloths.

Make sure the oven is filled with steam before putting in the loaves.

Bake the loaves at 240 °C (450 °F) for 15 to 20 minutes.

Be careful to not let the loaves dry out; they should be relatively soft-textured.

## Proofing

Allow the hands to rise on canvas cloths or on sheets of parchment paper. They should double in volume.

| ITALIAN-STYLE HAND BREAD | | | |
|---|---|---|---|
| **PREPARATION** | **15** min | **15** min | • calculate the temperatures<br>• prepare and weigh the raw ingredients |
| **KNEADING** | **10** min | **25** min | • knead the dough for 4 minutes (slow speed)<br>• knead for 6 minutes more on medium speed |
| **FIRST RISING** | **30** min | **55** min | • will depend on the strength of the dough<br>• protect the dough from air during rising |
| **SCALING** | **5** min | **1** hr | • fold the sections |
| **SHAPING** | **15** min | **1** hr **15** | • shape the dough to form the fingers |
| **PROOFING** | **1** hr | **2** hr **15** | • make sure the hand loaves are well proofed |
| **PREPARING FOR BAKING** | **5** min | **2** hr **20** | • bake the loaves directly on the oven floor or on sheet pans covered with parchment paper |
| **BAKING** | **20** to **25** min | **2** hr **40** | • loaves should be only lightly browned<br>• the loaves should be soft textured |
| **COOLING** | **5** min | **2** hr **45** | • arrange the breads on cooling racks |

**NOTE :** *The oil helps develop a delicate, crumbly crust with a bright, appealing sheen. The oil also improves the shelf life of the breads and gives the breads a soft crumb.*

# *Chapter 3*
# Elaborately Shaped Breads

### *A simple way to diversify your selections*

It is amazing how many differently shaped breads can be prepared using standard bread dough or country bread dough.

Twenty elaborately shaped breads are presented in this chapter. This completes the selection of breads presented in volume 1. Many of these distinctive breads are traditional breads from the regions of France where old style bread making is increasingly appreciated.

# A Wide Variety of Distinctive Breads

The French regional breads presented in the following pages are prepared from standard white bread dough or country bread dough.

Because of the striking appearance of these breads, they are especially well suited for birthdays and special occasions.

### Equipment

Long and crown shaped rising molds
Canvas rising cloths
Standard rolling pin + thin rolling pin (section of broom handle)
Pastry cutter (metal or plastic)
Medium pastry brush 3 to 4 cm. (1 to 1 1/2 in.) wide
Drum sieve
Sheet pans + parchment paper
2 flour boxes (the first is used for rice or rye flour used for certain regional breads, the second is filled with white flour and used for dusting the work surface and section of dough)
Oil (used to separate sections of certain loaves)
Round mold for baking crown loaves

### Baking

Baking methods for elaborately shaped breads vary according to region and the tastes of the clientele.

Certain shapes need to be more thoroughly baked than others. Breads with a large amount of crumb require more baking so that they don't sag or remain soggy after baking.

The best method for baking most larger loaves is to gradually lower the oven temperature. This method should not be used, however, for loaves with a small surface area such as baguettes and ficelles.

It is best to start baking at a high temperature to encourage the development of a crust and then to gradually lower the temperature to prevent excess coloring. During the last stage of baking, the loaves should be allowed to dry all the way through. There should be a 20 °C (40 °F) difference between the starting and ending baking temperatures.

## Chart of bread types

| Short preparation time | Long preparation time |
|---|---|
| **Round loaves** | |
| Seeded bun loaves | Bordeaux-style crown bread |
| Provençal-style bread | Daisy loaves |
| Pistolets | |
| Swiss-style split bread | |
| **Long loaves** | |
| Braided loaves | Chignon crown bread |
| Twisted bread | Rosary crown bread |
| Harness loaves | Four-part crown bread |
| Zigzag bread | Alsatian-style braided loaves |
| Rope bread | |
| **Flat loaves** | |
| Folded Brittany-style bread | Lyons-style sun bread |
| Portmanteau bread | |
| **Cut loaves** | |
| Sawtooth bread | Pillow loaves |

## Breads for eating or for presentation?

Different methods are used depending on whether the breads are part of a presentation or are going to be eaten.

The shape and design of presentation loaves should be very distinct, even exaggerated, so their shape holds up during baking.

For loaves which are to be eaten, however, the design and shape should be less exaggerated so that parts of the bread don't dry out and become unappealing.

Breads and pastries with sharp or pointed edges are unappealing to some people because the points dry out or even burn. On the other hand, many people enjoy pieces of very hard or even slightly burned crust. This is another example of where the baker should be receptive to the tastes and observations of the customer.

### Conclusion

Most loaves should be baked in an oven preheated to 240 °C (450 °F). Ten minutes after the start of baking, the oven should be turned down to 220 °C (425 °F).

### Steam

Bakers sometimes disagree on the amount of steam that should be used.
• *Large amount* of steam: shiny crust
• *Small amount* of steam: rustic, mat crust

**Miniature bread dough animals**

# Elaborately shaped breads presented in this volume

Pistolets     Rosary crown bread     Rope bread     Sawtooth bread

Swiss-style split bread     Chignon crown bread     Portmanteau bread     Harness loaves

Daisy loaves (with small rolls)     Bordeaux-style crown bread     Zigzag bread     Alsatian-style braided loaves

Daisy loaves (rolling pin method)     Twisted bread     Provençal-style bread     Pillow loaves

Four-part crown bread     Folded Brittany-style bread     Seeded bun loaves     Lyons-style sun bread

# Pistolets (Pain Pistolet)

**Place of origin:** Northeastern France and Belgium

## Preparation

These loaves can be prepared with standard white French bread dough or country bread dough.

Weigh the dough into 550 g. (19.5 oz.) sections. Gently shape the sections into round loaves. Let them rest for 10

minutes and shape them once again.

## Shaping the loaves

Dust the top of the raw loaves with rye or rice flour.

Using a European style rolling pin, press down on the center of the loaves to form a deep indentation running down the middle of each loaf. The depth of the indentations should be twice the thickness of the rolling pin.

Fold the two sides of each split loaf over themselves toward the center. Turn the loaves upside down to rise.

## Proofing

Allow the loaves to double in volume.

## Baking

Turn the loaves upright onto either the peel or the oven-loading conveyer. At this point, the pistolets can be again dusted with flour.

Inject steam into the oven before putting in the loaves. Preheat the oven to 250 ºC (475 ºF) and turn it down to 220 ºC (425 ºF) during baking.

Make sure the loaves are thoroughly baked before removing them from the oven so they don't sag once they have cooled.

## Note

Because of the dense crumb, pistolets keep better than French white bread baked in long loaves.

# Swiss-style Split Bread (Pain Vaudois)

**Place of origin:** French Savoy.

### Preparation

These loaves can be prepared from standard French white bread dough or country bread dough. Weigh the dough into 550 g. (19.5 oz.) sections. Remove an 80 g. (2.8 oz.) piece from each section. Roll both the large and small pieces into balls. Let them rest for 10 minutes and roll them again if necessary.

Let the rounded sections rest again for 20 minutes.

### Shaping the loaves

Take the large balls of dough, flour the tops with rice or rye flour and make deep indentations in two directions with a rolling pin. The loaves should be split in 4 parts. Place the small balls of dough in the center of each of the

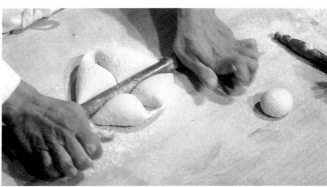

loaves. Bring together the loaves by gently pressing around their sides.

### Proofing

Turn the loaves upside down either directly on the baking surface or in canvas cloths. Proof until they double in volume.

### Baking

Flip the loaves upside right onto the baking surface or peel. Make sure there is plenty of steam in the oven before putting in the loaves.

### Note

Two methods can be used for shaping Swiss-style split bread:

1. When the loaves are being used for a presentation such as a shop window, the splits made with the rolling pin should be very deep.

2. If the loaves are being sold for eating, the splits should not be too deep or the bread will dry out during baking.

# Daisy Loaves (With Small Rolls)

## (La marguerite)

**Place of origin:** The area around Lyon in eastern France.

### Type of bread dough used

Standard white French bread dough or country bread dough.

### Preparation

Divide a 560 g. (20 oz.) section of dough into 7 parts weighing 80 g. (3 oz.) each.

Gently round the sections into mounds without overworking the dough.

Let the mounds of dough rest for 10 minutes.

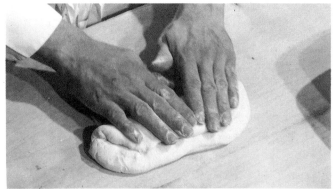

### Shaping the loaves

Round each of the seven mounds of dough. Place 1 loaf in the center and arrange the remaining 6 around the 1 loaf. Do not press on the loaves too firmly.

### Proofing

Turn the daisy loaf upside down on canvas cloths or in a canvas-lined rising mold. The loaves can also be placed upright on sheets of parchment paper which are then slid onto the peel or oven conveyor. Let the loaves proof until they have doubled in volume.

### Baking

See "Daisy loaves (rolling pin method)".

# Daisy Loaves (Rolling Pin Method)

**Shaping the loaves**

Shape the dough into a single, large round loaf. Sprinkle the top of the dough with rye or rice flour.

Using a thin rolling pin, press down on the round to divide it into 8 equal parts.

Place a 50 g. (1.7 oz.) ball of dough in the center of the loaf then gently press around the outside of the loaf.

**Proofing**

See " Daisy loaves (with small rolls).

**Baking**

Place the loaves on the peel or the oven conveyor. At this point, flour can be sprinkled on the tops of the loaves with a sieve and poppy seeds can be sprinkled over the miniature round loaf in the center.

Inject a large amount of steam into the oven before baking.

Be careful to avoid over baking the loaves so they don't dry out.

# Four Part Crown Bread (Couronne Fendue)

**Place of origin:** Central France and the Auvergne region.

### Type of dough used

Standard French white bread or country bread dough.

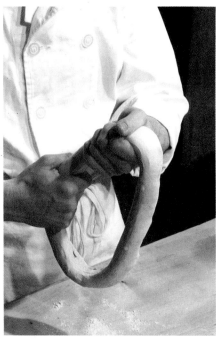

### Preparation

Weigh the dough into 550 g. (19.5 oz.) sections and roll them into balls. Let the balls of dough rest for 10 to 15 minutes.

### Shaping the loaves

Sprinkle the top of the balls of dough with flour, then press down through the center of each loaf with the elbow.

Gradually enlarge the hole in the center of the loaves being careful not to tear the dough. The dough can be allowed to rest periodically as the hole is being enlarged.

Once the center hole has been formed, place the loaves in canvas cloths, sprinkle them once more with flour, and make 4 indentations with a small rolling pin.

### Proofing

Turn the loaves upside down into rounded canvas cloths or on a baking surface.

Proof until the loaves have doubled in volume.

### Baking

Flip the loaves upside right onto the baking surface or peel. The loaves can be baked more or less depending on the consistency of the dough and the taste of the clientele.

The loaves should be baked approximately 30 minutes at 230 ºC (450 ºF).

# Rosary Crown Bread (Couronne Chapelet)

**Place of origin:**
Vosges mountains in eastern France.

**Preparation**

Divide standard French white bread dough into 550 g. (19.5 oz.) sections. Cut a 60 g. (2.1 oz.) piece from each of the sections. Make a long indentation in the large sections with a rolling pin.

Take the small sections of dough and roll them out into lengths the same size as the large, split sections.

With the side of the hand, roll the small strip of dough until it looks like a string of beads. Place it carefully in the split sections.

**Preparing for baking**

Three methods:
1. Bend the loaves into horseshoe shapes and place them on parchment paper.

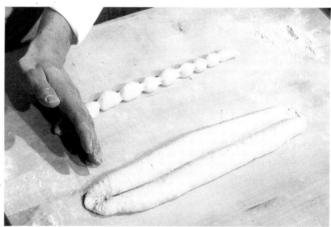

2. Place the loaves upside down in horseshoe shaped canvas cloths.

3. Shape the loaves into horseshoes and place them directly on the baking surface. A round wooden board facilitates transferring the loaves to the oven.

**Proofing**

Proof until the loaves have doubled in volume.

Bake the loaves upright. The parchment paper can be placed directly on the baking surface.

Use a large amount of steam during the beginning of baking.

**Variation: Braided crown bread**

Divide the dough into 550 g. (19.5 oz.) sections. Cut 3 30 g. (1 oz.) sections from each large section. Split the large sections in the way described for rosary crown bread. Roll each of the small sections into thin cords and braid them. Place the braid in the split sections.

# Chignon Crown Bread (Couronne Chignon)

## Preparation

Chignon crown loaves can be prepared from standard French white bread dough or country bread dough.

Section the dough, roll it into tight balls and let it rest for approximately 15 minutes.

## Shaping the loaves

Press through the center of each loaf with an elbow or the palm of the hand.

Gradually enlarge the hole in the center of the loaves in the same way as when preparing a crown bread split in 4 or a Lyon-style crown being careful not to tear the dough.

Once the center hole has been formed, lightly flour and flatten the loaves.

Place the loaves on a work surface and make 8 equidistant cuts around the outer perimeter of the loaves using a pastry cutter.

Make second cuts, 1 cm. (.4 in.) thick on the side of each of one of the 8 sections. Carefully roll out each one of these small sections between the palms of the hands. They should be rolled out into little ropes of equal length and thickness. Roll each of the little ropes in a snail-like, spiral pattern over the 8 larger sections of the loaves.

## Proofing

Proof in a proof box for approximately 1 hour.

## Baking

Bake the loaves on sheets of parchment paper placed directly on the oven conveyer or peel. Do not bake the loaves on sheet pans as they will rise less than when baked directly on the oven floor.

Use a large amount of steam during baking to encourage the development of a shiny, brown crust. Bake for 30 to 35 minutes in a 230 °C (450 °F) oven.

# Bordeaux-style Crown (Couronne Bordelaise)

**Place of origin:** Region of Bordeaux.

**Preparation**

Divide the dough into 540 g. (19.5 oz.) sections. Take each of the sections of dough and divide it into 9 equal pieces. Eight of the pieces are used in a series of buns baked as a single crown loaf and the extra piece is used to form a series of flaps that hold the loaf together.

Roll each of the 9 pieces into a tight ball. Let the balls of dough rest for 20 minutes.

**Shaping the loaves**

Take one of the balls of dough and roll it into a disk from 2 to 3 mm. (app. 1/8 in.) thick.

Brush the outer rim of the disk with a 3 cm. (1 in.) thick band of vegetable oil. Place the remaining 8 balls of dough around the outside edge of the disk.

Make a hole in the top center of each of the balls of dough as well as in the center of the disk. Stretch the disk over

each section of dough so that each of the round pieces is covered with a small flap.

**Preparing for baking**

Proof the crown loaves upside down in a crown shaped canvas rising cloth of the same type used for Lyons style crowns.

**Proofing**

Proof the loaves in a proof box.
Proof until they double in volume.

**Baking**

Flip the loaves upright onto the oven conveyor or peel. The little flaps over each section can be lightly floured at this point. Make sure there is a large amount of steam in the oven before starting to bake.

Bake for approximately 40 minutes at 230 °C (450 °F). Bordeaux style crowns need to be thoroughly baked or the flaps may detach from the sections of dough.

# Twisted Bread (Le Tordu)

**Place of origin:**

The Limousin and Charentes regions of France.

**Type of dough used**

French white bread dough, country bread dough, méteil (rye/wheat) dough, etc.

**Preparation**

Weigh the dough into 550 g. (19.5 oz.) sections. Round each of the sections into mounds and let them rest for approximately 15 minutes.

**Shaping the loaves**

Shape the sections of dough into thick, long loaves.

Dust each of the loaves with rice or rye flour and make 4 cm. (2 in.) wide in-

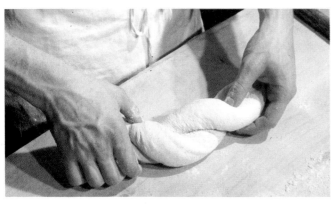

dentations lengthwise in the center of the loaves.

Fold one half of the loaf sideways over the other half until the two sides meet.

Twist the loaves by giving them three opposing turns.

Carefully place the loaves on sheet pans or canvas cloths so they hold their shape.

**Proofing**

Carefully transfer the loaves to the oven conveyor or peel. Be careful, so they hold their shape.

Inject a large amount of steam in the oven before baking and gradually decrease the temperature during baking.

Twisted loaves should not be baked at too high a temperature.

# Folded Brittanny-style Bread (Plié Breton)

**Place of origin:** Brittany.

**Type of bread dough used**

Standard French white bread dough based on previously fermented dough or semi-liquid starter.

**Note**

This bread is unusual in that it is folded after proofing.

**Preparation**

Divide the dough into sections weighing 550 g. (19.5 oz.) each. Round each of the sections into mounds.
Let the sections rest for 20 minutes.

**Shaping the loaves**

Roll the sections of dough into pear shapes. Place the pear-shaped dough on floured sheet pans with the seam facing down. The flour is to prevent the dough from sticking.

**Proofing**

The loaves should proof for about 1 hour. They should double in volume.

*Note:* Some bakers like to fold the breads 30 minutes before the end of proofing. This makes it possible to prolong the proofing time and results in less fragile loaves.

**Baking**

Place the loaves on the peel or oven conveyer.
Flatten the middle of the loaves which should first be dusted with rye or rice flour. Fold the pointed end of the pear over the middle of the loaf and press on it gently to attach it. The tip should detach slightly from the base during baking.

The oven temperature should be decreased gradually during the baking of the loaves.
Preheat the oven to 240 °C (475 °F) and let it decrease to 220 °C (425 °F) during baking.
Thoroughly bake the loaves with only a small amount of steam.

# Rope Bread (Bâtard Cordon)

**Place of origin:**

   Côte d'Or (Burgundy).

**Type of bread dough used**

   Standard French white bread dough, country bread dough, and peasant dough.

**Preparation**

   Weigh the dough into 550 g. (19.5 oz.) sections. Cut off a 50 g. (1.8 oz.) piece of dough from each of the sections. This small piece will be used for the decoration. Let the dough rest for 15 minutes.

**Shaping the loaves**

   Shape the large sections of dough into long thick loaves. Roll the small sections of dough into strands long enough to cover the length of the loaves. With the side of the hand, roll the strands until they form a series of beads.

   A variation of rope bread can be prepared by weighing 3, 25 g. (1 oz.) pieces of dough and rolling each into a strand. The strands are then woven into a braid slightly longer than the loaves. This braid is then attached to the top of the loaves with water.

**Proofing**

   Proof the loaves on a flat surface or upside down in canvas cloths. Continue proofing until the loaves have doubled in volume.

**Baking**

   Place the loaves on the oven conveyor or peel with the decorative strands on top. A decorative touch is to sift flour over the loaves while covering the strand running along the center of the loaf with a piece of cardboard. Bake the loaves in a medium oven.

# Portmanteau Bread (Pain Porte-manteau)

**Place of origin:**

Southwestern France (Toulouse).

**Type of bread dough used**

Standard white French bread dough, country bread dough, vegetable oil enriched dough.

**Preparation**

Weigh the dough into 550 g. (19.5 oz.) sections. Fold the sections over themselves lengthwise.

Let the sections of dough rest for 10 to 15 minutes.

**Shaping the loaves**

Roll out the loaves with a rolling pin starting one third from each end, without rolling the one third in the center.

Roll the two ends of the dough toward the center, leaving the center third of the dough unrolled.

Gently turn over the loaves for proofing. Be careful to keep the rolled ends intact.

**Proofing**

Let the loaves double in volume.

**Baking**

Turn the loaves upright onto the oven conveyor or peel.

The dough can be baked using one of two methods:

1. A large amount of steam can be used during baking so that the resulting bread has a soft texture. These breads can be used for presentations or for a clientele who likes this texture.

2. The loaves can be baked relatively long with little steam to please customers who like their bread crunchy.

# Zigzag Bread (Zig-zag Vivarais)

**Place of origin:** The Ardeche region in southeastern France.

### Type of bread dough used

Standard white French bread dough, country bread dough

### Preparation

Weigh the dough into 550 g. (19.5 oz.) sections and gently round them into mounds.

Let the sections rest for approximately 10 minutes.

### Shaping the loaves

Tightly shape the sections of dough into long thick loaves.

Thickly flour the tops of the loaves with rye or rice flour. A thick layer of flour is important to maintain the triangular shapes which are cut into the surface of the loaves.

Cut triangles into the surface of the loaves. The triangles should reach all the way down the sides of the loaves and run along the entire length.

### Proofing

Turn the loaves upside down on a flat surface and allow them to rise for approximately 1 hour and 20 minutes or until they have doubled in volume.

### Baking

Flip the loaves upside right onto the oven conveyor or peel.

Avoid using too much steam when baking zigzag bread so that the loaves cook thoroughly and have a rustic appearance.

This bread is especially appreciated by customers who like crunchy, well-cooked breads.

# Provençal-style Bread (Pain d'Aix)

**Place of origin:** Region of Marseille.

### Type of bread dough used

Standard French white bread dough, rye/wheat combination (méteil), and country bread dough.

### Preparation

Weigh the dough into 550 g. (19.5 oz.) sections.

Gently shape the sections into mounds and let them rest for approximately 10 minutes.

Shape the sections once again to make sure they are tight and well-rounded.

### Shaping the loaves

Dust the tops of the mounds of dough with rye or rice flour.

Roll out one fourth of each of the sections with a rolling pin so that a flap is formed (technique used for preparing pouches – Volume 1, p.121).

The flap should be large enough to completely cover the unrolled segment of the dough with a little left over to compensate for the eventual expansion of the thick part of the dough.

Brush 2 to 3 cm. (1/2 to 1 in.) of the inside edge of the flap with vegetable oil. This ensures that the edges of the flap detach in a decorative way during baking.

Fold the thick part of the loaf over the flap. Cut a notch out of the side of the loaves at the end of the flaps with a metal pastry cutter.

### Proofing

The loaves should be allowed to proof either upright or upside down on sheet pans. They should be allowed to double in volume.

### Baking

Place the Provençal-style bread on the oven conveyor or peel. The tops of the loaves can be dusted with flour at this point.

Inject a large amount of steam into the oven before baking. The temperature of the oven should be gradually allowed to decrease during baking (preheat to 240 °C/475 °F and allow to decrease to 220 °C/425 °F).

Be sure and thoroughly bake the loaves so they do not sag or remain damp after cooling.

# Seeded Bun Loaves (Pain Régence)

**Place of origin:** Northern France.

### Type of bread dough used

Standard white French bread dough, country bread dough. Originally, seeded bun loaves were prepared using a sponge starter.

### Preparation

Weigh the dough into 350 g. (12.5 oz.) sections.

Divide each of the sections into 5 smaller sections each weighing 70 g. (2.5 oz.)

Roll each of the small pieces of dough into balls. Let the dough rest for .approximately 15 minutes.

### Shaping the loaves

Roll the balls of dough one more time to make sure they hold together firmly.

Press the balls of dough together into strands.

### Proofing

Proof the loaves on sheet pans or on sheets of parchment paper.

When the loaves are finished proofing, brush them with water and sprinkle each one of the buns with seeds, alternating poppy seeds and sesame seeds.

### Baking

Put the loaves in a very hot oven so they are well browned but not too cooked on the inside.

These breads are appreciated by those who like rolls and other breads having a soft crumb.

# Sawtooth Bread (Pain Scie)

**Place of origin:**
The Rhone valley in eastern France.

**Type of bread dough used**

Standard French white bread dough, country bread dough

**Preparation**

Weigh the dough into 450 g. (16 oz.) sections.
Gently work the sections into round loaves and let them rest for approximately 10 minutes.

**Shaping the loaves**

Two methods can be used:

1. Roll the balls of dough into thick long loaves then flatten the loaves with a rolling pin. Cut 5 triangles out of each of the flattened loaves.

2. Cut the triangles directly out of the balls of dough by first flattening the dough and then cutting out 4 even triangles with a pastry cutter.

Attach the triangles by first moistening the corners and gently pressing them together in rows.
Be sure that the triangles are thick enough so they rise well during baking.

**Proofing**

Proof the loaves on sheet pans until they double in volume. The loaves will need approximately 1 hour of proofing before they are baked.

**Baking**

Place the sawtooth loaves on the oven conveyor or peel.
Inject a large amount of steam in the oven before baking.
Sawtooth bread should remain soft textured so it is imperative to not overcook it.
Bake the loaves in a very hot oven (240 °C/475 °F).

# Harness Loaves (Collier de Cheval)

**Place of origin:** Northern Provence.

### Type of bread dough used

Country bread dough, doughs which use a yeast starter.

### Preparation

There are three methods used by bakers to prepare harness loaves. The simplest, which requires the least amount of special equipment is presented here.

Weigh the dough into 550 g. (19.5 oz.) sections. Two sections will be used for each loaf. Gently round them into mounds and let them rest for approximately 10 minutes.

### Shaping the loaves

Shape the sections of dough into long loaves and let them rise. The loaves are assembled after proofing, otherwise they are unwieldy and take up too much space.

### Proofing

Place the loaves on flat surfaces for proofing. They should be dusted with rye or rice flour to give them a more rustic appearance.

The time needed for proofing depends on the type of bread dough used.

Proof the loaves until they have doubled in volume.

### Baking

Assemble the two loaves directly on the oven conveyor or peel. Moisten the ends of the loaves with water, wrap them around each other and flatten them slightly.

These loaves should be baked thoroughly so they have a well-cooked, crunchy texture.

# Alsatian Braided Loaves (Tressé Alsacien)

**Place of origin:**
The region of Alsace in eastern France.

**Type of bread dough used**

Standard white French bread dough, country bread dough.

**Preparation**

Weigh the dough into 450 g. (16 oz.) sections. Divide each of the sections in two.

**Shaping the loaves**

Roll each of the 2 half sections of dough into thin strands of equal length. The strands should taper slightly at each end.

Place two of the strands over one another in a cross. One of the strands should run vertically while the other runs horizontally. (It is helpful to continue to visualize this cross during the braiding).

The strands are braided by continuously crossing them in opposite directions. The top strand is folded down and the bottom strand is folded up so they switch places on the cross. Then the left is folded to the right and the right crossed over to the left. The vertical strands are then crossed again, followed by the horizontal strands. Continue this process until all the dough has been used.

**Proofing**

Place the loaves on sheet pans and proof until they have doubled in volume.

**Baking**

Place the loaves on the oven conveyor or peel.
Inject a large amount of steam into the oven before baking.
Bake the loaves for approximately 30 minutes at 230 °C (450 °F). Do not overcook the loaves; both the crumb and crust should be soft textured.

# Pillow Loaves (Le " Subrot ")

**Place of origin:**
Alsace, in eastern France.

**Type of bread dough used**

Standard white French bread or country bread dough made with a starter or dough which has been fermented for at least 4 hours at 20 °C (68 °F).

**Preparation**

For each loaf, weigh 2 sections of bread dough weighing 1.5 kg. (53 oz.) each.

Roll each of the sections into squares 2.5 cm. (1 in.) thick.

Brush the top of the first section with vegetable oil or melted butter and then dust it with flour. Place the second rolled out section on top of the first.

Gently roll over the sections with a rolling pin to attach them.

**Shaping the loaves**

Cut the doubled squares of dough into lozenges measuring from 10 to 12 cm. (4 to 5 in.) on the longest side. Pay close attention to the size of the lozenges; they should all be exactly the same size. Attach the lozenges end to end in pairs.

**Proofing**

Let the dough rise in canvas cloths with deep folds to help keep them upright during proofing.

Count on approximately 1 hour for proofing.

**Baking**

Place the loaves, in groups of 2 pairs, on the oven conveyor or peel. Start baking the loaves in a very hot oven (250 °C/475 °F) so that they color properly and then lower the oven temperature to 235 °C/450 °F and cook the loaves for 15 to 20 minutes to make sure they are cooked throughout.

The loaves should have a relatively soft crust and crumb.

# Lyon-style Sun Bread (Les Soleils)

**Place of origin:**
The region around Lyon in eastern France.

**Type of bread dough used**

Standard white French bread dough, country bread dough, brié bread dough.

### Preparation

Weigh the dough into 550 g. (19.5 oz.) sections. Gently round the sections into mounds without overworking the dough.

Let the mounds of dough rest for 10 minutes. Flatten the rounds to form disks about 6 mm. (1/4 in.) thick. Transfer the disks to baking sheets.

### Shaping the loaves

Place an inverted glass on the center of each of the disks of dough and flour the rest of the disks using a drum sieve.

Working around the glass, divide the disks in 4 parts, then 8 parts, and finally into 16 parts.

At this stage, one of two methods can be used to finish the loaves:

1. Twist each of the 16 segments of dough several times.

2. Give each of the segments a quarter turn so each side rests flat against the baking surface.

Remove the glass which serves as a guide and also prevents the center from being floured and helps it to stand out.

### Proofing

Let the dough proof for approximately 1 hour.

### Baking

The proofed sun loaves should be baked on sheets of parchment paper. Slide the parchment paper with the loaves onto the oven conveyor or peel.

Avoid over baking the loaves or they will dry out.

Lyon-style sun bread should have a relatively soft crust and crumb.

# Bread Dough Animals

## Introduction

The miniature animals presented here are each made with 400 g. (14 oz.) of bread dough. The designs have been taken from children's books.

Miniature animals are primarily used as decoration in bakery windows but can also be used to decorate buffets. Tortoises, lobsters, crabs, and crocodiles are especially popular for buffets because they can be used to hold canapés.

## Equipment

Sheet pan, chef's knife and paring knife, scissors with pointed tips, rolling pastry cutter, brush, razor blades.

## The bread dough

The bread dough used for preparing animals is enriched with oil and uses fermented dough from a previous batch.

The oil softens the dough and makes it easier to shape.

The fermented dough shortens the time required for kneading and the length of the first rising.

After they are baked, bread dough animals have an excellent shelf life. The dough is smooth, resistant to moisture, and holds together without crumbling.

## Tips for preparing the animals

Before shaping the animals:

• prepare a list of the various types,

• assemble and prepare the equipment and raw ingredients.

Work the dough gently and with a minimum of flour to avoid tearing the dough.

After each sheet pan is completed, place it immediately in a 20 °C (68 °F) proof box to prevent a crust from forming.

## Kneading

Use a base temperature of 60 to 64 °C (204 to 211 °F) when the work area temperature is between 23 and 24 °C (73 and 75 °F).

Combine all the ingredients (flour, salt, fermented dough, water, and oil) in the bowl of the electric mixer.

Knead the dough for 10 minutes on slow speed, until it is relatively firm.

The temperature of the dough after kneading should be: 24 °C (75 °F).

Cover the dough after kneading to prevent a skin from forming.

## First rising

The dough should be allowed to rise for 15 minutes unless more than 10 animals are being made in which case it is no longer necessary.

## Scaling

The dough for the animals can be sectioned by hand or with an automatic dough divider (for large quantities).

Divide the dough into sections weighing 400 g. (14 oz.) for decorative animals or into 1 kg. (35.5 oz.) sections for buffets.

Once the dough has been sectioned and rounded, cover or place the sections in the rising area (proof box or steam chamber) to prevent a skin from forming.

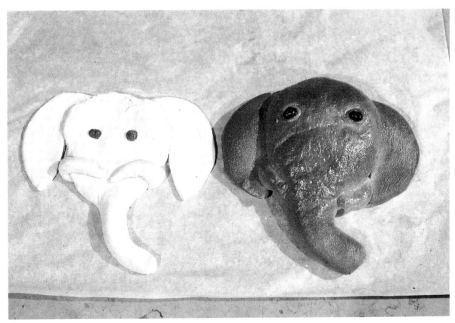

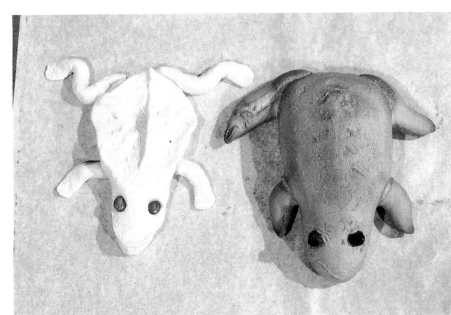

93

# Bread Dough Animals

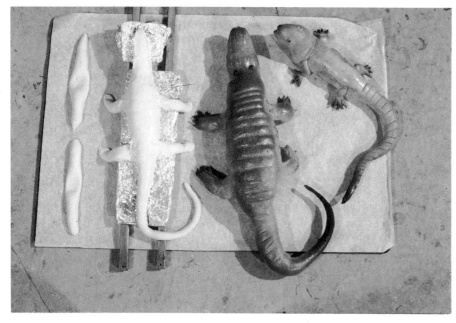

**Bread dough containing oil**

1 kg. flour (35.5 oz.)
1 kg. fermented dough (2 to 3 hours fermentation with 20 g./4 tsp. yeast)
20 g. salt (4 tsp.)
50 ml. oil (1.7 fl. oz.)
450 ml. water (15 fl. oz.)

## Proofing

This is a very important stage. Avoid overproofing the animals -- excess proofing will distort their shape.
Proof the animals for 1 hour at 20 °C (68 °F).

## Preparing the animals for baking

Many bread dough animals require finishing touches before they go in the oven. Eyes made of hazelnuts or raisins are usually added.

***Snake***
Use hazelnuts for the eyes. Sprinkle the length of the snake, except for the head, with poppy seeds.

***Lizard***
Use hazelnuts for the eyes. Score the top with a sausage cut using a razor blade (see lobster).

***Frog***
Use hazelnuts for the eyes. Make cuts for the webbed feet.

***Stingray***
Use hazelnuts for the eyes.

***Fish***
Use hazelnuts for the eyes. Lightly sprinkle the fish with sesame seeds.

***Bird***
Use hazelnuts for the eyes. Score the dough using a pair of scissors to define the wings and feathers.

***Elephant head***
Use hazelnuts for the eyes.

***Crab***
Use hazelnuts for the eyes.
Lightly pinch around the sides of the dough and then make little cuts with the tip of a pair of scissors.

***Star fish***
Cut around the star with the tip of a pair of scissors. Finish with little cuts on the top.

## Lobster

Use hazelnuts for the eyes. Make sideways, sausage cuts with a razor blade. Make cuts to form the claws with scissors.

## Ladybug

Use hazelnuts for the eyes. Make distinctive markings on the surface of the dough with poppy seeds. It is useful to apply the seeds with a pastry bag tip which acts as a funnel.

## Owl

Use hazelnuts for the eyes. Use a razor blade to form the wings and a pair of scissors to make the center feathers.

## Baking

When the animals are completed, bake them in an oven preheated to 210 °C (400 °F) using a large amount of steam.

Bake for approximately 20 minutes.

Keep a close watch on the animals during baking; some require more baking than others.

## Storage

Once the animals have been baked, they have an excellent shelf life.

After baking they can be coated with gelatin sealer or with starch glaze.

To prepare the starch glaze: dissolve 1 tablespoon cornstarch in 100 ml. (3.5 fl. oz.) of water. Bring the mixture to a boil and brush it on the baked animals while still hot.

# Chapter 4

# Viennese Yeast-Raised Pastries

## The aristocrats of baked products

*Although the sale of freshly baked bread comprises most of a successful bakery's business, freshly baked Viennese pastries are constantly gaining in popularity and will enhance a bakery's reputation.*

*Because the reputation of a bakery is often based on the quality of its croissants, a large segment of this chapter is dedicated to a variety of excellent methods and recipes for making these popular pastries. Also included are methods for preparing a wide selection of brioches and Danish pastries.*

# Introduction to Viennese Pastries

## A - Croissants

Because croissants are the most popular of all Viennese pastries, it is essential to a bakery's success to make the best quality croissants with a minimum of expense. For this reason, we have included six methods that can be used for producing croissants and have explained the advantages and disadvantages of each.

**Method A: Straight-dough method croissants**

**Method B: Controlled fermentation croissants**

**Method C: Croissants with slow-risen dough**

**Method D: Croissants with a sponge starter**

**Method E: Croissants with combined method**

**Method F: Croissants with a mixed starter**

## B - Danish and croissant pastries

These pastries are excellent when served as morning or afternoon snacks as well as at teas.

Danish pastry dough can be used to prepare a variety of miniature pastries which are especially popular with children who love both their flavor and appearance.

| | |
|---|---|
| Windmills | Bats |
| Bow ties | Bear claws |
| Danish fruit squares | Twisted fruit rolls |
| Danish pastry horns | Chocolate rolls |
| Danish sweet rolls | Sweet pretzels |
| Danish tartlets | Candied fruit strips |
| Medallions | |

## C - Brioches

Brioches are often considered the best of all Viennese pastries. The methods used for preparing and presenting brioches are extremely diverse and often depend on the region or country where they are baked. Presented here is a selection of the most classic methods.

Also included are miniature brioche animals that will delight children and brighten the bake shop window.

| **Brioches** | **Miniature brioches** |
|---|---|
| Classic butter brioche | Individual brioches with dried fruit |
| Star brioche | and nuts |
| Russian-style braided brioche | Individual chocolate brioches |
| Brioche crowns | Cream-filled individual brioches |
| Vendée-style brioche | Bresse-style tarts with pastry cream |
| Nice-style crown brioche | Mice |
| Bordeaux-style crown brioche | Frogs |
| Craquelins | Elephant heads |
| Anise loaves | **Exception: bread sticks** |
| Swiss-style brioche | The bread sticks presented here are |
| Layered brioche | made with milk bread dough. |

# A - Croissants

## The history of croissants

The first croissants were baked in 1683 while Austria was under siege by the Turks. When they reached Vienna, the attackers, who were tiring of the siege, dug themselves a series of underground tunnels. The Viennese bakers who were up all night working in their underground bakeries heard the attackers who were then caught by surprise and driven from the city.

Vienna's bakers were rewarded with special privileges including the right to sell certain pastries at high prices. They soon developed the croissant which mocked the crescent moon on the Turkish flag.

It wasn't until a hundred years later that the croissant was introduced in France by Marie-Antoinette.

The leafy croissants that we appreciate today were introduced in France at the beginning of this century but did not become popular until 1920.

The airy texture of croissants results from two factors:

- the use of fat
- turning the dough

The dough is given a series of "turns". Because each layer of dough is separated by fat, moisture causes the layers to puff up. Gas produced by the yeast also contributes airiness to the finished croissants.

By combining these two approaches, a well prepared croissant should be made up of a series of fragile layers and have a light and airy texture.

## Methods for making croissants

*The chart on the following two pages is designed to illustrate the advantages of different croissant making methods.*

*In addition to the method used, the type of fat used in the croissants will have an important effect on the finished product.*

**Fats:**

The best croissants are made with **butter.** Butter croissants have a better flavor, texture, and shelf life than croissants made with other fats. Butter is the most nutritious of all animal fats because of the vitamins A and D that it contains.

The most economical croissants are made with **margarine** which is easier to work with and requires less refrigeration.

Whichever fat is used, certain ingredients can be added that will improve the quality of the finished croissants:

*Eggs:* Because of the lecithin they contain, eggs soften the gluten in the flour, improve the shelf life of the croissants, stimulate yeast activity, and contribute to a softer textured crumb.

*Powdered milk:* Contributes to lactic acid fermentation as well as to normal fermentation. Care should be taken not to use too much or the flavor of the croissants will be disagreeably altered.

*Malt:* Speeds fermentation because of the sugar it contains. In doing so, it causes the croissants to rise more and also helps them color more during baking.

*Butter:* Additional butter will soften the dough and produce a finer crust. It also improves the shelf life.

## Which method to use?

A sponge starter or mixed starter causes the development of up to three or four times the amount of volatile acid in the croissant dough than when the straight-dough method is used. Because the dough is allowed to rise before kneading, no more time is required when using these starters.

The use of starters is especially helpful when strong, high-gluten flour is unavailable. Dough made with weaker flours tends to sag and not hold well during baking.

The addition of starters at the beginning of fermentation provides stronger dough with better rising potential. The finished croissants will have a more leafy and fine textured crumb.

# Comparison of Six Methods

| **Straight-dough method (+ autolysis)** | **Controlled fermentation method** | **Slow-risen dough method** |
|---|---|---|
| **Recipe** | **Recipe** | **Recipe** |
| No preliminary fermentation. It is recommended to let the dough rise sufficiently to make sure it is well fermented. | Fermented dough (25%) from a previous batch is added to the fresh dough. Additional sugar is used to compensate for the fermented dough. | No preliminary fermentation. A long first rising is used. Relatively high hydration. |
| **Work schedule** | **Work schedule** | **Work schedule** |
| Practical but somewhat time consuming. Very commonly used. | This method makes it possible to better distribute the work load. Croissants which are shaped in the morning can be baked the same night. | Long and slow first fermentation resulting in the development of volatile acids. Overall, this method is relatively long. |
| **Characteristics** | **Characteristics** | **Characteristics** |
| Medium textured honeycombed crumb<br>Good leafy layers<br>Good flavor due to long first rising<br>Good rising | Good results<br>Well textured honeycombed crumb<br>Good flavor<br>Good leafy layers | Very good results<br>Crumb has even, honeycombed texture<br>Same characteristics as croissants made with a sponge starter |
| Because it is quick and practical, the straight-dough method is by far the most commonly used for preparing croissant dough. No advance preparation is needed in the same way as dough prepared with a starter.<br><br>When using the straight-dough method, it is essential that the dough be given adequate rising time. If not, the finished croissants will lack flavor and will have a poor shelf life.<br><br>Autolysis (fermentation before the completion of kneading) improves the texture of the kneaded dough and reduces the time required for kneading by 1/4. It also improves the rising of the finished croissants and makes the dough easier to turn and roll out. | This method makes it possible to distribute the work required for making croissants over a longer period. Croissants which are shaped in the morning can be baked the following night. When using this method, it is essential to let the dough rise before shaping the croissants.<br><br>When preparing controlled fermentation croissants, avoid excess proofing. Reduce the oven temperature by 10 °C (20 °F) to prevent the croissants from becoming too dark. | The slow first rising causes a large quantity of volatile acids to develop which improves the flavor and shelf life of the croissants.<br><br>The slow-risen dough method is useful for increasing the strength and tenacity of the dough.<br><br>Croissants made using the slow-risen dough method have an appealing honeycombed crumb, and a light, leafy texture. |

# Used for Making Croissants

| Sponge starter method | Combined method | Mixed starter method |
|---|---|---|
| **Recipe**<br><br>The starter is fermented for approximately 2 hours before the preparation of the dough. The time required for fermenting the starter depends on the amount of yeast used. | **Recipe**<br><br>A natural, sourdough starter is used. An extremely small quantity of yeast and sugar is added. | **Recipe**<br>Fermented dough from a previous batch is added to the dough. (20 to 30% fermented dough to flour contained in dough.)<br>A higher percentage of liquid ingredients is used (higher hydration).<br>Extra sugar is added to compensate for the use of previously fermented dough. |
| **Work schedule**<br><br>The use of a sponge starter makes it possible to reduce the time required for the first rising. Preparing croissants with a sponge starter is more time consuming than other methods. | **Work schedule**<br><br>Time consuming and delicate to prepare. | **Work schedule**<br><br>Quick method.<br>The use of fermented dough from a previous batch makes it possible to decrease the time for the first rising. |
| **Characteristics**<br>Very good results.<br>Excellent honeycombed crumb.<br>Well defined leafy crumb with appealing texture in the mouth.<br>Croissants color well during baking.<br>Good flavor.<br>Dough rises extremely well.<br>Very good shelf life. | **Characteristics**<br><br>Well honeycombed crumb.<br>Excellent shelf life.<br>A pronounced tangy flavor.<br>Rise less than croissants made with other methods. | **Characteristics**<br>Very good results.<br>Excellent honeycombed crumb.<br>Well defined leafy crumb with an appealing texture in the mouth.<br>Good shelf life.<br>Colors well during baking. Good flavor.<br>Rises well. |
| The results are very similar to croissants made with fermented dough from a previous batch.<br>Croissants made with a sponge starter have a leafy, honeycombed texture and an excellent shelf life. The fermentation of the starter before the preparation of the final dough makes it possible for the baker to shorten the time for the first rising.<br>Using a sponge starter also improves the flavor of the croissants. | This method is time consuming and can be very difficult to do properly.<br>Croissants made using the combined method will have an excellent flavor and shelf life.<br>Croissants made in this way can be sold as "all natural" or "organic". | This excellent method allows the baker to use dough from a previous batch. The previously fermented dough should be allowed to ferment at least 4 hours in the open air before being incorporated into the new batch. From the time the fermented dough is added to the new batch, the time required to finish the croissants is the shortest of all the methods. It also gives excellent results.<br>Add 20 to 30% fermented dough for a given weight of flour used in the dough. Because the fermented dough has already developed flavor, the time allowed for the first rising can be diminished. Fermented dough improves the texture, flavor, and shelf life of the finished croissants. |

# Straight-Dough Method Croissants

### Introduction

The straight-dough method is widely used for both breads and croissants because it can be carried out both quickly and simply.

To obtain good quality croissants using the straight-dough method (without using a starter or dough from a previous batch), it is essential that sufficient time be allowed for the first rising.

A long first fermentation causes an increase in the quantity of alcohol, volatile acids, and carbon dioxide which contribute to the strength and holding power of the dough. The finished croissants have improved flavor and shelf life.

The exact amount of time required for the first rising depends on the amount of yeast which is added to the dough.

The quality of croissants is improved by using a small quantity of yeast and a long first rising.

Example:

30 g. (1 oz.) yeast: 2 hour first rising
40 g. (1.4 oz.) yeast: 1 1/4 hours first rising

## Ingredients

1 kg. good quality flour (35.5 oz.)
20 g. salt (4 tsp.)
140 g. sugar (5 oz.)
35 g. yeast (1.2 oz.)
1 egg
50 g. butter or margarine (1.8 oz.)
20 g. powdered milk (4 tsp.)
520 ml. cool water (17.5 fl. oz.)

The butter incorporated during the turns should weigh 1/4 the weight of the dough (in this case 500 g./17.5 oz.).

These ingredients will produce 38 croissants made from 60 g. (2.1 oz.) of dough or 46 croissants made from 50 g. (1.8 oz.) of dough.

## Procedure (straight-dough method)

*Kneading:* 4 minutes on slow speed and 4 minutes on medium speed.
The dough should be 23 °C (73 °F) after kneading.

*First rising:* 1 hour 30 minutes to 2 hours.

*Turning:* 1 double turn + 1 single turn or 3 single turns with a 10 minute rest between the last 2 turns.

*Chilling:* 15 minutes of refrigeration cools the dough and causes it to relax.

*Cutting*

*Proofing:* 2 hours to 2 hours 30 minutes at 27 °C (81 °F) in a proof box.

*Baking:* Approximately 15 minutes at 230 °C (450 °F).

## Results

The straight-dough method produces good results but the finished croissants rise less and do not have as leafy a structure as croissants made with a starter or with previously fermented dough.

# STRAIGHT DOUGH METHOD CROISSANTS

| PREPARATION | 10 min | 10 min | • calculate the temperatures<br>• prepare and weigh the ingredients |
|---|---|---|---|
| KNEADING | 8 min | 18 min | • knead the mixture for 4 minutes on slow speed and 4 minutes on medium speed |
| FIRST RISING | 1 hr 30 to 2 hr | 1 hr 50 | • make sure the dough is well covered<br>• the dough can be refrigerated depending on the preparation method<br>• roll out the dough before putting it in the refrigerator so it chills all the way through |
| TURNING | 5 min to 20 min | 2 hr | • 1 double turn + 1 single turn or 3 single turns with a 10 minute rest between the last 2 |
| RESTING | 15 min | 2 hr 15 | • rest the dough in the refrigerator |
| CUTTING AND SHAPING | 10 min | 2 hr 25 | • avoid over rolling the dough. If it is too thin, the individual layers can be damaged |
| PROOFING | 2 hr 30 to 3 hr | 5 hr 10 | • brush the croissants with egg wash |
| PREP. FOR BAKING | 5 min | 5 hr 15 | • do not inject steam into the oven |
| BAKING | 15 min | 5 hr 30 | • carefully watch the coloring of the croissants |
| COOLING | 5 min | 5 hr 35 | • be sure the croissants have completely cooled before stacking |

**STORAGE :** *Straight dough croissants can be sold up to 1 day after baking. They should be eaten no longer than 1 day after baking.*

### Straight-dough method with autolysis

A short resting period near the beginning of kneading (autolysis) reduces the time required for kneading while improving the quality of the finished dough. Autolysis also makes the dough easier to roll out when the butter is being incorporated.

# STRAIGHT DOUGH METHOD CROISSANTS (WITH AUTOLYSIS)

| PREPARATION | 10 min | 10 min | • calculate the temperatures<br>• prepare and weigh the ingredients |
|---|---|---|---|
| KNEADING AND AUTOLYSIS | 22 min | 32 min | • knead the dough for 3 minutes on slow speed<br>• let the mixture rest for 15 minutes (autolysis)<br>• continue kneading for 4 minutes on medium speed |
| FIRST RISING | 1 hr 30 to 2 hr | 2 hr 10 | • make sure the dough is well covered<br>• the dough can be refrigerated depending on the preparation method<br>• roll out the dough before putting it in the refrigerator so it chills all the way through |
| TURNING | 5 min to 10 min | 2 hr 20 | • 1 double turn + 1 single turn or 3 single turns with a 10 minute rest between the last 2 |
| RESTING | 15 min | 2 hr 35 | • rest the dough in the refrigerator |
| CUTTING AND SHAPING | 10 min | 2 hr 45 | • avoid over rolling the dough. If it is too thin, the individual layers can be damaged |
| PROOFING | 2 hr 30 to 3 hr | 5 hr 30 | • brush the croissants with egg wash |
| PREP. FOR BAKING | 5 min | 5 hr 35 | • do not inject steam into the oven |
| BAKING | 15 min | 5 hr 50 | • carefully watch the coloring of the croissants |
| COOLING | 5 min | 5 hr 55 | • be sure the croissants have completely cooled before stacking |

**STORAGE :** *Good shelf life.*

# Preparing croissants using controlled fermentation

## Introduction

Controlled fermentation techniques allow the baker to slow or completely stop the fermentation of croissant dough during proofing.

Excellent results can be obtained by allowing a relatively long period for proofing croissants as well as using one of a variety of starters such as sponge starter, yeast starter, or dough from a previously fermented batch. Both long proofing and using a starter contribute to the strength and holding power of the dough while augmenting the accumulation of organic acids which improves both the flavor and shelf life of the finished breads.

When preparing croissants, it is advisable to use a good quality patent flour or a strong, high gluten flour. Because of the long rising time used with controlled fermentation and the high fat content of the dough, a strong gluten structure is necessary to support the croissants during proofing and baking.

If good quality patent flour or flour with the necessary strength is unavailable, additives such as ascorbic acid can be incorporated into the dough to improve the rising and flakiness of the croissants.

Avoid allowing the dough to become overheated at any point.

## Ingredients

1 kg. good quality patent flour or strong, high-gluten flour (35 oz.)
20 g. salt (4 tsp.)
150 g. sugar (a relatively large amount to compensate for long fermentation)
35 g. yeast (5.5 oz.)
1 egg
520 ml. cool water (17.5 fl. oz.)
250 g. fermented dough (9 oz.) (4 hours rising at 20 °C/68 °F or 18 hours at 6 °C/ 43 °F.)

The butter which is incorporated into the dough should represent about one fourth of the total weight of the finished dough (i.e. 520 g./17.5 oz. when used with the ingredients given above).

The quantities given will produce approximately 42 croissants weighing 60 g. (2.1 oz.) or 50 croissants weighing 50 g. (1.8 oz.).

*Resting (in refrigerator):* 20 minutes for pure butter croissants.

*Turning:* Give the dough one double turn followed by one single turn.

*Resting:* Allow the dough to rest in the refrigerator for 15 minutes.

*Cutting:* When the croissants have been shaped, they should be placed in a refrigerator or fermenting chamber set to 2 °C/36 °F for 12 hours.

The fermentation should then be continued for 4 hours at 24 °C/75 °F.

*Baking:* 15 minutes in a 220 °C/425 °F oven.

Avoid letting the dough over proof. Over proofing will detract from the flakiness of the dough.

# CROISSANTS USING CONTROLLED FERMENTATION

| | | | |
|---|---|---|---|
| PREPARATION | 10 min | 10 min | • calculate the temperatures<br>• prepare and weigh the ingredients |
| KNEADING | 8 min | 18 min | • knead for 3 minutes on slow speed followed by 5 minutes on medium speed. Add the fermented dough halfway (medium speed) |
| FIRST RISING | 1 hr to 2 hr | 1 hr | • let rise for 1 hour at room temperature<br>• refrigerate the dough to firm the butter it contains |
| TURNING | 5 min to 20 min | 2 hr | • 1 double turn + 1 single turn or 3 single turns with a 10 minute rest between the last two |
| RESTING | 15 min | 2 hr 15 | • rest the dough in the refrigerator |
| CUTTING AND SHAPING | 10 min | 2 hr 25 | • do not roll the dough out too thinly or the individual layers may break |
| HOLDING | | | • hold the dough at 2 °C (36 °F) (optional) |
| PROOFING | 4 hr | 6 hr 25 | • do not let the dough over proof or the individual layers may be damaged |
| BEFORE BAKING | 5 min | 6 hr 30 | |
| BAKING | 15 min | 6 hr 45 | • bake in a 220 °C (425 °F) oven |
| COOLING | 5 min | 6 hr 50 | • be sure the croissants have completely cooled before stacking them |

**STORAGE :** *Controlled fermentation croissants can be sold up to 2 days after baking. They should be eaten within 2 days of baking.*

# Croissants with slow-risen dough

## Introduction

These croissants are made with dough which has undergone a slow fermentation before they are shaped and proofed.

There are several advantages to using slow-risen dough.

Slow-risen dough has less elasticity, a smoother texture, and greater strength and holding power than other types of dough.

During the long first rising, carbon dioxide is formed from the action of the yeast on the sugar contained in the dough. The carbon dioxide then becomes trapped in the gluten structure of the dough and along with the alternating layers of butter and flour gives the dough its flaky texture and porous crumb.

Slow-risen dough results in the formation of a relatively large amount of alcohol in the dough which improves the flavor of the croissants.

A long first rising allows organic acids to accumulate in the dough which improve the flavor and shelf life of the croissants.

Croissants made from slow-risen dough are convenient for bakers who like to turn, cut, and bake their croissants all in the same night. Because the dough has already undergone sufficient fermentation, less time is required for finishing the croissants.

When the croissant dough has been kneaded, it can be allowed to partially rise at room temperature before being transferred to a 6 °C (43 °F) refrigerator or fermenting chamber or the room temperature stage can be skipped, and the kneaded dough placed immediately in a 7 °C (45 °F) refrigerator or fermenting chamber. When large quantities are being chilled, fermentation will be quicker at the beginning because the center of the dough takes longer to cool off.

## Ingredients

The ingredients listed below will produce 39 croissants weighing 60 g. (2.1 oz.) or 47 croissants weighing 50 g. (1.8 oz.).

The amount of butter used for the layers should weigh one fourth as much as the rest of the dough. (In this case 450 g./16 oz.)

1 kg. good quality flour (35 oz.)
20 g. salt (4 tsp.)
140 g. sugar (5 oz.)
35 g. yeast (1.2 oz.)
1 egg
50 g. butter (1.8 oz.)
20 g powdered milk (4 tsp.)
560 ml. cold water (19 fl. oz.)

**Procedure**

*First rising:* 1 hour at room temperature followed by 12 hours at 6 to 7 °C (43 to 45 °F).

*Kneading:* Knead for 4 minutes at slow speed followed by 4 minutes at medium speed.

The temperature of the kneaded dough should be 23 °C/73 °F.

*Turning:* One double turn followed by one single turn.

*Resting (in refrigerator):* 15 minutes

*Cutting*
As usual for croissants.

*Baking:* 15 minutes
Oven temperature: 220 °C (425 °F)

*Results:*
Honeycombed, porous crumb
Flaky with layered texture
Good shelf life
Light brown crust
Melting texture in the mouth.

## CROISSANTS WITH SLOW RISEN DOUGH

| | | | |
|---|---|---|---|
| **PREPARATION** | **10** min | **10** min | • calculate the temperatures<br>• prepare and weigh the ingredients |
| **KNEADING** | **8** min | **18** min | • 3 min. slow speed and 5 min. medium sp. |
| **FIRST RISING** | **13** hr | **13** hr **18** | • let rise for 1 hour at room temperature followed by 12 hours at 6 to 7 °C (43 to 45 °F)<br>• make sure the dough is well covered |
| **TURNING** | **5** to **29** min | **13** hr **30** | • 1 double turn + 1 single turn or 3 single turns with a 10 minute rest between the last two |
| **RESTING** | **15** min | **13** hr **45** | • rest the dough in the refrigerator |
| **CUTTING AND SHAPING** | **10** min | **13** hr **55** | • do not roll the dough into too thin a sheet<br>• make sure the croissants are long enough but not too wide so they can easily be given turns |
| **PROOFING** | **2** hr **30** | **16** hr **25** | • in a proof box at 27 °C (81 °F)<br>• brush the croissants with egg wash |
| **BEFORE BAKING** | **15** min | **16** hr **45** | • do not inject steam into the oven |
| **BAKING** | **15** min | **16** hr **45** | • carefully watch the browning of the croissants |
| **COOLING** | **5** min | **16** hr **50** | • place the croissants on cooling racks<br>• be sure the croissants have completely cooled before stacking them |

**STORAGE :** *Croissants based on slow risen dough can be sold up to 2 days after baking. They should be eaten within 2 days of baking.*

# Croissants with a sponge starter

## Introduction

Viennese bakers were the first to develop this method for making croissants. It was introduced in France around 1820.

From the time they were first made in France until about 1920, croissants were always made using a sponge

starter. Gradually this method was abandoned in favor of the more efficient straight dough process where all the ingredients are mixed at one time.

Today, as interest in traditional baking techniques is on the rise, many bakers are returning to making croissants using a sponge starter.

A sponge is a semi-liquid starter made with baker's yeast, water, and flour. The amount of water used for making the starter can vary from 1/3 to 4/5 the total amount of water used for the dough. In general, the amount of flour used in the starter is equal to the amount of water by weight except when strong, high gluten flours are used, in which case less flour is used. The time needed for the rising of the sponge depends on the amount of yeast used in its preparation.

The amount of yeast needed is determined as follows:

| Rising Time | Weight of yeast per kg. (2.2 lb.) flour |
|---|---|
| 2 hours | 20 g. (4 tsp./.7 oz.) |
| 3 hours | 15 g. (3 tsp./.5 oz.) |
| 5 hours | 8 g. (1 1/2 tsp./.3 oz.) |

The sponge should triple in volume and begin to sag in the middle before it can be used as a starter for the finished dough.

***Ingredients for the sponge starter for dough are based on 2 kg. (4.4 lb.) of flour (the sponge starter uses 1/2 of the total water from the recipe).***

Base temperature: 68 °C/219 °F.

Combine 15 g. (3 tsp.) yeast with 550 ml. (18.5 ml.) water and add 550 g. (19.5 oz.) flour. The sponge can be made by hand or in an electric mixer.

Make sure the ingredients are well combined. Let the sponge rise for approximately 2 hours.

When the top of the sponge is sagging in the middle, add the remaining water called for in the recipe (in this case, an additional 550 ml./18.5 fl. oz.). Pour the water around the sides of the starter so that it can be easily transferred to the bowl of the mixer. The water can also be added to the sponge after it has been transferred to the mixer bowl.

**Remaining ingredients**

1.45 kg. good quality flour (51 oz.)
240 g. sugar (8.5 oz.)
40 g. salt (1.4 oz.)
55 g. yeast (1.9 oz.)
2 eggs
40 g. powdered milk (1.4 oz.) (optional)
100 g. butter (3.5 oz.) (optional)
20 g. malt (4 tsp.)
550 ml. water (18.5 fl. oz.)
The butter used in the turns should weigh one fourth the amount of the dough.

The ingredients given above can be used to prepare 78, 60 g. (2.1 oz.) croissants or 93, 50 g. (1.8 oz.) croissants.

**Procedure**

*Kneading:* 4 minutes at slow speed fol-lowed by 5 minutes at medium speed. The temperature of the fermented dough should be 23 °C (73 °F).

*First rising:* Let the dough rise at room temperature for 1 hour. Transfer it to the refrigerator for 20 minutes before incorporating the butter.

*Turning:* One double turn followed by a single turn, or 3 single turns with a 10 minute rest between the second and last turns.

*Resting (in refrigerator):* 15 minutes

*Cutting*

*Proofing:* 2 hours and 30 minutes at 27 °C (81 °F).

*Baking:* 15 minutes at 225 °C (425 °F).

**Results**

Croissants rise well due to the sponge starter and have an excellent flavor. Croissants made using a sponge starter have a beautifully textured crumb and a very good shelf life.

# CROISSANTS WITH A SPONGE STARTER

| PREPARATION | 5 min | 5 min | • prepare and weigh the ingredients |
|---|---|---|---|
| KNEADING THE SPONGE | 5 min | 10 min | • mix thoroughly with a whisk or the hands |
| FERMENTING THE SPONGE | 2 hr | 2 hr 10 | • rising time depends on temperature of the rising area |
| PREPARING THE FINAL DOUGH | 10 min | 2 hr 20 | • calculate the temperatures<br>• prepare and weigh the ingredients |
| KNEADING | 8 min | 2 hr 28 | • pour the rest of the water over the sponge to detach it from the rising container<br>• put the sponge in the bowl of the electric mixer with the rest of the ingredients<br>• 3 min. slow speed and 5 min. medium speed |
| FIRST RISING | 1 hr | 3 hr 28 | • make sure the dough is well covered<br>• the dough may be chilled depending on whether butter or margarine is being used |
| TURNING | 5 to 20 min | 3 hr 40 | • 1 double turn + 1 single turn or 3 single turns with a 10 minutes rest between the last two |
| RESTING | 15 min | 3 hr 55 | • rest the dough in the refrigerator |
| CUTTING AND SHAPING | 10 min | 4 hr 05 | • do not roll the dough into too thin a sheet or the individual layers may be damaged |
| PROOFING | 2 hr | 6 hr 05 | • in a proof box at 28 °C (82 °F) |
| BEFORE BAKING | 5 min | 6 hr 10 | • do not inject steam into the oven |
| BAKING | 15 min | 6 hr 25 | • carefully watch the browning |
| COOLING | 5 min | 6 hr 30 | • place the croissants on cooling racks<br>• be sure the croissants have cooled |

**STORAGE :** *Sponge based croissants can be sold up to 2 days after baking. They should be eaten within 2 days of baking.*

# Croissants with combined method

### Introduction

The method of preparing breads using both a natural starter and commercial yeast began soon after yeast was first discovered and isolated. It is an excellent method which takes advantage of the benefits of a natural starter while reducing the rising time needed by adding a small amount of commercial yeast to the dough. The amount of yeast used in the combined method ranges from 3 to .8% of the total amount of flour used in the finished dough.

Croissants made using a natural yeast starter alone are time consuming to prepare and often rise inadequately because of their small size. For this reason, sourdough breads and breads based on a natural starter are usually baked in large long or round loaves.

Making croissants using yeast in combination with a natural starter takes time and requires careful attention but if the workload is carefully organized, the results are well worth the effort. Croissants made using the combined method have an excellent flavor and long shelf life.

Croissants made with the combined method are best:

• for serious bakers who wish to make the highest quality croissants possible,

•for a clientele who appreciates baked goods made from organic flours

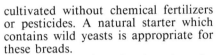

cultivated without chemical fertilizers or pesticides. A natural starter which contains wild yeasts is appropriate for these breads.

When preparing dough using the combined method the amount of commercial yeast added must be gaged to the amount of natural starter incorporated into the dough:

6 g. (.6%) yeast + 450 g. (16 oz.) starter per kg. (35 oz.) of flour

8 g. (.8%) yeast + 370 g. (13 oz.) starter per kg. (35 oz.) of flour

### Ingredients

1 kg. flour (35 oz.)
20 g. salt (4 tsp.)
160 g. sugar (5.5 oz.) (large amount to compensate for the starter)
6 g. yeast (1 tsp./.2 oz.)
1 egg
520 ml. cool water (17.5 fl. oz.)
450 g. natural starter (16 oz.)

The butter incorporated during the turns should weigh one fourth the total weight of the dough (i.e. 550 g./19.5 oz.).

The ingredients given above will produce 47 croissants weighing 60 g. (2.1 oz.) or 56 croissants weighing 50 g. (1.7 oz.).

### Procedure

**Kneading:** 12 minutes on slow speed. Temperature of the finished dough: 23 °C (74 °F).

**First rising:** 5 hours.

**Resting (in refrigerator):** 20 minutes (before incorporating butter).

**Turning:** 1 double turn followed by one single turn.

**Resting (in refrigerator):** 15 minutes.

### Cutting

**Proofing:** Proof in a proof box for 5 hours at 28 °C (82 °F).

**Baking:** 15 minutes in a 225 °C (425 °F) oven.

### Results

Flaky croissants with a porous, honeycombed crumb, and an appealing golden crust. They have a delicately tangy flavor and a very good shelf life.

## CROISSANTS WITH COMBINED METHOD

| PREPARATION | 10 min | 10 min | • calculate the temperatures<br>• prepare and weigh the ingredients |
|---|---|---|---|
| KNEADING | 12 min | 22 min | • knead 12 minutes on slow speed. Add the starter halfway through the kneading |
| FIRST RISING | 4 hr<br>5 hr | 5 hr 50 | • the dough may be chilled depending on whether butter or margarine is being used |
| TURNING | 5<br>or 20 min | 6 hr | • time needed depends on turning method<br>• 1 double turn + 1 single turn or 3 single turns with a 10 minute rest between the last two |
| RESTING | 15 min | 6 hr 15 | • rest the dough in the refrigerator |
| CUTTING AND SHAPING | 10 min | 6 hr 25 | |
| PROOFING | 5 hr | 11 hr 05 | |
| BEFORE BAKING | 5 min | 11 hr 30 | • do not inject steam into the oven |
| BAKING | 15 min<br>to 20 min | 11 hr 45 | • bake in an 225 °C (420 °F) oven (approximately) |
| COOLING | 5 min | 11 hr 50 | • be sure the croissants have cooled |

STORAGE : *Combined method croissants can be sold up to 2 days after baking. They should be eaten within 2 days of baking.*

# Croissants with a mixed starter

## Introduction

Croissant dough made with a mixed starter contains fresh yeast and a piece of fermented dough from a previous batch. The fermented dough, which contributes strength and holding power, also supplies organic acid-producing bacteria which improve the flavor of the bread. In doing so, it reduces the time needed for proofing the croissants, and improves their shelf life and texture.

To avoid over kneading the fermented dough, do not add it to the fresh batch until halfway through the kneading.

Using a mixed starter is an excellent method not only because it is quick but because it requires little extra effort. The baker needs only save a piece of dough from the last batch.

When preparing a fresh batch of dough, use from 200 to 300 g. (7 to 10.5 oz.) of fermented dough per kg. (35 oz.) of flour. Remember to compensate for the fermented dough by adding extra sugar.

## Ingredients

1 kg. high gluten bread flour (35 oz.)
20 g. salt (4 tsp.)
150 g. sugar (5.5 oz.)
35 g. yeast (1.2 oz.)
1 egg
50 g. butter (1.8 oz.)
20 g. powdered milk (4 tsp.)
10 g. malt (2 tsp.)
550 ml. cool water (18.5 fl. oz.)
300 g. fermented dough (10.5 oz.)

The butter used for the turns should weigh one fourth the weight of the dough. (i.e. 550 g./19.5 oz.)

These ingredients will produce 44 croissants weighing 60 g. (2.1 oz.) each or 53 croissants weighing 50 g. (1.8 oz.) each.

## Procedure

*Kneading:* Knead the dough in the electric mixer for 4 minutes on slow speed followed by 4 minutes at medium speed. If a kneading machine is being used, knead for 4 minutes on slow speed followed by 8 minutes on medium speed.

Temperature of the dough after kneading: 23 °C (73 °F).

*First rising:* 1 hour.

*Resting (in refrigerator):* 15 to 20 minutes for all-butter croissants.

*Turning:* One double turn followed by a single turn or 3 single turns with a 10 minute rest between the last two turns.

*Resting (in refrigerator):* Chilling the dough makes it easier to cut.

*Cutting:* 10 minutes.

*Proofing:* 2 hours.

*Baking:* Approximately 15 minutes. Oven temperature: 225 to 230 °C (425 to 450 °F).

### Results

Very good.
Good rising with flaky texture and well structured crumb.
Attractive light brown crust.
Good shelf life.

## CROISSANTS WITH A MIXED STARTER

| | | | |
|---|---|---|---|
| **PREPARATION** | 10 min | 10 min | • calculate the temperatures<br>• prepare and weigh the ingredients |
| **KNEADING** | 8 min | 18 min | • knead the mixture for 3 minutes on slow speed and 5 minutes on medium speed. Add the starter halfway through the kneading |
| **FIRST RISING** | 1 hr | 1 hr 18 | • make sure the dough is well covered<br>• the dough can be refrigerated depending on whether butter or margarine is being used |
| **TURNING** | 5 or 20 min | 1 hr 30 | • time needed depends on turning method<br>• 1 double turn + 1 single turn or 3 single turns with a 10 minute rest between the last two |
| **RESTING** | 15 min | 1 hr 45 | • rest the dough in the refrigerator |
| **CUTTING AND SHAPING** | 10 min | 1 hr 55 | • avoid over rolling the dough. If it is too thin, the individual layers may be damaged |
| **PROOFING** | 2 hr to 2 hr 30 | 4 hr 10 | • use a proof box set to 27 °C (81 °F) |
| **BEFORE BAKING** | 5 min | 4 hr 15 | • do not inject steam into the oven |
| **BAKING** | 15 min | 4 hr 30 | • carefully watch the coloring of the croissants |
| **COOLING** | 5 min | 4 hr 35 | • be sure the croissants have cooled |

**STORAGE :** *Croissants made with a mixed starter can be sold from 1 to 2 days after baking. They should be eaten within 2 days of baking.*

# Walnut Croissants

## An added attraction

Traditionally, croissants are served at breakfast with coffee. Walnut croissants, however, can be eaten at other times during the day, such as at teas or as afternoon snacks. Walnut croissants are rich enough that they can even be served as a substitute for small cakes and petits fours.

## Ingredients

A batch of dough based on 1 kg. (35 oz.) of flour will produce 40 croissants weighing 55 g. (1.9 oz.) each.

Type of dough used: croissant dough or Danish pastry dough (couques).

## *Walnut batter*

250 g. fondant (9 oz.)
150 g. butter (5.5 oz.)
500 g. walnuts (17.5 oz.)
    Confectioner's sugar (to stiffen batter)

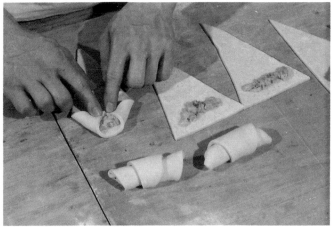

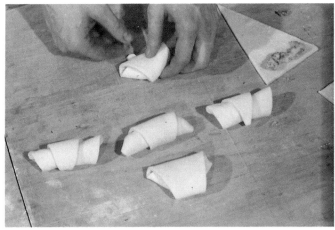

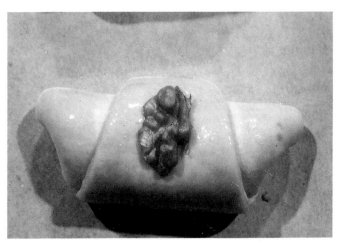

## Procedure

Roll the dough 4 mm. (between 1/8 and 1/4 in.) thick.

## Cutting and shaping

Two methods can be used for cutting and shaping walnut croissants. The first method is the traditional one used for regular croissants. The second method, given below, is designed to seal the filling in the center of the croissants.

Cut a strip of croissant dough into triangles. Pipe a strip of the walnut batter on each triangle using a pastry bag with a 10 mm. (.4 in.) tip.

Fold the two corners of the base of the triangle over the walnut batter, then roll the rest of the dough around the center.

Place the croissants on baking sheets.

Brush the croissants with egg wash and put them in a proof box or steam chamber at 28 °C (82 °F).

## Proofing

Proof for approximately 1 hour.

When the croissants are finished proofing, brush them a second time with egg wash and place a half walnut on the center of each one.

## Baking

Bake for approximately 17 minutes in a 220 °C (425 °F) oven.

As soon as the croissants come out of the oven, brush them with warm (30 °C/86 °F) sugar syrup.

# Two-dough rolled pastries

**An original pastry roll**

These specially shaped rolls are made with two types of dough. They are especially tasty because of the butter and sugar that are rolled in all the way to the center.

**Type of dough used**

Croissant dough combined with brioche dough or Danish pastry dough combined with brioche dough.

**Procedure**

Roll the croissant dough or Danish pastry dough into a rectangle measuring 30 by 20 cm. (12 by 8 in.).

Roll a rectangle of brioche dough to the same size and place it over the rectangle of croissant dough.

Roll the rectangle to 4 mm. (between 1/8 and 1/4 in.) thick sheets using a dough sheeter.

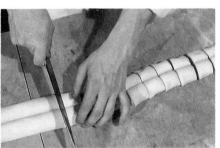

Cut the double roll of dough into 3 cm. (1 in.) wide sections. Turn one side of each of the sections around so that what was the top is now facing down. Place the pastries on buttered sheet pans.

Brush the pastries with egg wash and place them in a proof box or steam chamber at 28 °C/82 °F.

## Proofing

Proof the pastries for approximately 1 hour.

## Baking

Brush the pastries a second time with egg wash, then bake them for 18 minutes in a 220 °C (425 °F) oven.

Let the pastries cool. Some bakers like to glaze the pastries after baking.

## Shaping

Brush the surface of the laminated dough with melted butter and sprinkle it with crystallized sugar.

Roll the dough from two sides to form two adjacent cylinders. Press on the pastry to make sure it is tightly rolled and to prevent it from unravelling during baking.

# Miniature Viennese Pastries

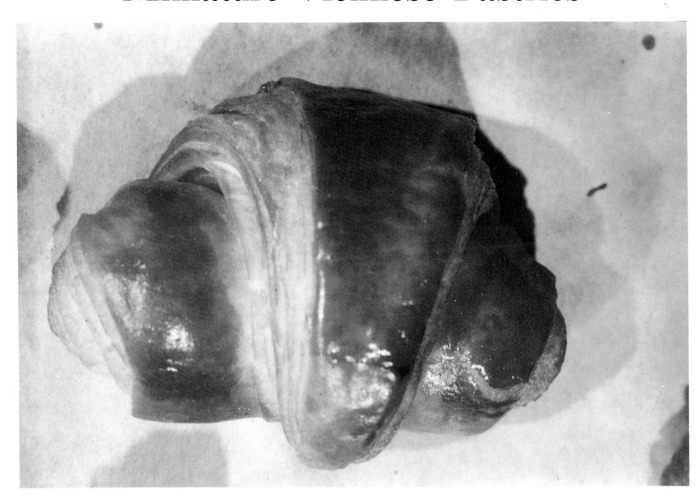

### Introduction

Miniature Viennese pastries are a recent innovation among French bakers. Because of their size, they can be offered in an assortment of fanciful shapes.

Some bakeries sell these miniature pastries in groups of 3 to accompany brunch. A typical assortment might include a miniature croissant, a chocolate roll (pain au chocolat), and a raisin roll (pain aux raisins).

Miniature pastries are gaining in popularity in Europe where the traditional 3 meals a day are gradually giving way to a less structured pattern of continual snacking.

These miniature pastries can be sold in cafes as an accompaniment to coffee.

### Procedure

Miniature Viennese pastries are prepared in the same way as standard size pastries. The only difference is that they weigh about 1/3 as much, i.e. 15 to 20 g. (.5 to .7 oz.).

### Cutting and shaping
#### *Croissants*

Roll out the croissant dough somewhat thinner than when making full-size croissants but do not roll it too thinly or the layers will break.

Cut the thin sheet of croissant dough into 8 cm. (3 in.) wide strips. Stack the strips 3 high to save time and cut them into triangles 5.5 cm. (2 in.) at the base. Shape the croissants in the same way as full size croissants.

#### *Chocolate rolls (Pains au chocolat):*

Cut a sheet of croissant dough into rectangles 5 by 7 cm. (2 by 3 in.) using a dough cutter. Insert a strip of chocolate before rolling.

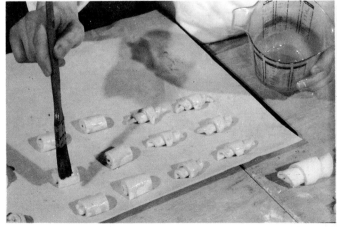

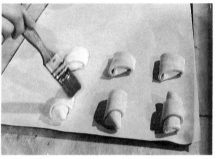

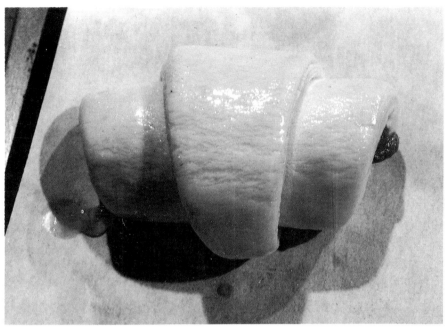

***Raisin rolls (Pains aux raisins):*** Cut out 15 cm. (6 in.) long strips from a sheet of croissant dough.

Spread the sheets with the cream filling, sprinkle them with raisins and roll them into cylinders.

Slice the cylinders into 2 cm. (1 in.) rolls.

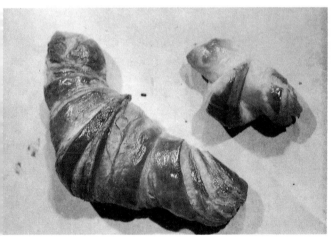

119

# B – Danish and Croissant Pastries

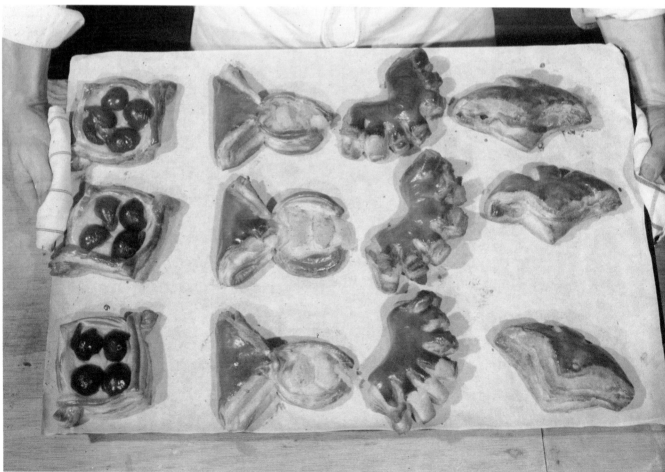

# A Wide Assortment of Pastries

*Danish pastry dough (pâte à couques) can be used to make a variety of baked goods with an assortment of shapes and fillings. Because it contains eggs, Danish pastry dough is soft textured and easy to work with.*

*Well made Danish pastries have a soft, leafy texture with an appealing yellow crumb and a rich flavor. The finished pastries are attractive and appetizing.*

# Danish Pastry Dough (Pâte à Couques)

The ingredients and methods used for preparing Danish pastry dough are similar to those used for making croissant dough. The main difference is that Danish pastry dough contains eggs.

Danish pastry dough is richer than croissant dough and because of its shorter kneading time is more quickly made.

## Ingredients

The percentages of salt, sugar, and butter added during the turns is the same as for croissant dough. The following ingredients, however, should be added:

• 4 to 5 eggs per kilogram (35.5 oz.) of flour. The eggs give a softer, airier texture to the dough and also give it an appealing yellow hue. Because of the lecithin contained in eggs, they also make the dough easier to work with.

• 400 ml (14 fl. oz.) of milk per kilogram (35.5 oz.) of flour. The milk enrichens the dough, contributes to its soft texture, and improves the fermen-

tation because of the natural sugars it contains.

### Kneading

Kneading times are relatively short: 7 minutes on slow speed in an electric mixer; 4 minutes on slow speed followed by 3 minutes on medium speed in a kneading machine.

**Turning the dough:** 1 double turn + 1 single turn or 3 single turns.

**Temperature of the kneaded dough:** 23 to 25 °C (73 to 77 °F).

**First rising:** 1 hour at 23 °C (73 °F) or 12 hours at 4 °C (39 °F).

### Recipe
500 g bread flour (17.5 oz.)
500 g. high gluten flour (patent flour) (17.5 oz.)
400 ml. milk (14 fl. oz.)
50 g. yeast (1.8 oz.) - 20 g. salt (4 tsp.)
4 to 5 eggs - 100 g. sugar (3.5 oz.)
Butter for turning (1/4 the weight of the dough)

## DANISH PASTRY DOUGH

| | | | |
|---|---|---|---|
| **PREPARATION** | **10** min | **10** min | • *calculate the temperatures*<br>• *prepare and weigh the raw ingredients* |
| **KNEADING** | **7** min | **17** min | • *7 minutes slow speed (electric mixer)*<br>• *4 minutes slow speed followed by 3 minutes medium speed (a kneading machine)* |
| **FIRST RISING** | **1** hr to **12** hr | **1** hr **20** | • *1 hour at 23 °C/73 °F or 12 hours at 4 °C/39 °F*<br>• *when working with butter, chill the butter before turning* |
| **REFRIGERATING THE DOUGH** | **30** min | | • *optional* |
| **TURNING** | **10** min | **1** hr **30** | • *1 double turn + 1 single turn or 3 single turns with a 15 minute resting period between the last 2 turns* |
| **REFRIGERATING THE DOUGH** | **20** min | **1** hr **50** | |
| **SHAPING** | **20** min | **2** hr **10** | • *use a rolling croissant cutter for regularity*<br>• *form into the desired shape* |
| **PROOFING** | **1** hr | **3** hr **10** | • *in a proof box at 27 °C/81 °F* |
| **PREP. FOR BAKING** | **10** min | **3** hr **20** | • *brush the pastries with egg wash before baking* |
| **BAKING** | **15** min to **18** min | **3** hr **35** | • *bake in a 230 to 240 °C/450 to 475 °F oven* |
| **COOLING** | **5** min | **3** hr **40** | |
| **FINISHING THE PASTRIES** | **10** min | **3** hr **50** | • *the finished pastries can be brushed with sugar and water glaze or with fondant* |

**STORAGE** : *Danish pastries should be sold within a day after baking.*

# General Procedure

## 1. Rolling out the dough

The following shapes can be cut from a rectangular sheet of dough:

- 10 by 10 cm. (4 by 4 in.) squares for windmills, bow ties, Danish fruit squares, Danish sweet rolls, Danish tartlets, medallions, bats, and bear claws;

- rectangles for twisted fruit rolls and candied fruit strips;
- long, narrow strips for sweet pretzels;
- triangles for Danish pastry horns;
- rectangles rolled into cylinders for chocolate chip rolls.

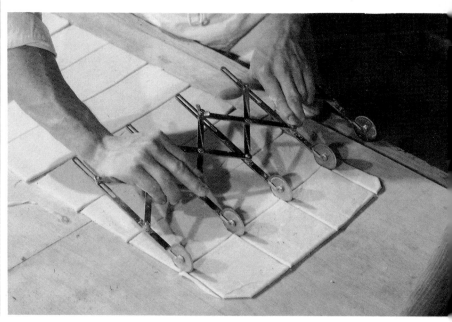

## 2. Shaping miniature pastries

It is best to cut sheets of dough for miniature pastries with a dough cutter to save time.

It is most efficient to prepare the pastries in groups based on the same size and shape of cut out pastry - squares, rectangles etc.

The wide variety of miniature pastries which are available makes it possible for bakers to offer a constantly changing selection to their clientele.

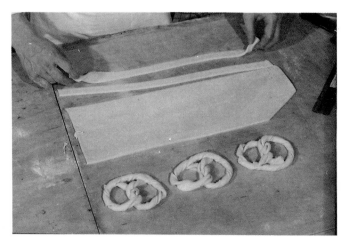

# 3. Glazing and garnishing the pastries

Glaze the pastries and garnish them with pastry cream and poached or canned fruits such as apricots, pears, plums, oranges, etc.

Make sure that the fruit is well placed on the pastries so it doesn't fall off when the pastries rise in the oven.

Do not add too much pastry cream or fruit or the pastries will be heavy.

Some pastries can be coated with slivered almonds or crystallized sugar after baking. The choice will depend on the tastes and age of the clientele.

# 4. Baking and finishing

When the pastries come out of the oven, glaze them according to the recipe.

Do not try to remove sweet pretzels or twisted fruit rolls from the sheet pans until they have completely cooled or the pastry cream may cause them to stick.

The tops of sweet pretzels and twisted fruit rolls can be coated with a mixture of blueberries and cold glaze after baking.

# Windmills

**Type of dough used**

Danish pastry dough or croissant dough.

**Preparation**

Cut the dough into 4 to 5 mm. (between 1/8 and 1/4 in.) thick squares measuring 10 cm. (4 in.) on each side.

**Shaping**

Make 4 cm. (1 in.) cuts moving from each corner toward the center of the squares. Fold every other corner over the center of the crosses.

Brush the pastries with egg wash and place them in a 28 °C (82 °F) proof box or steam chamber.

**Proofing**

Approximately 1 hour.

**Baking**

Pipe a dollop of pastry cream in the center of each of the windmills using a pastry bag with a 10 mm. (3/8 in.) plain tip. Place a piece of poached or canned fruit over the dollop of pastry cream; apricot halves work especially well for this. Brush the pastries a second time with egg wash.

Bake for 15 minutes in a 220 °C (425 °F) oven.

Brush the pastries with sugar syrup as soon as they come out of the oven.

# Bow ties

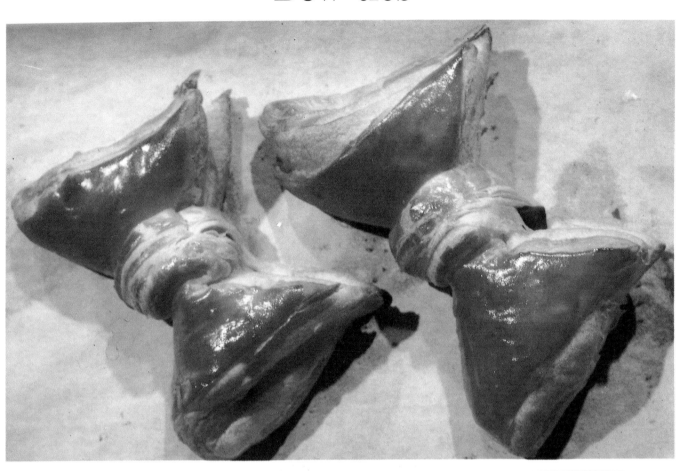

**Preparation**

Cut the dough into 4 to 5 mm. (between 1/8 and 1/4 in.) thick squares measuring 10 cm. (4 in.) on each side.

**Shaping**

Brush the edges of one half of each of the squares with egg wash. Place a strip of chocolate diagonally through the center of the squares.

Fold the squares over themselves so they form triangles. Press firmly on the

edges to form a seal. Cut a thin strip (3 to 4 mm./1/8 in. wide) of pastry starting at the point of the triangle and running three fourths of the way to the base.

Bend the base of the triangle to obtain a butterfly shape. Wrap the strip of dough around the middle of the two triangles to create a bow tie effect. Brush the pastries with egg wash and put them in a 28 °C (82 °F) proof box or steam chamber to rise.

**Proofing**

Proof the pastries for approximately 1 hour and brush them a second time with egg wash.

**Baking**

Bake for 18 to 19 minutes in a 220 °C (425 °F) oven. As soon as the bow ties come out of the oven, brush them with warm sugar syrup (30 °C/86 °F).

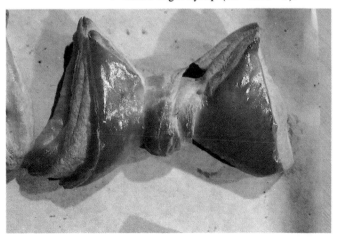

# Flemish fruit squares

**Type of dough used**
Danish pastry dough or croissant dough

**Preparation**

Cut the dough into 4 to 5 mm. (between 1/8 and 1/4 in.) thick squares measuring 10 cm. (4 in.) on each side.

**Shaping**

Brush the center of each of the squares with egg wash. Turn each of the corners into the center and press to seal them.

Brush the pastries with egg wash and place them in a 28 °C (82 °F) proof box or steam chamber.

Pipe a dollop of pastry cream in the center of each of the pastries using a pastry bag with a 10 mm. (3/8 in.) plain tip. Place a piece of poached or canned fruit over the dollop of pastry cream; apricot halves work especially well for this.

**Proofing**

Proof the pastries for about 1 hour.

**Baking**

Brush the pastries a second time with egg wash. Bake for 18 minutes in a 220 °C (425 °F) oven.

Brush the pastries with sugar syrup as soon as they come out of the oven.

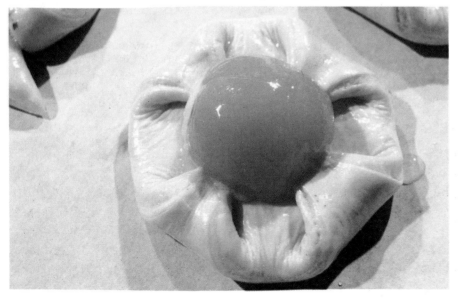

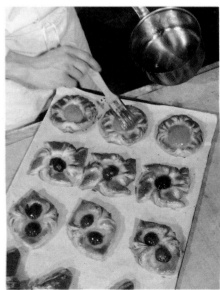

# Danish pastry horns

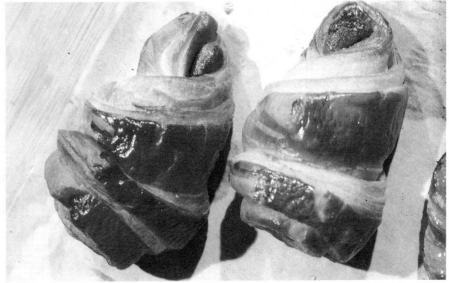

### Type of dough used

Flemish pastry dough or croissant dough.

### Preparation

Roll the dough into a sheet 4 mm. (between 1/8 and 1/4 in.) thick.

### Shaping

Cut the dough into triangles the same way as when making croissants.

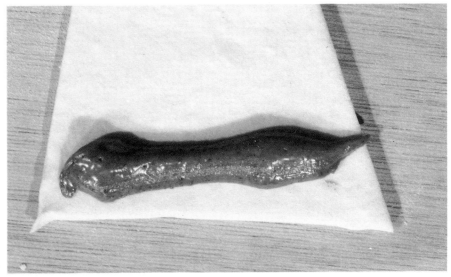

Pipe a strip of praline paste, pastry cream, or almond cream along the base of each of the triangles using a pastry bag with a 10 mm. (3/8 in.) plain tip.

Carefully roll the triangles around the cream filling using one hand for rolling and the other to gently stretch the dough. Avoid pressing down on the pastries so none of the filling seeps out.

The finished pastries look like cream-filled croissant halves.

### Proofing

Proof the pastries for approximately 1 hour.

Brush the pastries with egg wash when they have finished proofing.

### Baking

Bake the pastries for 17 minutes in a 220 °C (425 °F) oven.

Brush the pastries with warm (30 °C/86 °F) sugar syrup as soon they come out of the oven.

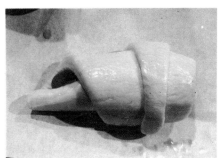

# Danish sweet rolls

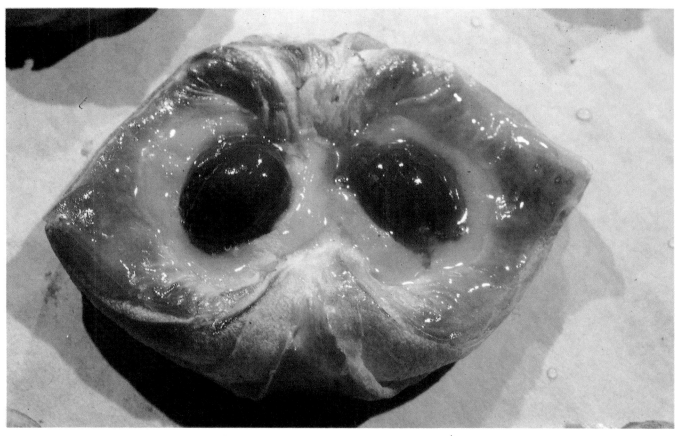

### Type of dough used
Danish pastry dough or croissant dough.

### Preparation
Cut the dough into 4 to 5 mm. (between 1/8 and 1/4 in.) thick squares measuring 10 cm. (4 in.) on each side.

### Shaping
Fold 2 opposing corners into the center of the square of pastry. Press firmly to seal them. Brush the pastries with egg wash and place them in a 28 °C (82 °F) proof box or steam chamber.

### Proofing
Proof the pastries for approximately 1 hour.

### Baking
Use a pastry bag with a 10 mm. (3/8 in.) tip to place a dollop of pastry cream on each side of the pastries. Place an apricot or plum half over each of the dollops. Brush the exposed parts of the pastry with egg wash. Bake the pastries for 18 minutes in a 220 °C (425 °F) oven.

Brush the pastries with sugar syrup as soon as they come out of the oven.

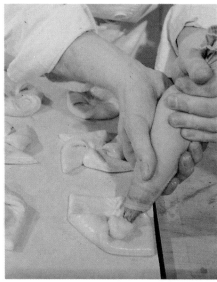

# Danish tartlets

**Type of dough used**

Danish pastry dough, croissant dough, or puff pastry.

**Preparation**

Cut the dough into 4 to 5 mm. (between 1/8 and 1/4 in.) thick squares measuring 10 cm. (4 in.) on each side.

**Shaping**

Fold the squares in half to form triangles.

Use a pastry cutter to cut strips on 2 sides of the triangles leading three quarters of the way to the apex.

Open the triangles into squares.

Brush the edges of the squares with egg wash and fold the strips to the opposite sides.

Brush again with egg wash and transfer the pastries to sheet pans for proofing. Place the pastries in a 28 °C (82 °F) proof box or steam chamber.

**Proofing**

Approximately 1 hour.

When the pastries are sufficiently proofed, brush them once again with egg wash and fill the insides with pastry cream. Different types of poached or canned fruits such as cherries, plums, and apricot halves can then be placed over the pastry cream.

**Baking**

Bake the tartlets for approximately 17 minutes in a 220 °C (425 °F) oven. As soon as the tartlets come out of the oven, they should be brushed with sugar syrup.

# Medallions

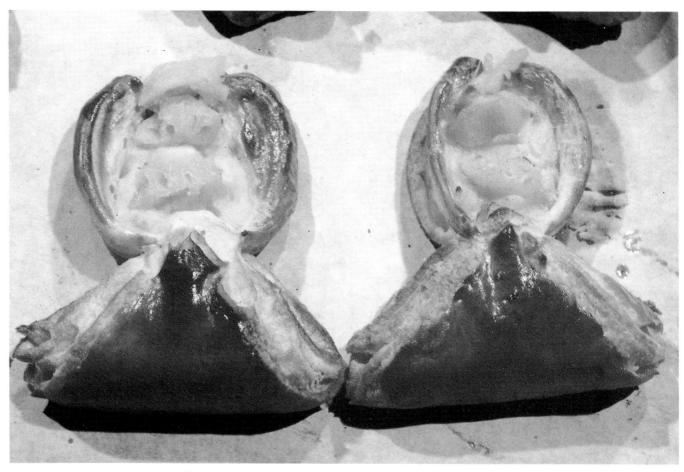

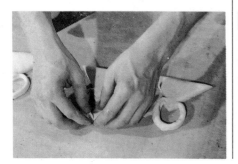

### Type of dough used

Danish pastry dough or croissant dough.

### Preparation

Cut the dough into 4 to 5 mm. (between 1/8 and 1/4 in.) thick squares measuring 10 cm. (4 in.) on each side.

### Shaping

Brush two opposite sides of the squares with egg wash and then fold the squares in half to form triangles. Press gently on the edges of the triangles to make sure they are well sealed. Some bakers like to put a strip of chocolate or a dollop of pastry cream or almond cream in the center of the squares before forming the triangles.

Use a pastry cutter to cut two 4 to 5 mm. (between 1/8 and 1/4 in.) wide strips on two sides of the triangles leading almost all the way to the apex. Each of these strips is then bent around and attached to form a heart shape. Brush the pastries with egg wash and put them in a 28 °C (82 °F) proof box.

### Proofing

Proof the pastries for approximately 1 hour. Fill the hearts with pastry cream and candied fruit.

### Baking

Bake the medallions for approximately 15 minutes in a 220 °C (425 °F) oven.

Be careful to not let the medallions dry out in the oven. Let them cool while still on the baking sheets or the hot pastry cream will cause them to stick.

As soon as the medallions come out of the oven, they should be brushed with 30 °C (86 °F) sugar syrup.

# Bats

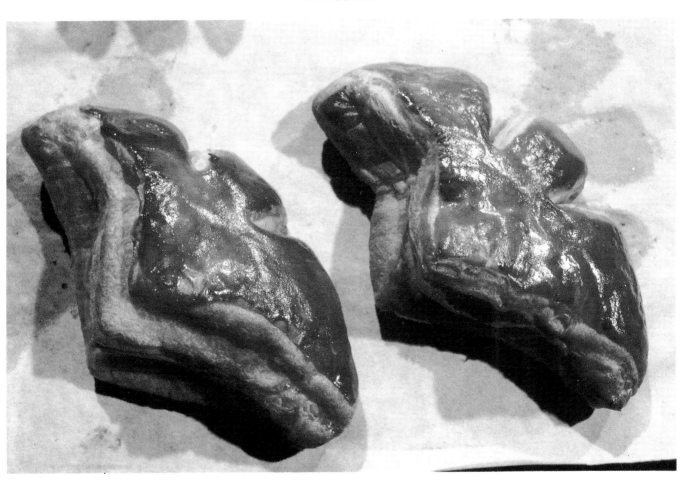

### Type of dough used

Danish pastry dough or croissant dough.

### Preparation

Cut the dough into 4 to 5 mm. (between 1/8 and 1/4 in.) thick squares measuring 10 cm. (4 in.) on each side.

### Shaping

Brush 2 opposite sides of the squares with egg wash.

Place a thin bar of chocolate diagonally across the squares.

Fold the squares in half to obtain triangles. Press firmly on the edges to make sure they are well sealed.

Using a pastry cutter, make two 1 cm. cuts into the base of the triangles. Turn the bottom corners of the triangles downward.

Brush the pastry bats with egg wash and place them in a 28 °C (82 °F) proof box or steam chamber.

### Proofing

Proof the bats for approximately 1 hour.

Brush the bats a second time with egg wash after proofing.

### Baking

Bake the bats for approximately 17 minutes in a 220 °C (425 °F) oven.

As soon as the pastries come out of the oven, brush them with sugar syrup.

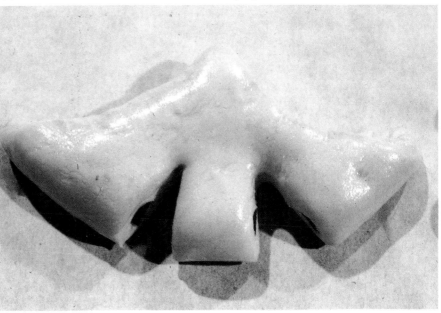

# Bear claws

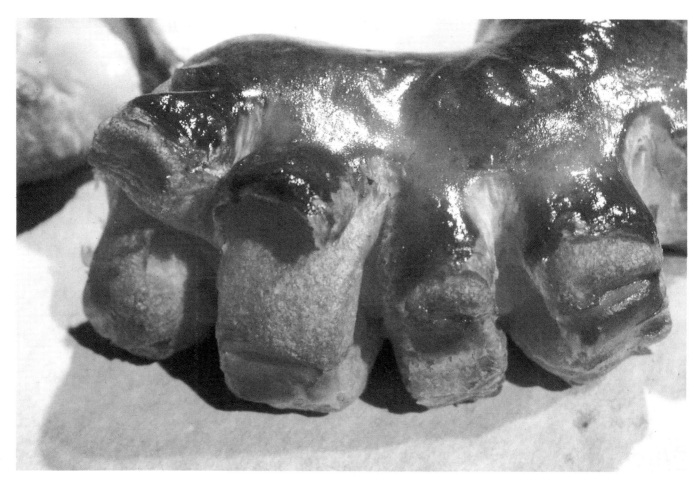

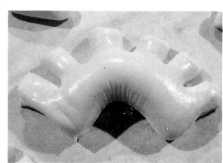

**Type of dough used**

Danish pastry dough or croissant dough.

**Preparation**

Cut the dough into 4 to 5 mm. (between 1/8 and 1/4 in.) thick squares measuring 10 cm. (4 in.) on each side.

**Shaping**

Roll over the middle of each of the squares. This thins the center, leaving more room for the cream filling, and also lengthens the squares.

Fill a pastry bag with a 10 mm. (3/8 in.) plain tip with pastry cream or almond cream.

Pipe a strip of either cream down the middle of the squares. Do not go all the way to the ends.

Brush one of the two sides of the pastry with water.

Fold the squares in half to enclose the filling. Using a pastry cutter, make 5, 2 cm. (1 in.) cuts into the sides of the pastries.

Bend the base of the bear claws downward to spread open the cuts.

Brush the bear claws with egg wash and place them in a 28 °C (82 °F) proof box or steam chamber.

**Proofing**

Proof the bear claws for approximately 1 hour.

Brush them a second time with egg wash at the end of proofing.

**Baking**

Bake the bear claws for approximately 17 minutes in a 220 °C (425 °F) oven.

Brush the bear claws with 30 °C (86 °F) sugar syrup as soon as they come out of the oven.

# Twisted fruit rolls

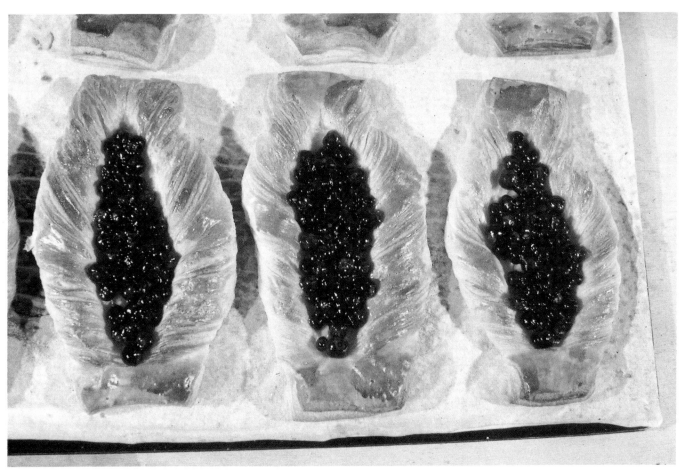

**Preparation**

Cut the dough into strips 4 by 13 cm.

**Shaping**

Using a pastry cutter, make a cut down the center of the strips. Make sure to leave each side of the strips attached at the ends. Take the sides of the strips and twist them in opposite directions; one should be twisted inward, the other outward.

Place the pastries on sheet pans. Be careful to keep the two sides apart.

Brush the fruit rolls with egg wash and place them in a 28 °C (82 °F) proof box or steam chamber.

**Proofing**

Proof the pastries for approximately 1 hour. Brush the pastries a second time with egg wash before baking.

Using a pastry bag, fill the insides of the rolls with pastry cream.

**Baking**

Bake the pastries in a 220 °C (425 °F) oven for approximately 15 minutes.

When the pastries have finished baking, let them cool on the baking sheets before trying to lift them off, otherwise the hot pastry cream will cause them to stick.

As soon as the pastries come out of the oven, place berries (blueberries are shown here) on top of the cream filling. Brush the pastries with sugar syrup.

If fruit is unavailable, these rolls can be prepared with pastry cream alone.

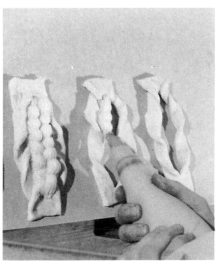

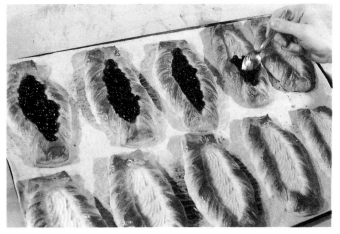

# Chocolate chip rolls

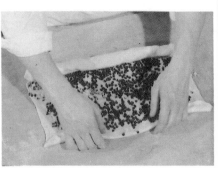

### Type of dough used

Danish pastry dough or croissant dough.

### Preparation

Roll out 4 mm. (between 1/8 and 1/4 in.) thick sheets of dough using a dough sheeter or rolling pin.

### Shaping

Spread the sheet of dough with a thin layer of pastry cream then sprinkle the surface with chocolate chips.

Roll two opposite sides of the dough to obtain two equal size cylinders. Press gently on the double rolls to make sure they hold together during baking.

Cut the double rolls into 2 cm. (in.) thick slices.

Brush the slices with egg wash and place them in a 28 °C (82 °F) proof box or steam chamber.

## Proofing

Proof the rolls for approximately 1 hour.

## Baking

Brush the rolls a second time with egg wash and bake in a 220 °C (425 °F) oven for approximately 18 minutes.

When the rolls have cooled, sprinkle them with confectioner's sugar.

# Sweet Pretzels

**Type of dough used**

Danish pastry dough or croissant dough.

**Preparation**

Roll the pastry into 4 or 5 mm. (between 1/8 and 1/4 in.) thick sheets. Cut the sheets into 40 by 2 cm. (16 by 1 in.) strips.

**Shaping**

Twist the strips of dough by turning them in opposite directions at each end.

Bring both ends of the strip toward the center and wrap the two ends around each other. Attach the two ends to the bottom of the pretzels.

Brush the pretzels with egg wash and place them in a 28 °C (82 °F) proof box or steam chamber.

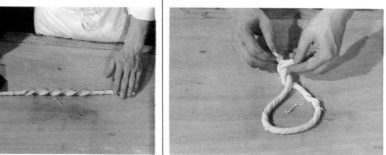

## Proofing

Proof the pretzels for approximately 1 hour.

When the pretzels have finished proofing, brush them a second time with egg wash and fill the empty spaces with pastry cream.

## Baking

Bake the pretzels in a 220 °C (425 °F)

oven for approximately 15 minutes. Be careful to not let them dry out.

When the pretzels have finished baking, don't try to remove them from the baking sheets before they are completely cool. Otherwise, the still hot pastry cream may cause them to stick.

Brush the pretzels with 30 °C (86 °F) sugar syrup as soon as they come out of the oven.

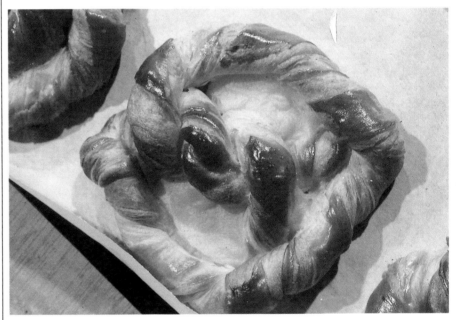

# Candied fruit strips

**Type of dough used**

Danish pastry dough or croissant dough.

## Preparation

Cut sheets of dough into rectangles 25 by 30 cm. (10 by 12 in.).

Spread half the width of the sheets with a thin layer of pastry cream leaving a 2 cm. (1 in.) border. Sprinkle the pastry cream with cubes of candied fruit.

Brush the border with egg wash and fold the uncoated side over the layer of fruit and pastry cream.

Cut the pastry into 3 cm. (1 in.) thick slices and transfer them to baking sheets.

Brush the fruit strips with egg wash and place them in a 28 °C (82 °F) proof box or steam chamber.

## Proofing

Proof the pastries for approximately 1 hour.

Brush the strips a second time with egg wash after proofing.

## Baking

Bake the candied fruit strips in a 220 °C (435 °F) oven for 15 minutes.

Prepare a glaze with confectioner's sugar and water or fondant and water to brush on the pastries after baking.

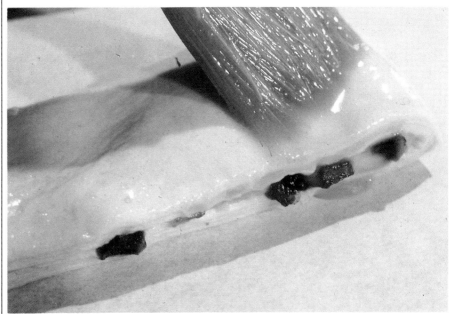

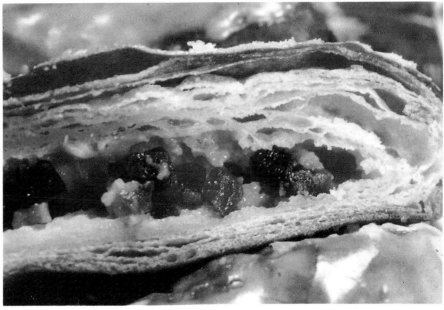

# C – Brioches

### The effect of added ingredients

Ingredients such as milk, butter, shortening, eggs, and sugar will often improve the quality of the finished breads depending on the quantities that have been used.

These additional ingredients also affect the quality of the dough and the rising potential of the dough during baking.

Most brioche is unflavored, but certain special recipes contain orange flower water or other traditional flavorings.

Brioche is often prepared with dried fruit, pralines, chocolate, raisins, lemon zest and crystallized sugar.

*Fresh milk:*
- slightly decreases rising of the dough during baking,
- increases browning,
- contributes to the development of a soft shiny crust, and a fine regular crumb,
- improves flavor.

*Butter or shortening*
- slightly decreases rising of the dough during baking,
- increases browning and contributes to a bright, shiny crust,
- butter improves the flavor,
- contributes to the development of a soft crust and a fine, regular crumb.

*Eggs*
- help emulsify the dough,
- help fats combine with the water in the dough and contribute to the retention of carbon dioxide,
- increase browning and contribute to the development of a soft brown crust and a fine regular crumb.

*Sugar*
- causes the dough to color more quickly during baking,
- improves flavor.

Because fresh milk, butter, and eggs slow down the fermentation, it is often necessary to increase the amount of yeast.

# A Large Variety of Brioches

## The long history of brioche

*Traditionally, special pastries such as brioche are eaten only on special occasions, but today they are becoming staples for both breakfast and snacks.*

*It is easy to imagine how brioche originated – man has long known that milk, butter, and eggs can be added to the daily bread for a richer, cake-like loaf.*

*The first brioche was most likely prepared by adding eggs and butter to already fermented bread dough and probably resembled a " fougasse ", a type of bread still prepared today. There is a version of " fougasse " (galette vendéenne) where butter, eggs, and sugar are added to already fermented dough.*

*In France, a version of brioche prepared around Easter is still made using the old technique of adding butter, eggs, and sugar to already fermented dough.*

*No one knows for sure when brioche was invented but we do know that brioche is the oldest type of bread in which sugar is added to the dough.*

Classic butter brioche

Star brioche

Russian-style braided

## Miniature brioches

Individual

Dried fruits

Chocolate

Cream-filled

Bresse-style

Mice

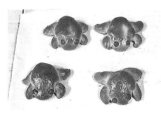

Frogs

Elephants

## Regional brioches

Brioche crowns

Vendée-style

Nice-style crown

Bordeaux-style crown

Craquelins

Anis loaves

Swiss-style

Layered brioche

# Classic Butter Brioche

## Introduction

Classic butter brioche dough can be used to prepare a variety of breads prepared in standard bakeries and pastry shops. Some more typical preparations are large round brioches (brioches à tête), braided loaves, crown loaves, and daisy loaves.

For these preparations, Parisian-style brioche which is particularly rich in butter, eggs, and often milk, is also sometimes used.

The smell and flavor of classic butter brioche are largely due to the type and quality of the raw ingredients used in its preparation.

It is important when preparing brioche to use a high quality, high gluten flour (patent flour is good) either alone or combined with an equal amount of ordinary bread flour. Make sure also that the butter has an appealing smell and flavor and that the milk, if it is used, is perfectly fresh.

Classic brioche is not flavored in the same way as certain regional brioches so that the flavor and fragrance of the raw ingredients is not masked.

### Uses of classic butter brioche dough

*1. Classic shaped brioches*
*2. Braided loaves*
*3. Miniature loaves and rolls*

Classic butter brioche can be used to prepare:
Round brioche with dried fruits
Bresse-style sugar tart
Bresse-style cream and apricot filled tart
Round chocolate brioche
Cream filled round brioches with fruit added after baking
Miniature animals: mice, frogs, elephant heads etc.
Classic butter brioche can be prepared with the additional fermented dough from a previous batch or with a yeast starter.

### Ingredients

1 kg. high gluten flour (patent) (35 oz.)
20 g. salt (4 tsp.)
35 g. yeast (1.2 oz.)
120 to 150 g. sugar (4 to 5.5 oz.)
500 to 600 g. eggs (17.5 to 21 oz.) and 100 ml. milk (3.5 fl. oz.)
400 to 500 g. butter (14 to 17.5 oz.)

A small amount of ascorbic acid (20 mg. to 1 kg./35 oz. of flour) can be added to stabilize the gluten structure and increase the holding power of the dough. This is especially important if

the flour seems weak in gluten or if previously fermented dough is not being used.

The time needed to prepare brioche dough is considerably reduced if fermented dough from a previous batch is used; the first rising will be shortened.

### Kneading

Several methods can be used.

Gently knead together flour, salt, sugar, and eggs on slow speed (frasing) for 4 to 5 minutes. Two of the eggs can be held in reserve and added once the dough begins to firm up.

The yeast can be added along with the liquid ingredients or after the initial kneading (frasing).

When fermented dough or a yeast starter is being used, it should be added halfway through the kneading – after the frasing but before the butter is added.

Do not begin to add the butter until the dough begins to pull away from the sides of the mixing bowl. The dough should be smooth and homogenous.

It is also possible to let the dough rest after the first stage of kneading (frasing) and then continuing the kneading 30 minutes later on medium speed. This reinforces the gluten structure of the dough and reduces the total time required for actual kneading. In short: gently knead the flour, sugar, eggs, and the milk (frasing); let the mixture rest for 15 to 30 minutes; add the yeast, the ascorbic acid, the salt, and the fermented dough or yeast starter and continue kneading. When the dough starts to pull away from the sides of the mixing bowl, the butter can be incorporated.

### Kneading times

With an electric mixer (paddle blade): 4 minutes at slow speed, 10 minutes at medium speed (without butter) or 7 minutes at slow speed (with butter).

With a kneading machine: 4 minutes at slow speed, 13 minutes on medium speed (without butter) or 8 minutes on slow speed (with butter).

The temperature of the dough should be 23 °C (73 °F) after kneading.

**First rising:** 2 1/2 hours

### Punching down

The dough should be " punched down " or given a turn once or twice during the rising depending on the recipe or chosen work method. This punching down helps improve the strength of the dough.

Punch down the dough the first time after 50 minutes and once again after 1 hour 40 minutes.

### Refrigerating

It is best to refrigerate the dough in a 5 to 6 °C (41 to 43 °F) refrigerator for several hours before it is used. The preliminary cooling improves the consistency and body of the dough.

### Scaling (20 min.)

Miniature loaves are best prepared 10 at a time.

For miniature round brioches (brioches à tête), weigh a 500 g. (17.5 oz.) section of dough and cut it into 10, 50 g. (1.8 oz.) sections.

This method saves time.

Round the individual pieces of dough and let them rest.

**Resting:** 10 to 15 minutes.

**Shaping:** 20 minutes depending on the chosen size and shape.

**Proofing:** 1 hour 40 minutes in a proof box or steam chamber at 27 to 28 °C (81 to 82 °F).

### Baking

Bake the brioches in a relatively hot oven (the actual temperature will depend on the amount of sugar in the recipe.): 225 to 230 °C (425 to 450 °F) for miniature brioches. For larger brioches, lower the oven temperature by approximately 10 to 20 °C (20 to 40 °F) to about 210 °C (400 °F).

*Baking times:*

13 to 16 minutes for 50 g. (1.8 oz.) brioches and 16 to 18 minutes for 300 g. (14 oz.) brioches.

## CLASSIC BUTTER BRIOCHE

| | | | |
|---|---|---|---|
| **PREPARATION** | **15** min | **15** min | • calculate the temperatures<br>• prepare and weigh the raw ingredients |
| **KNEADING**<br>**(kneading machine)** | **21** min | **31** min | • knead 4 minutes on slow speed (frasing)<br>• 13 minutes medium speed without butter or 8 minutes slow speed with butter<br>• add the butter when the dough starts to pull away from the sides of the mixing bowl |
| **FIRST RISING** | **2** hr | **2** hr **30** | • punch down the dough after 50 minutes<br>• punch down again after 1 hr 40 min |
| **REFRIGERATING**<br>**THE DOUGH** | **12** hr | **14** hr **30** | • refrigerate at 5 to 6 °C (41 to 43 °F)<br>• refrigeration stiffens the dough |
| **SCALING** | **20** min | **14** hr **50** | • divide the dough and round the sections<br>• let the rounded sections rest |
| **RESTING** | **10** to **15** min | **15** hr | |
| **SHAPING** | **20** min | **15** hr **20** | • gently work the dough into the desired shape |
| **PROOFING** | **1** hr **40** | **17** hr | • proof in a proof box at 27 °C (81 °F) |
| **PREPARING**<br>**FOR BAKING** | **10** min | **17** hr **10** | • brush the loaves with egg wash and score them with scissors depending on their shape<br>• add sugar |
| **BAKING** | **13** to **18** min | **17** hr **25** | • do not let the brioches get too brown<br>• do not let the brioches dry out |
| **COOLING** | **5** min | **17** hr **30** | • let the brioches cool before arranging them on trays or cooling racks |

**NOTE :** *When preparing brioche with a mixed starter (using already fermented dough), use a piece of brioche from the day before (400 g./14 oz. of fermented dough per 1 kg./ 35.5 oz. flour). A piece of fermented standard bread dough can also be used (300 g./ 10.5 oz. of fermented dough per 1 kg./35.5 oz. flour).*

# Star Brioche (Brioche Étoile)

## *Braided loaves*

Even though a wide variety of braided loaves is found throughout Europe, they are relatively little appreciated in France and the United States. The braided loaf has its origins in the grim tradition that required a woman to be sacrificed if her husband died before her. When this tradition finally died out, it was replaced with the wife's ritualistic cutting of her long braids so that they could be buried with her husband. Greek literature is filled with numerous examples of this practice. A similar custom was recorded among the ancient Germans who imposed closely cropped hair on their servants and slaves. The ritual clipping

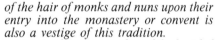

of the hair of monks and nuns upon their entry into the monastery or convent is also a vestige of this tradition.

Eventually, the sacrifice of the braided hair was replaced by symbolic preparation of braided breads and as Christianity spread through Europe, the bread was distributed to the poor rather than thrown in the tomb. This tradition still exists in Europe where braided loaves are given to the poor on feast days such as All Saints Day and the New Year.

As braided breads came to be appreciated on their own merits, other varieties such as star and crown loaves were developed.

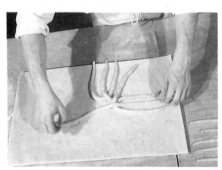

## Introduction

With a little skill and imagination bakers can diversify their products and

constantly offer new and different types of breads to their clientele. Braided loaves can be offered throughout the year but they are especially appreciated on holidays.

Braided loaves which are prepared with brioche dough have a somewhat different appearance than braided loaves prepared with either standard bread dough or Viennese bread dough (see volume 1). Brioche dough tends to be softer than either of these.

### Scaling

Divide the dough into 60 g. (2.1 oz.) sections or prepare a 540 g. (19 oz.) section and divide it in three equal parts.

### Shaping

Roll the pieces of dough until they all have the same length, 35 cm. (14 in.). Make sure the middle is thicker and the strands are thinner near the ends.

Once the sections of dough have all been rolled into stands, place them in a circle. They should overlap i.e. the first strand should be half covered by the second etc.

### Braiding

Braid the strands in groups of three. In this way you will obtain 6 braids containing 3 strands each. Each braid should be perfectly even; there should be no single strands remaining at the ends. (see photos).

The six braids of three strands each are braided in the following way: The first group is braided upright: bring the left strand to the middle (it now becomes the center strand) then move the right strand to the middle. Repeat the process until the braid is completed.

The second group is braided underneath; the strands are passed under each other instead of over. Lift the center strand and bring the left one under so it now becomes the center. Lift this center strand and bring the right strand under and so forth until the braid is finished.

Braid the third group of strands overhand, the fourth group underhand, the fifth group overhand and the sixth group underhand.

This method makes it possible to present a perfectly braided star brioche.

Star brioche is easy to prepare after a little practice. At the beginning, it is necessary to find the 3 strands that go together. This is very simple: if you start with the wrong strand you will have the impression of having turned it around and the center of the star will be unbalanced.

Place the star on a baking sheet covered with a sheet of parchment paper. The points of the star can be left straight or folded according to taste.

### Proofing

Proof the loaves for 1 hours. Do not let them over proof.

Brush the star with egg wash before baking.

### Baking

The brioche stars can be left on the parchment paper and slid directly onto the conveyor or peel without using a baking sheet.

Bake for 30 minutes in a 210 °C (400 °F) oven.

# Russian-style Braided Loaves

# (Tresse Russe)

## Introduction

These appetizing loaves are relatively simple to prepare and can be served at family dinners.

Using classic butter brioche greatly improves the quality of the finished loaves. Coat a sheet of the dough with a layer of pastry cream and sprinkle the cream with raisins or candied fruit.

Tightly roll the dough and then cut it in two and braid it.

When the braid is complete, brush it with glaze then sprinkle it with crystallized sugar or slivered almonds.

Because this loaf takes awhile to prepare, it is usually made in large loaves.

## Preparing the brioche dough

Prepare a classic butter brioche and let it rise.

## Scaling and resting

Weigh the dough into 200 g. (7 oz.) sections (or larger if desired).
Gently work them into oval shapes and let them rest for 10 to 15 minutes. Make sure they are protected from drafts.

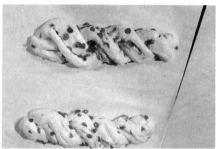

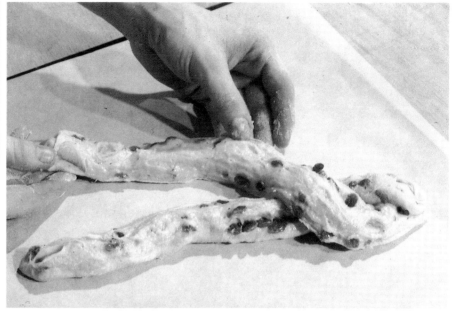

## Shaping

Roll the sections of dough into 3 or 4 mm. (1/8 to 1/4 in.) thick rectangles.

Spread each rectangle with pastry cream and sprinkle the cream with raisins or candied fruits.

It is also possible to cover the rectangles with almond cream sprinkled with slivered almonds.

Roll up the rectangles and cut them in two lengthwise.

Place the two lengths in a cross and braid them.

Place the braided dough on sheet pans or in rectangular molds.

## Proofing

2 hours to 2 1/2 hours in a proof box at 27 °C (81 °F).

Brush the loaves with egg wash before baking.

## Baking

Bake the loaves for 25 minutes at 220 °C (425 °F).

When the loaves are finished baking they should be brushed with glaze. This also improves their shelf life.

Sprinkle the loaves with slivered almonds or crystallized sugar.

# Miniature Brioches (Petites Pièces)

Using the brioche dough, different types of miniature brioches can be prepared:
• Individual brioches with dried fruits
• Chocolate brioches
• Cream-filled individual brioches
• Bresse-style tarts
• Individual brioches with pastry cream
• Animals: mice, frogs, elephants, etc.

Individual brioches can also be classified into:

1) Miniature brioches
2) Cream-filled individual brioches

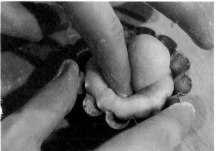

# Individual Brioches with dried fruit and nuts (walnuts, hazelnuts, raisins)

Incorporate the dried fruit and nuts into the brioche dough either at the end of kneading or after refrigerating the dough. Use 250 g. (9 oz.) of fruit and nuts per 1.5 kg. (53 oz.) of dough.

Dried fruits improve the flavor and shelf life of the brioche. When dried fruits are added to brioche dough, the first rising can be carried out more quickly.

On the other hand, when dried fruits and nuts are added to the dough, it becomes more fragile and difficult to shape.

### Dried fruits and nuts

Rinse off the raisins in cold water then soften them for several hours in water to which some flavorful liqueur or brandy has been added. Drain them in a strainer before incorporating them into the dough.

Do not chop the nuts or hazelnuts too finely or their flavor and texture will be lost.

### Procedure

*Scaling:* Weigh the dough into 500 g. (17.5 oz.) sections. Divide each of the sections into equal parts. Round each of the sections and let them rest.

*Shaping:* Round the sections of dough a second time and place them on sheet pans to rise.

*Proofing:* Approximately 1 hour.
Do not let the dough overproof. Brush with egg wash just before baking.

Score a cross on the top of the individual brioches and place a half a walnut in the center of the cross

*Baking:* Bake the individual brioches in a 220 °C (425 °F) oven for 15 to 18 minutes.

## Individual chocolate brioches

Weigh the dough into 500 g. (9 oz.) sections. Divide each of the sections equally into 10 pieces.

Round each of the individual sections and place them upside down on sheet pans so the seam is on top.

Drop-shaped chocolate chips are then applied to the outside of the individual brioches.

Gently press about 12 chocolate chips onto the surface of the brioches without puncturing the dough.

Carefully round the brioches a second time.

**Proofing:** Allow the dough to proof for 1 or 2 hours at 27 °C (81 °F).

Brush the brioches with egg wash just before baking. Score the tops of the brioches with a cross shape and place a few chocolate chips on the center of the cross.

Bake for 15 minutes at 220 °C (425 °F).

## Cream-filled individual brioches

Weigh the dough into 500 g. (17.5 oz.) sections. Divide each of the sections into 10 equal parts.

Round each of the individual sections and let them rest for 10 to 15 minutes.

Round the individual brioches a second time and let them proof for about 1 hour. Brush them with egg wash.

Just before baking, fill a pastry bag fitted with a 10 mm. (.4 in.) tip with pastry cream. Insert the tip halfway down into each of the brioches and squeeze in 10 to 15 g. (about a tablespoon) of pastry cream into each one until it swells slightly.

When injecting the pastry cream, make sure that the tip of the pastry bag is as close to the center of each of the brioches as possible. If it is too close to the top or bottom, the cream will ooze out during baking.

Bake the cream-filled brioches for 16 minutes in a 220 °C (425 °F) oven.

As soon as the brioches come out of the oven, place candied orange rinds on the tops.

The brioches can also be glazed with a glaze combined with some blueberry jelly and a teaspoon of blueberry preserves placed in the hole left by the pastry bag.

# Bresse-style tarts (Bressannes)

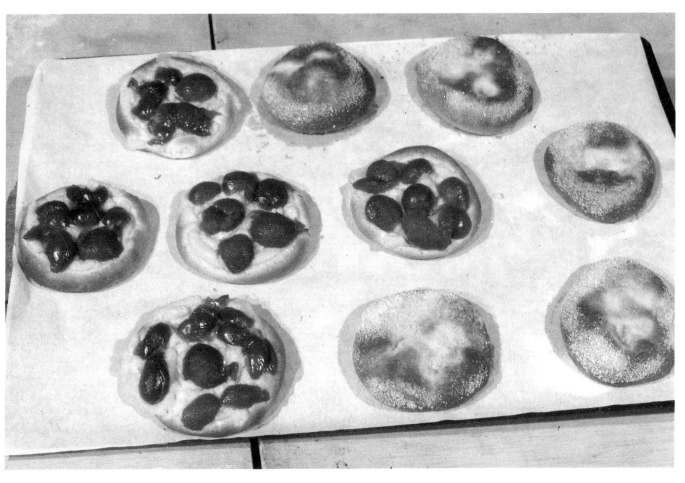

Weigh the dough into 500 g. (17.5 oz.) sections. Divide each of the sections into equal parts.

Round the sections and let them rest.

Roll the individual sections of dough into flat disks and place them on sheet pans to rise.

**Proofing:** Approximately 1 1/2 hours.

Sprinkle the outer rim of each of the disks with granulated sugar just before baking.

Make indentations in the center of each of the disks with the tips of the fingers. Place a spoonful of crème fraîche or several pieces of butter on top of the disks so it is held by the indentations.

Bake the tarts in a 220 to 230 °C (425 to 450 °F) oven for approximately 10 minutes.

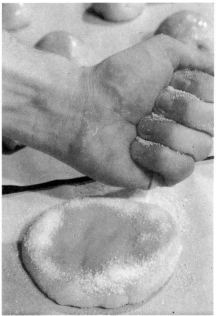

# Bresse-style tarts with pastry cream

 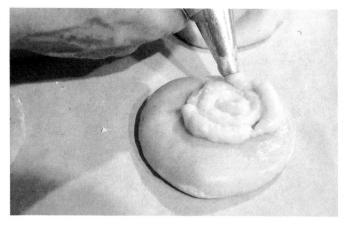

Prepare the disks for Bresse-style tarts in the same way as described above.

Before baking, coat 3/4 of the surface of each of the tarts with pastry cream using a pastry bag. Sprinkle the outside rim of the cakes with granulated sugar and place 2 apricot halves in the center of the pastry cream.

Glaze the cakes after baking.

# Miniature Brioche Animals

## Mice

Preparation time: 1 minute.

Divide a 500 g. (17.5 oz.) section of dough into 10 equal parts.

Round each piece of dough. Let them rest for approximately 15 minutes.

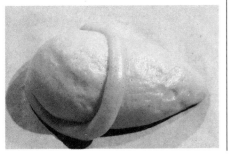

The dough can be shaped using 1 of 2 methods:

a) Take a 5 cm. (2 in.) length of brioche dough and roll out one end so that it forms a 6 cm. (2 1/2 in.) tail. Bring the tail around so that it meets the center of the dough.

b) Take a 10 g. (1/3 oz.) piece of dough off each 50 g. (1.8 oz.) section. Shape the remaining 40 g. (1.4 oz.) pieces of dough into 5 to 6 cm. (2 to 2 1/2 in.) long individual loaves. Roll out the small piece of dough to form a 6 cm. (2 in.) tail. Attach the tail to the larger piece of dough; leave the end of tail tucked under the dough.

**Proofing:** 1 hour at 27 °C (81 °F).

Just before baking, brush the mice with egg wash. Place slivered almonds on the mice to form ears and raisins for the eyes.

Bake for 18 minutes in a 225 °C (425 °F) oven.

The mice loaves can be coated with a mixture of butter, sugar, and flour (streusel) to give them a natural, mottled appearance.

### Coating ingredients

100 g. butter (3.5 oz.)
100 g. sugar (3.5 oz.)
100 g. flour (3.5 oz.)

Combine the ingredients by rubbing them together with the fingers until irregular lumps are formed.

# Frogs

Divide a 500 g. (17.5 oz.) section of dough into 10 equal parts.

Gently round each of the sections and let them rest for 10 to 15 minutes.

Remove two 8 g. (1/4 oz.) pieces of dough from each of the sections for making the legs and claws.

Roll the small pieces of dough into miniature sausage shapes. Flatten the ends with the forefinger to form the claws.

Take the larger section of dough and roll along part of it so that one extremity becomes the head. Thin the opposite end to form the tail.

Widen the loaves with a small rolling pin but leave the head in a round shape.

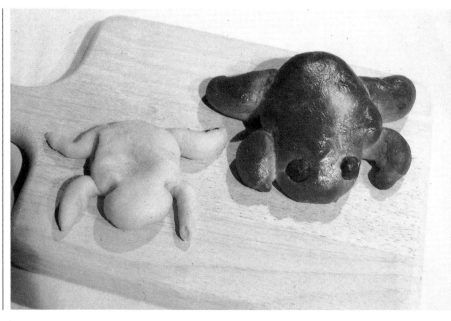

Place the legs and claws on sheet pans and set the bodies of the frogs on top.

**Proofing:** 1 1/2 hours.

Brush the frog brioches just before baking. Attach two raisons to make eyes. Make slits in the claws for a realistic effect.

Bake the frogs for 18 minutes in a 225 °C (450 °F) oven.

The frogs can be coated with crystallized sugar after baking.

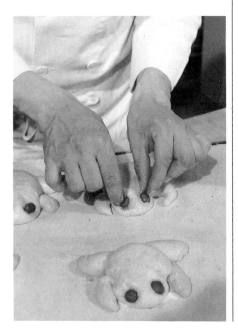

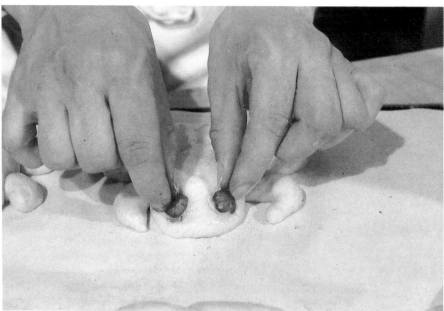

# Elephant heads

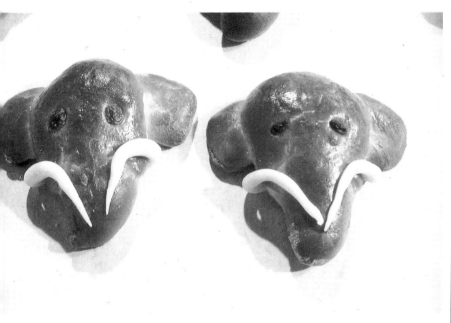

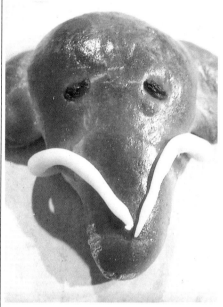

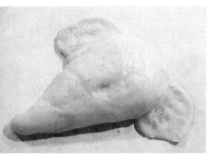

Preparation time: 2 minutes

Divide a 500 g. (17.5 oz.) of dough into 10 equal parts. Reserve two 10 g. (1/3 oz.) pieces out of each section for the ears.

Work the larger piece of dough into a pear shape and roll each of the small sections into balls.

Place the sections on a sheet pan, roll out the ears and brush them with egg wash.

Attach the ears to the head by first brushing one end with egg wash. The narrow part of the dough represents the elephant's trunk.

Brush the elephant heads with egg wash and attach two raisins to form the eyes.

Bake the heads for 17 minutes in a 225 °C (425 °F) oven.

After baking, attach two tusks made with almond paste to the front of each head.

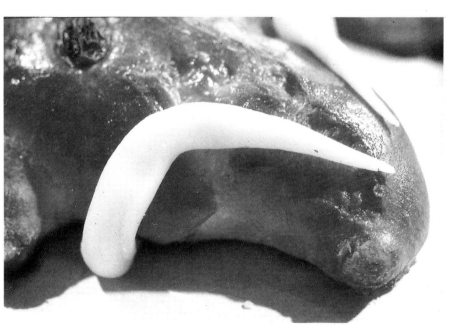

# Brioche Crowns (Pognes de Romans)

### Introduction

These brioches originated when home bakers reserved a piece of bread dough that they would enrich with eggs, butter, and other ingredients to be served on feast days and special occasions. "Poignée" means "handful" in French and provides us with the origin of the French name "pognes de Romans".

As tradition has it, once extra butter and eggs were added to the dough, it was worked into a crown shape and baked along with the everyday breads.

Crown brioche is most often found in the south of France, primarily in the regions of the Drôme and the Ardèche. Originally it was based on a natural sourdough starter but nowadays a yeast starter is most commonly used. Yeast starter gives a satisfactory result and shortens the total rising time required for the dough.

One characteristic of crown brioche is that flavorings such as orange flower water and lemon zest are frequently used.

Almonds or pralines are often incorporated into brioche crowns. They can be added directly to the dough just after kneading, just before it is shaped into crowns, or placed on the crowns at the last minute.

If regular bread flour is used for the brioche crowns rather than a special high gluten variety such as patent flour, a small amount of ascorbic acid can be added to the dough to contribute to the development of the gluten structure.

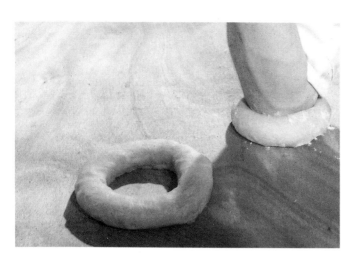

## Recipe for yeast starter

350 g. high quality flour (12.5 oz.)
210 ml. water (7 fl. oz.)
5 g. yeast (1 tsp.)

Knead the starter for 12 minutes on slow speed.

Let the starter rise for 6 hours at 22 °C (72 °F) or for 15 hours at 5 °C (41 °F).

## Recipe for crown brioche

1 kg. high quality flour (35 oz.)
20 g. salt (4 tsp.)
40 g. yeast (1.4 oz.)
100 g. yeast (3.5 oz.)
400 g. eggs (14 oz.)
280 g. butter (10 oz.)
50 ml. orange flour water (1.7 fl. oz.)
1 lemon zest
565 g. yeast starter (20 oz.)

## Kneading

Knead the dough for 4 minutes at slow speed and then for 15 minutes more at medium speed.

Begin the kneading with all the ingredients except for the butter, the starter, and the orange flower water.   Add the yeast starter to the dough halfway through the kneading – when the dough has started to pull away from the sides of the bowl.

Be careful not to over knead the dough which would detract from the flavor of the finished brioche crowns.

## First rising

Let the dough rise at room temperature for 3 to 4 hours.

Punch down the dough (give it a turn) after 1 hours and a second time after 2 hours.

**NOTE:** *If the pralines have been incorporated in the dough, the surface of the loaves can be sprinkled with crystallized sugar.*

## Scaling

Divide the dough into 400 to 500 g. (14 to 17.5 oz.) sections.

Round the sections once or twice depending on the strength of the dough. Pralines can be added at this time.

**Resting:** 10 minutes

## Shaping

Pierce the center of each of the rounded sections of dough with the palm of the hand or the elbow.

Place both hands in the center hole and turn the brioche several times until the center has the desired size to form the crown. Make sure the crown is even; be careful not to tear it.

**Proofing:** Approximately 3 hours.

**Baking:** Bake in a relatively low oven.

| BRIOCHE CROWNS | | | |
|---|---|---|---|
| **PREPARATION** | 10 min | 10 min | • *calculate the temperatures*<br>• *prepare and weigh the raw ingredients* |
| **KNEADING** | 18 min | 28 min | • *knead for 4 minutes slow speed (frasing)*<br>• *continue kneading for 14 minutes medium speed* |
| **FIRST RISING** | 4 hr | 4 hr 28 | • *punch down the dough one or two times* |
| **SCALING AND ROUNDING** | 10 min | 4 hr 38 | • *divide and weigh the dough in sections of the desired size* |
| **RESTING** | 10 min | 4 hr 48 | |
| **SHAPING** | 15 min | 5 hr 03 | • *gently work the dough into smooth and regular crown shapes* |
| **PROOFING** | 3 hr 00 | 8 hr 03 | • *proofing time will depend on the temperature* |
| **PREPARING FOR BAKING** | 5 min | 8 hr 08 | • *brush with egg wash and add the pralines* |
| **BAKING** | 20 to 25 min | 8 hr 30 | • *bake in a relatively low oven (200 to 220 °C (400 to 425 °F)* |
| **COOLING** | 5 min | 8 hr 35 | • *let cool on racks to prevent from becoming soggy* |

**STORAGE:** *Brioche crowns have a fairly good shelf life. They can be sold up to 2 days after baking.*

# Vendée-style Brioche (Brioche Vendéenne)

# Introduction

In the wooded areas of western France – the Vendée and Mauges – two special brioche cakes, " galettes paquaudes " and "alises " were traditionally prepared the Saturday before Easter Sunday.

These breads required a special starter which was long the responsibility of the village baker to prepare. The starter for these breads had to be incorporated at exactly the right time for the breads to have their traditional compact texture and flavor.

Even though these traditional brioches were prepared the day before Easter, they were not served until after the afternoon Easter feast when relatives and friends went from farm to farm tasting the different " paquaudes ".

Today, the traditional " alises " and "paquaudes " have been replaced with braided brioches and crown brioches.

It was also in western France that a bride's godparents had prepared a special brioche wedding cake. The wedding cake was so large – 1.5 m./5 ft. wide – that the opening to the oven had often to be enlarged to bake it. The cake was brought to the wedding by men who held it up while dancing the quadrille. The wedding cake was then divided by the bride and groom and distributed to the guests.

## Preparing Vendée-style brioche

Vendée-style brioche which has become very popular in France was traditionally prepared with a natural, sourdough starter. Nowadays it contains less butter and more sugar than classic brioche and is usually prepared with a yeast starter or a mixture of fermented dough and commercial yeast.

It is typically presented in 3-strand braided loaves.
Vendée-style brioche can be baked in a variety of shapes including large crown loaves for special occasions.

Vendée-style brioche is often baked in refractory molds.
Avoid over kneading Vendée-style brioche dough which will cause it to rise higher during baking but will detract from the quality of the finished product.

It is essential to use high quality, high gluten flour when preparing Vendéeßstyle brioche. If the flour contains no additives, a pinch of ascorbic acid can be added to the dough to encourage the development of the gluten and improve the strength of the dough.

A leavening such as a yeast starter or a piece of fermented dough from a previous batch should be added to the dough during kneading. Allow time for a slow, long first rising.

## Ingredients

1 kg. high quality flour (patent) (35.5 oz.)
280 g. sugar (10 oz.)
6 eggs
240 ml. milk or water (9.5 fl. oz.)
Flavoring (optional): 50 ml. rum (1.7 fl. oz.)
50 to 60 g. yeast (1.8 to 2.1 oz.)
20 g. salt (4 tsp.)
400 g. fermented brioche dough (from the day before) (14 oz.)
350 g. butter (12.5 oz.)

## Kneading

Knead the dough for 4 to 5 minutes on slow speed (frasing) and allow it to rest for 30 minutes. This resting period reduces the total kneading time and strengthens the gluten structure while preventing the dough from oxidizing. Both of these factors improve the flavor of the brioche.

Add the yeast at the beginning of the second stage of kneading and the salt 1 minute later.
Add the fermented dough 5 minutes before the butter.
If fermented brioche dough is unavailable, fermented standard bread dough which has fermented for at least 4 hours at 20 °C (68 °F) can be used instead. Be sure and add more sugar to compensate for using bread dough instead of brioche.
Add the butter to the dough as soon as it begins to pull away from the walls of the mixing bowl during kneading.
The dough should be smooth and not sticky; the temperature of the dough should be approximately 28 °C (82 °F) at the end of kneading.

### Kneading times:
Kneading machine: 5 minutes at slow speed and 20 minutes at medium speed.
Electric mixer: 4 minutes at slow speed and 14 minutes at medium speed.

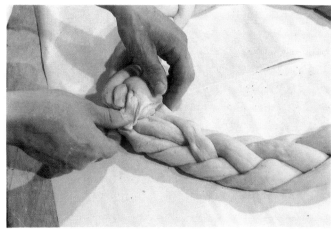

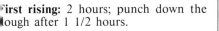

**First rising:** 2 hours; punch down the dough after 1 1/2 hours.

**Scaling and resting:** Weigh a 360 g. (12.5 oz.) section of dough and divide it into 3 equal pieces to form the strands for braiding.

Let the dough rest for 20 minutes.

**Shaping:** Prepare braided loaves with the 3 strands of dough and place them on sheet pans or in molds. Avoid braiding the strands too tightly.

**Proofing:** Proof the loaves for 4 to 5 hours depending on the amount of sugar in the dough; sugar slows fermentation.

The loaves can also be sprinkled with crystallized sugar before baking.

**Baking:** Bake the loaves in a low oven (180 to 190 °C/350 to 375 °F).

A brioche loaf weighing 800 g. (28 oz.), requires approximately 30 minutes baking time.

| VENDEE-STYLE BRIOCHE | | | |
|---|---|---|---|
| **PREPARATION** | **10** min | **10** min | • calculate the temperatures<br>• prepare and weigh the raw ingredients |
| **KNEADING** | **48** min | **58** min | • knead for 4 minutes slow speed (frasing)<br>• let the dough rest for 30 minutes<br>• continue kneading the dough for 14 minutes |
| **FIRST RISING** | **2** hr **30** | **3** hr **30** | • punch down after 1 hour 30 minutes |
| **SCALING** | **10** min | **3** hr **40** | • divide and weigh the dough in sections |
| **RESTING** | **10** min | **3** hr **50** | |
| **SHAPING** | **15** min | **4** hr **05** | • divide the sections of dough into 3 strands<br>• braid them in groups of three |
| **PROOFING** | **4** hr **30** (approx.) | **8** hr **30** | • proofing time will depend on the temperature<br>• make sure the loaves are well proofed |
| **BEFORE BAKING** | **5** min | **8** hr **35** | • brush the loaves with egg wash |
| **BAKING** | **20** to **30** min | **9** hr | • bake in a 180 °C (350 °F) oven<br>• the baking time will depend on the size |
| **COOLING** | **5** min | **9** hr **05** | • let the brioches cool on racks |
| **STORAGE :** *Vendee-style brioches have a very good shelf life. They can be sold up to 3 days after.* | | | |

# Nice-style Crown Brioche (Couronne Niçoise)

## Introduction

The Nice-style crown brioche is similar to the "gâteau des rois" served almost everywhere in France to celebrate the Epiphany. Practically every region in France has its own version, the most famous being from Bordeaux and Paris.

Nice-style crown brioche loaves are much richer than similar crown loaves typically made in the south of France.

Nice-style crown brioches are usually fermented using a yeast starter augmented with commercial yeast. A long first rising is required because of the richness of the dough. The dough must also be punched down once or twice every hour during the first rising before being refrigerated.

Nice-style crown brioche is traditionally served with hot chocolate. It is glazed after baking and then decorated with candied fruits and crystallized sugar.

Some bakers like to save time and avoid glazing by decorating the crown loaves before baking. When this method

is used, the crown loaves weigh less; the price is reduced accordingly.

## Ingredients

### Yeast starter

250 g. high quality flour (9 oz.)
50 g. yeast (1.8 oz.)
150 ml. water (5 fl. oz.)
  Let the starter ferment for 2 to 3 hours at room temperature.

### Brioche dough

750 g hiqh quality flour (26.5 oz.)
580 g. eggs (20.5 oz.)
80 g. salt (2.8 oz.)
125 g. sugar (4.5 oz.)
650 g. softened butter (23 oz.)
400 g. chopped candied orange rinds or mixed candied fruits (14 oz.)
Zest and juice of 3 lemons
50 ml. orange flower water (1.7 fl. oz.)

## Kneading

Knead the dough with an electric mixer for 4 minutes at slow speed (frasing) and for 13 minutes more at medium speed.

It is recommended to let the dough rest for 15 minutes between the two kneading stages.

As soon as the dough begins to pull away from the sides of the mixing bowl, add the softened butter, the chopped candied fruit, and the lemon zest.

Continue kneading until all the ingredients are evenly distributed.

## First rising

Let the dough rise for 1 hour and punch it down.

Let the dough rise for 1 hour more and then put it in the refrigerator for 12 hours.

## Scaling

Weigh the dough into sections weighing from 200 to 500 g. (7 to 17.5 oz.). Round the sections and flatten them slightly.

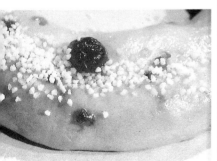

## Resting

Let the sections rest for 10 minutes.

## Shaping

Dust the center of each of the sections of dough with flour. Make a hole in the centers and gradually enlarge it with both hands.

Continue shaping the crown until it is smooth and even.

## Proofing

Let the loaves proof for 4 to 5 hours at 25 °C (77 °F).

Brush the loaves with egg wash and place the candied fruit and crystallized sugar on top before baking.

## Baking

Bake the crown loaves in a 210 to 220 °C (400 to 425 °F) oven for 25 to 35 minutes depending on the size of the loaves.

If the loaves have not been decorated before baking, the crystallized sugar and candied fruits can be attached to the crowns with glaze after baking.

## NICE-STYLE CROWN BRIOCHE

| | | | |
|---|---|---|---|
| PREPARING THE YEAST STARTER | 5 min | 5 min | • calculate the temperatures<br>• prepare and weigh the raw ingredients |
| KNEADING | 12 min | 17 min | |
| FERMENTATION | 2 hr | 2 hr 17 | |
| PREPARING THE CROWNS | 10 min | 2 hr 27 | • calculate the temperatures<br>• prepare, weigh, and measure ingredients |
| KNEADING | 17 min | 2 hr 44 | • knead until the dough is smooth |
| FIRST RISING AND REFRIGERATION | 12 hr | 14 hr 44 | • refrigerate the dough after punching it down twice. Allow dough to rise for 1 hour between each punching down |
| SCALING | 5 min | 14 hr 49 | • divide and weigh the dough in sections |
| RESTING | 10 min | 14 hr 59 | • cover the dough to protect them from air |
| SHAPING | 10 min | 15 hr 09 | • shape into smooth and regular crowns |
| PROOFING | 2 hr 30 | 17 hr 39 | • proof the loaves in a warm and humid rising area: 27 °C (81 °F) |
| PREPARING FOR BAKING | 5 min | 17 hr 44 | • brush the loaves with egg wash<br>• decorate the tops of the loaves with candied orange rinds and crystallized sugar |
| BAKING | 20 to 35 min | 18 hr 10 | • the baking time will depend on the size of the loaves |
| COOLING | 5 min | 18 hr 15 | • let the brioches cool on racks |

STORAGE : Nice-style crown brioches have a good shelf life. They can be sold up to 2 days after.

# Bordeaux-style Crown Brioche

# (Gâteau des Rois de Bordeaux)

### Introduction

This brioche which has long been a tradition of the city of Bordeaux, was first introduced by the Romans who used it to celebrate " Basilinda ", a feast day named after the word " Basileus ", meaning king.

Bordeaux-style crown loaves contain a large proportion of eggs and butter. The dough is usually prepared with a yeast starter which has been allowed to ferment from 2 to 3 hours.

In France today, crown loaves are prepared with either brioche dough or puff pastry (pâte feuilletée). Preparing the loaves with both types of dough allows the baker to offer a wider variety to his or her clientele.

Bordeaux-style crown loaves can be baked in large or individual size loaves.

## Ingredients

### Yeast starter

250 g. high quality flour (9 oz.)
40 g. yeast (1.4 oz.)
160 ml. water (5.5 fl. oz.)

Knead the ingredients for 2 minutes on slow speed and for 5 minutes more on medium speed.

Let the starter ferment for 2 to 3 hours depending on the temperature of the rising area (24 to 25 °C/75 to 77 °F).

### Brioche dough

750 g. flour (26.5 oz.)
18 g. salt (3 tsp.)
10 eggs
250 g. sugar (9 oz.)
60 g. crystallized sugar (2.1 oz.)
60 ml. orange flour water (2 fl. oz.)
200 g. candied citron or mixed fruits (7 oz.)
Zest of 1 lemon
400 g. butter (14 oz.)
Cognac (optional)

## Kneading

Knead all the ingredients except the candied fruits and the butter for 3 minutes on slow speed. Continue the kneading for 14 minutes more on medium speed.

Add the butter to the dough as soon as the dough begins to detach from the sides of the mixing bowl.

Continue kneading for 4 to 5 minutes more after adding the butter until the dough is smooth.

To quickly smooth the dough, the mixer can be turned up to high speed at the end of kneading but in no case should the dough be kneaded for longer than a total of 20 minutes.

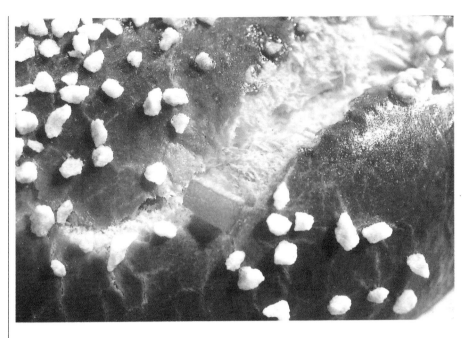

## First rising

Punch down the dough after 1 hour of rising.

Let the dough rise for 1 hour more, punch it down, and refrigerate it for 12 hours.

## Scaling

Weigh the dough into 300 to 600 g. (10.5 to 21 oz.) sections.

Round the sections of dough until they are perfectly smooth.

## Resting

Cover the dough with plastic wrap and let it rest for 10 minutes.

## Shaping

See " Nice-style crown brioche "

## Proofing

Proof the loaves for 2 to 2 1/2 hours in a proof box or steam chamber set to 27 °C (81 °F).

Brush the proofed loaves with egg wash, sprinkle them with crystallized sugar, and arrange the candied fruits on top before baking.

## Baking

Bake the crown loaves for 20 to 30 minutes in a 210 °C (400 °F) oven. The exact baking time will depend on the size of the loaves.

## BORDEAUX-STYLE CROWN BRIOCHE

| | | | |
|---|---|---|---|
| PREPARING THE YEAST STARTER | 5 min | 5 min | • calculate the temperatures<br>• prepare and weigh the raw ingredients |
| KNEADING | 12 min | 17 min | |
| FERMENTATION | 2 hr 30 | 2 hr 47 | • Let the starter double in volume |
| PREPARING THE CROWNS | 10 min | 2 hr 57 | • calculate the temperatures<br>• prepare, weigh, and measure ingredients |
| KNEADING | 17 min | 3 hr 14 | • knead until the dough is smooth |
| FIRST RISING | 3 hr 30 | 6 hr 44 | • cover the dough to prevent a skin from forming |
| SCALING AND ROUNDING | 5 min | 6 hr 49 | • divide and weigh the dough in sections<br>• be careful not to tear the dough during |
| RESTING | 10 min | 6 hr 59 | |
| SHAPING | 10 min | 7 hr 09 | • shape into smooth and regular crowns |
| PROOFING | 2 hr 30 | 9 hr 39 | • proof the loaves in a warm and humid rising area 27 °C (81 °F) |
| PREPARING FOR BAKING | 6 min | 9 hr 45 | • brush with egg wash and decorate with candied orange rinds and crystallized sugar |
| BAKING | 20 min | 10 hr 05 | • bake the crowns in a relatively low oven |
| COOLING | 10 min | 10 hr 15 | • let the brioches cool on racks |

STORAGE : Good shelf life. They can be sold up to 2 days after baking.

# Craquelins (Craquelins)

## Introduction

Craquelins are popular in northern European countries such as Belgium, Holland, and northern France.

Because of the ingredients and methods used in their preparation, craquelins are very sweet and very fragile.

Craquelin dough is actually more like sweetened and flavored milk bread dough (pâte à pain au lait) than it is like brioche.

## Ingredients

1 kg. flour (35.5 oz.)
20 g. salt (4 tsp.)
60 g. yeast (2.1 oz.)
50 g. sugar (1.8 oz.)
50 g. powdered milk (1.8 oz.)
1 egg
150 g. butter (5.5 oz.)
500 to 550 ml. water (17 to 18.5 fl. oz.)
25 g. lemon zest (.9 oz./1 tbsp. + 2 tsp.)

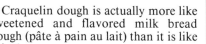

## Kneading

Electric mixer: Knead the dough for 4 minutes on slow speed and for 8 minutes more on medium speed.

Kneading machine: Knead the dough for 5 minutes on slow speed and for 14 minutes on medium speed.

Add the lemon zest to the dough 1 minute before the end of kneading.

The temperature of the dough should be 24 to 25 °C (75 to 77 °F).

## First rising

Allow the dough to rise for 30 minutes. Make sure it is protected from drafts.

## Scaling

Weigh out 6, 140 g. (5 oz.) sections of dough. To the remainder of the dough, add 500 g. (17.5 oz.) sugar and 100 g. (3.5 oz.) finely chopped candied cherries and candied orange peel.

Thoroughly mix the ingredients.

Divide the dough into 6 sections weighing 295 g. (10.5 oz.) each. Round the sections and let them rest.

## Shaping

Roll the unsweetened, 140 g. (5 oz.) sections of dough into ovals.

Place the sweetened sections of dough on the ovals which should envelope them completely.

Place the craquelins on sheet pans with the seams on the bottom.

## Proofing

Proof the craquelins for 1 hour and 20 minutes to 1 hour and 40 minutes in a 26 °C (79 °F) proof box or steam chamber.

Brush the surface of the craquelins with egg wash and make a short incision on the top of each of the loaves. The incision can then be sprinkled with crystallized sugar before baking.

## Baking

Bake the loaves at approximately 210 °C (400 °F).

Closely watch the craquelins during baking to make sure they don't become too dark. The outer envelope of dough should protect the sweetened section in the middle of each craquelin.

# CRAQUELINS

| PREPARATION | 10 min | 10 min | • calculate the temperatures<br>• prepare and weigh the raw ingredients |
|---|---|---|---|
| KNEADING | 12 min | 22 min | • knead 4 minutes on slow speed (frasing)<br>• continue kneading the dough for 8 minutes on medium speed<br>• add the lemon zests at the end of kneading |
| FIRST RISING | 30 min | 55 min | • protect the dough from drafts |
| SCALING | 10 min | 1 hr 05 | • divide 1/3 of the dough into 140 g. (5 oz.)<br>• prepare the mixture with crystallized sugar, candied cherries, and orange rinds |
| RESTING | 10 min | 1 hr 15 | • let the dough rest |
| SHAPING | 12 min | 1 hr 37 | • wrap sections of the candied fruit mixture in the plain dough so that it is well sealed |
| PROOFING | 1 hr 20 to 1 hr 40 | 3 hr | • proof the craquelins in a proof box at 27 °C (81 °F) |
| PREPARING FOR BAKING | 5 min | 3 hr 05 | • score and brush with egg wash<br>• crystallized sugar can also be used |
| BAKING | 20 min | 3 hr 25 | • bake in a 210 °C (400 °F) oven |
| COOLING | 5 min | 3 hr 30 | • let the craquelins cool before placing them on cooling racks |

**STORAGE** : Craquelins have a good shelf life and can be sold up to 3 days after baking.

# Anise Loaves (Pastis Landais)

### Introduction

These anise loaves were developed in the Landes, a region in southwestern France famous for its rustic, full-flavored cooking. These anise loaves share certain characteristics with specialties of the neighboring Béarn and Périgord regions.

Anise loaves are rustic, full-flavored breads which contain anisette, vanilla, and sometimes orange flower water and lemon zest.

Anise loaves are often baked in extremely large sizes: 4 and 5 pound loaves are typical.

In southwestern France, Anise loaves can always be found on the family table for feast days and weddings.

These loaves can be traced back to the 14th century. A quotation survives from 1363 when Jean d'Armagnac responded to the threats of the Prince de Galles by promising him a giant anise loaf.

There are several recipes and techniques which are used for making anise loaves.

To prepare successful anise bread:

Avoid over kneading the dough so that the flavor, aroma, and texture of the breads stays intact.

Use a high quality, high gluten flour such as patent flour.

Use only the best butter.

Allow for a long first rising which improves the shelf life of the breads.

Prepare a yeast starter using 1/3 of the flour in the recipe.

## Recipe

### Yeast starter

300 g. flour (10.5 oz.)
20 g. yeast (4 tsp.) dissolved in 185 ml. warm milk (6 fl. oz.)

Knead together the ingredients for the starter for 10 minutes at slow speed.

Let the starter ferment for 1 1/2 hours at 22 °C (71 °F) or for 8 hours at 5 °C (41 °F).

### Anise bread recipe

(As prepared by Marcel Larché in Biscarosse)

### Preparing the syrup

Combine 350 g. (12.5 oz.) butter, 250 g. (9 oz.) sugar, 200 ml. (7 fl. oz.) milk, and 25 ml. (1 fl. oz.) anisette liqueur in a saucepan. Gently heat the mixture to between 30 and 35 °C (85 and 95 °F) maximum.

When the syrup is warm and the butter has melted, beat 5 eggs and combine them with the syrup.

### Kneading

Place the following ingredients in the bowl of the electric mixer: 700 g. (24.5 oz.) flour, 20 g. (4 tsp.) salt, 6 g. (1 tsp.) powdered vanilla, and the anisette syrup.

Knead the dough until it begins to pull away from the sides of the bowl.

Halfway through the kneading, add the starter and 25 g. (.9 oz.) of yeast.

Knead the dough for 5 minutes on slow speed followed by 5 minutes on medium speed.

### First rising: 3 hours

Fill the molds 1/3 of the way up with the dough.

### Proofing

Proof the loaves for approximately 1 hour – until the dough rises 2/3rds of the way up the sides of the molds.

Brush the tops of the loaves with egg wash (half egg, half milk). Sprinkle the loaves with crystallized sugar.

### Baking

Bake the anise loaves for 20 to 30 minutes depending on their size.

Check if the loaves are done by inserting a wooden skewer deep into the loaves and pulling it out. If it comes out with no dough adhering, the loaves are done.

Allow the loaves to cool.

## ANISE LOAVES

| | | | |
|---|---|---|---|
| **PREPARING THE YEAST STARTER** | **5** min | **5** min | • calculate the temperatures<br>• prepare and weigh the raw ingredients |
| **KNEADING** | **10** min | **15** min | • knead the starter on slow speed |
| **FERMENTATION** | **1** hr **30** | **1** hr **45** | • the time required for the first rising depends on the temperature of the work area |
| **PREPARING THE FINISHED DOUGH** | **15** min | **1** hr **50** | • calculate the temperatures<br>• prepare, weigh, and measure ingredients |
| **KNEADING** | **10** min | **2** hr **10** | • 5 min. slow speed and 5 min. more medium speed. Do not overknead the dough<br>• add the yeast starter and the commercial yeast halfway through the kneading |
| **FIRST RISING** | **3** hr | **5** hr **10** | • a long and slow first rising improves flavor and shelf life and shortens proofing time |
| **DOUGH IN MOLDS** | **5** min | **5** hr **15** | • fill the molds 1/3 full with the dough |
| **PROOFING** | **1** hr | **6** hr **15** | • proof the dough until it comes 2/3rds up |
| **PREPARING FOR BAKING** | **6** min | **9** hr **45** | • brush the loaves with egg wash |
| **BAKING** | **20** to **30** min | **6** hr **50** | • baking times will depend on the size of the loaves |
| **COOLING** | **5** min | **6** hr **55** | • let the brioches cool on racks |

**STORAGE :** Anise loaves have a very good shelf life and will keep for several days in the open air. They should be sold within 12 hours after baking.

# Swiss-style Brioche (Brioche Suisse)

## Introduction

Swiss-style brioche is popular not only in Switzerland but in eastern France where it is served for dessert or as an afternoon snack.

Swiss-style brioche is made with pastry cream and raisins which are rolled up in the brioche dough and baked in cake pans.

## Recipe

Prepare a classic butter brioche dough and a batch of pastry cream.

Macerate raisins in rum for 4 hours ahead of time. Drain them well.

The brioche dough is used as soon as the first fermentation is completed.

## Shaping

Line the cake pans with a thin sheet of brioche dough.

Spread a layer of pastry cream over the layer of brioche.

Roll another sheet of brioche 4 mm. (1/8 in.) thick into a rectangular shape. (this is the same technique used for raisin loaves.)

Spread a layer of pastry cream over the rectangle of dough and sprinkle with the macerated raisins, with candied fruit, or a mixture of the two.

Roll the dough into a tight cylinder and cut it into 1.5 cm. (1/2 in.) thick slices. Arrange the slices in the brioche-lined cake pan. Place a slice in the center and carefully arrange the remaining slices around. Do not arrange the slices too tightly.

The number of slices needed to fill the cake pan will of course depend on the pan's size.

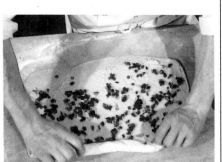

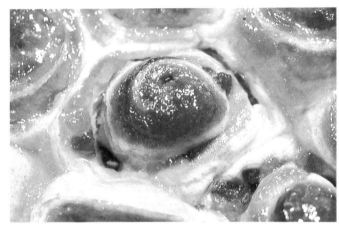

### Proofing

Proof the loaves for 1 to 2 hours. Brush with egg wash before baking.

### Baking

Bake the loaves in a 200 °C (400 °F) oven for approximately 40 minutes.

### After baking

The loaves can be finished in several ways:

a) Thickly brush the loaves with white fondant and decorate them with candied cherries and toasted almonds.

b) Brush them with apricot glaze.

c) Prepare a water glaze (water and confectioners' sugar) and brush the loaves as soon as they come out of the oven.

# SWISS-STYLE BRIOCHE

| | | | |
|---|---|---|---|
| **PREPARATION** | **10** min | **10** min | • calculate the temperatures<br>• prepare and weigh the raw ingredients |
| **KNEADING** | **21** min | **30** min | • 4 minutes on slow speed (frasing)<br>• continue 10 minutes medium speed (without butter) or 5 minutes slow speed (with butter)<br>• add the butter |
| **FIRST RISING** | **2** hr | **2** hr **30** | • punch down the dough after 50 minutes<br>• punch down again after 1 hour 40 minutes |
| **REFRIGERATING THE DOUGH** | **4** hr | **6** hr **30** | • refrigerate at 5 to 6 °C (41 to 43 °F)<br>• refrigerating makes the dough easier to work |
| **LINING THE MOLDS** | **5** min | **6** hr **35** | • line the cake pans with a thin sheet of brioche-dough |
| **ROLLING OUT THE DOUGH** | **5** min | **6** hr **40** | • roll the dough into 4 mm (1/8 in.) thick rectangles |
| **SPREADING THE PASTRY CREAM** | **5** min | **6** hr **45** | • spread a layer of pastry cream over the rectangles. Sprinkle with raisins |
| **ROLLING AND CUTTING** | **10** min | **6** hr **55** | • roll the dough into a tight cylinder<br>• cut the cylinder into slices<br>• arrange the slices in the lined cake molds |
| **PROOFING** | **1** hr **30** to **2** hr | **8** hr **25** | • proof the brioche in a proof box at 27 °C (81 °F) |
| **BEFORE BAKING** | **5** min | **8** hr **30** | • brush with egg wash before baking |
| **BAKING** | **40** to **50** min | **9** hr **10** | • bake at 200 to 210 °C (400 to 425 °F)<br>• time will vary depending on the size<br>• after baking, coat the brioches with white fondant or water glaze |

**STORAGE** : Swiss-style brioches can be sold up to 2 days and can be eaten for up to 3 days.

# Layered Brioche (Brioche Feuilletée)

## Introduction

Layered brioche is prepared using the same method as croissant dough. A series of turns – 3 single, 1 simple + 1 double, or two doubles – is given to the dough to create a flaky, layered effect.

The basic dough used for layered brioche is less rich than classic butter brioche dough but extra butter is incorporated into the dough when it is given turns.

Several methods can be used for preparing layered brioche dough. The simplest method is to remove some dough from a batch of classic brioche before adding the butter so that it isn't necessary to prepare two batches completely from scratch.

The dough can then be finished with the correct amount of butter.

Layered brioche dough provides delicate, flaky pastries.

Ingredients such as praline paste and pastry cream can be incorporated into layered brioche dough for a variety of effects.

## Recipe

1 kg. high quality flour (35.5 oz.)
20 g. salt (4 tsp.)
35 g. yeast (1.2 oz.)
150 g. sugar (5.5 oz.)
11 eggs
100 ml. milk (3.5 fl. oz.)
200 g. butter (7 oz.)

## Kneading

Knead the dough in an electric mixer for 4 minutes at slow speed and 10 minutes more at medium speed (without butter) or for 5 minutes at slow speed (with butter).

Add the butter when the dough is completely smooth and starts to pull away from the sides of the mixing bowl.

The dough should be 23 °C (73 °F) at the end of kneading.

## First rising

Let the dough rise for a total of 2 hours. Punch down the dough after 40 minutes and again after 1 hours.

Refrigerate the dough for several hours after rising to make it firm and easier to work with.

## Scaling

Weigh the dough into 685 g. (24 oz.) sections.

Prepare 135 g. (5 oz.) sections of butter.

## Turning

Turn the sections of butter into the dough with 3 single turns. Allow the dough to rest for 10 minutes between the second and final turns.

## Shaping

Allow the dough to rest in the refrigerator for 20 minutes and then roll it into a 4 mm. (1/8 in.) thick rectangle.

The size and shape of the rectangle depends on the baking molds. If a wide, low mold is being used, the rectangle should be long but not too wide. If molds with high sides are being used, the rectangle should be correspondingly wider.

Roll the rectangles of dough into cylinders.

It is also possible to spread a layer of pastry cream or praline paste over the surface of the rectangle before it is rolled.

Insert the cylinders, seam up in the buttered molds.

After shaping, layered brioches can be baked in a variety of molds including savarin molds and round brioche molds (brioches à tête).

## Proofing

Proof the loaves for 2 1/2 to 3 hours. Brush the loaves with egg wash before baking.

## Baking

Bake the layered brioches in a 210 to 220 °C (400 to 425 °F) oven for 20 to 40 minutes depending on their size.

Unmold the brioches as soon as they come out of the oven.

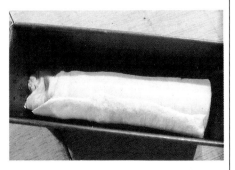

# LAYERED BRIOCHE

| PREPARATION | 10 min | 10 min | • calculate the temperatures<br>• prepare and weigh the raw ingredients |
|---|---|---|---|
| KNEADING | 19 min | 30 min | • for 4 minutes on slow speed (frasing)<br>• continue 10 minutes medium speed (without butter) or 5 minutes slow speed (with butter) |
| FIRST RISING | 2 hr | 2 hr 30 | • punch down after 10 minutes of rising<br>• a second time after 1 hour 30 minutes |
| REFRIGERATING THE DOUGH | 5 hr | 7 hr 30 | • refrigerate at 5 to 6 °C (41 to 43 °F) |
| SCALING | 5 min | 7 hr 35 | • weigh the dough into 685 g. (24 oz.) sections. Prepare 135 g. (5 oz.) pieces of butter |
| TURNING | 20 min | 7 hr 55 | • give the dough 3 single turns. Let it rest for 10 minutes between the last two turns |
| RESTING | 20 min | 8 hr 15 | • let the dough rest in the refrigerator |
| SHAPING | 8 min | 8 hr 23 | • roll the dough into rectangles<br>• roll each of the rectangles into cylinders<br>• place in molds with seam on the bottom |
| PROOFING | 2 hr 30 to 3 hr | 10 hr 53 | • make sure the brioche is well proofed before baking |
| BEFORE BAKING | 2 min | 10 hr 55 | • brush the loaves with egg wash |
| BAKING | 20 to 40 min | 11 hr 15 | • baking time depends on the shape and size of the loaves |
| COOLING | 5 min | 11 hr 20 | • unmold as soon as out of the oven |

**STORAGE** : Layered brioche can be sold up to 2 days after baking.

173

# Bread Sticks (Longuets)

### Introduction

Bread sticks are excellent when served at cocktail parties where dry, salty foods make an excellent accompaniment to drinks.

Bread sticks are prepared from a type of milk bread dough (pâte à pain au lait) which is cut in 20 to 60 g. (.7 to 2.1 oz.) sections. These sections are then rolled into strips and baked in one of two ways:

Each section of dough is rolled out to the length of a standard sheet pan (40 by 60 cm./16 by 24 in.). They are then arranged in rows with 3/4 inch spaces left between each strip.

The dough is rolled into strips and allowed to rise in special bread stick pans. These pans consist of a series of gullies which contain the bread sticks.

Quick rising doughs are used for preparing bread sticks.

Bread sticks have a good shelf life and can be served at breakfast, as afternoon snacks and with before-dinner drinks.

The best way to keep and present bread sticks is to tie them into bundles and leave them uncovered. They will keep for several days in the open air.

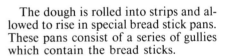

## Recipe

1 kg. mixture high gluten flour and
   regular bread flour (35.5 oz.)
20 g. salt (4 tsp.)
40 g. yeast (1.4 oz.)
85 g. butter (3 oz.)
50 g. sugar (1.8 oz.)
50 g. powdered milk (1.8 oz.)
50 g. malt (1.8 oz.)
520 ml. water (17.5 fl. oz.)

*Note:* The powdered milk can be replaced with fresh milk.

## Kneading

Use a base temperature of 65 °C/
213 °F.
   Knead the dough for 4 minutes at
slow speed followed by 6 minutes at medium speed.

## First rising

Let the dough rise for approximately
1 1/2 hours.
   Punch down the dough after 45 minutes of rising.
   The time required for the first rising
will depend on the strength of the
flour, and the temperature and humidity of the work area.

## Scaling

Weigh the dough into 850 g. (30 oz.)
sections. Divide each of the sections
into 10 equal parts.
   Round the sections into balls or
short, elongated shapes.

## Resting

Allow the rounded pieces of dough to
rest for approximately 20 minutes.

## Shaping

Roll each of the sections of dough
into strips which correspond to the
length of the sheet pan or bread stick
mold being used for baking.
   When using standard 40 by 60 cm.
(16 by 24 in.) sheet pans, attach the
ends of the strips to the sheet pan by
pressing the dough against the edge.
   Make sure the bread sticks are
smooth and have an even shape.

## Proofing

Proof the bread sticks for about
1 1/2 hour. Cover them to protect them
from air which would cause a skin to
form on their surface.

   Brush the bread sticks with egg wash
before baking.

## Baking

Bake the bread sticks in a 210 °C
(400 °F) oven for 14 to 15 minutes.

# BREAD STICKS

| | | | |
|---|---|---|---|
| **PREPARATION** | **10** min | **10** min | • *calculate the temperatures*<br>• *prepare and weigh the raw ingredients* |
| **KNEADING** | **10** min | **20** min | • *knead until smooth and homogenous* |
| **FIRST RISING** | **1** hr **30** | **1** hr **50** | • *the time required for the first rising will de-pend on the strength and consistency of the dough* |
| **SCALING AND ROUNDING** | **15** hr | **2** hr **05** | • *weigh into 850 g. (30 oz.) sections*<br>• *divide each into 10 parts. Round each part* |
| **RESTING** | **20** min | **2** hr **25** | • *cover the dough to prevent a skin from form-ing* |
| **SHAPING** | **10** min | **2** hr **35** | • *make sure the loaves are compact* |
| **PROOFING** | **1** hr **30** | **4** hr **05** | • *proof the bread sticks in a warm and humid rising area 28 °C (82 °F)* |
| **BEFORE BAKING** | **5** min | **4** hr **10** | • *brush with egg wash before baking* |
| **BAKING** | **15** min | **4** hr **25** | • *bake the loaves in a 210 °C (400 °F) oven* |
| **COOLING** | **5** min | **4** hr **30** | • *place the brioches on cooling racks so they don't become soggy* |

**STORAGE :** *Bread sticks have a very good shelf life. They will keep for several days in the open air. Their shelf life is further improved if they are tied into bundles after baking.*

# Chapter 5
# Decorating Methods and Techniques

## Perfecting Decorating Techniques

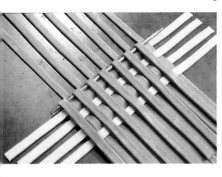

The basic techniques for using decorating dough were presented in Volume 1 of "Special and Decorative Breads".

A variety of presentations such as grape vines, sheaves of wheat, scrolls, and ribbons were also illustrated and described.

In the chapter that follows, Alain Couet and Eric Kayser have expanded the presentations and techniques shown and described in Volume 1.

# Chapter Organization

### 1. Decorating doughs

Alain Couet and Eric Kayser present six types of decorating dough and compare their uses and relative merits.

### 2. Modeling (animals, fruit,...)

These animals and fruits are modeled with salt-based decorating dough and can be used in shop windows or as part of larger presentation pieces.

### 3. Ribbons, braiding

This is an expanded section on braiding which presents a variety of new techniques. Multi-colored ribbons are also presented.

### 4. Miniature flowers, fruits, and leaves

Presentation of miniature flowers and fruits which are extremely useful for decorative presentations.

### 5. Decorated breads

Decorated breads are the main reason that most bakers are interested in decorating methods and techniques. As "gourmet" breads come to be appreciated by an ever widening clientele, their appearance and presentation is more and more important.

### 6. Decorated plates and platters

These plates and platters are presentation pieces in themselves. The examples shown here enable the reader to make the most out of decorating techniques.

# Decorating Dough

## Coloring Methods for Decorating Dough

### Rye flour

Some recipes for decorating dough call for rye flour. Rye flour, depending on the amount used, will darken the dough. When preparing decorating dough, it is extremely important to balance the various flours to obtain a dough with the desired color. A dough that is too dark after kneading will be even darker after baking and may even appear burnt.

### Egg yolks and food coloring

Egg yolks, food coloring, or dough containing glucose can be added to a decorating dough near the end of kneading to give finished designs such as leaves and flowers the appropriate color. Egg yolks and food coloring can also be used to color the finished objects. Be very careful when coloring decorating dough to not use too much color.

### Coffee extract

Coffee extract is sometimes used to color sugar syrup-based decorating dough. It should be added near the end of kneading and should be used cautiously.

When the coffee extract is incorporated into the dough, the dough should be pale beige.

Coffee extract can also be used for braiding with different colored strands as well as for staining objects after they are baked.

### Tips for using decorating dough

All types of decorating dough must be covered with plastic wrap and stored in the refrigerator immediately after kneading to prevent a skin from forming on their surface.

When objects made from decorating dough are finished baking, they can be stored in the open air or they can be frozen. In no case should they be covered with plastic wrap or moisture may collect on the surface of the decoration and cause it to discolor. This is especially true for dough that has been colored with coffee extract.

*Compare two decorated breads*

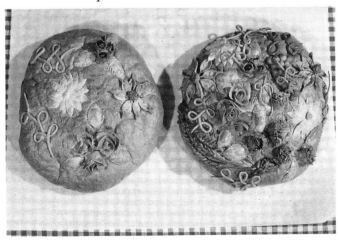

*The bad example*

*The right example*

# Comparison of

## Long-keeping inert decorating dough

### Ingredients

1 L. water (34 fl. oz.)
2 kg. sugar (70.5 oz.)
1.8 to 2 kg. all purpose white flour (63.5 to 70.5 oz.)

### Procedure

Combine the sugar and water and bring the mixture to a simmer. As soon as the mixture starts to boil, combine it with the flour and knead the mixture for 5 minutes on slow speed. The finished dough should be stiff and perfectly smooth.

### Baking

Once the dough has been shaped or molded, the shapes should be allowed to dry out for 2 to 3 days so that the dough is completely relaxed and does not change shape during baking. If small blisters form on the surface during baking, the oven is too hot.

Once shaped, the dough should be baked in an 80 to 100 °C (175 to 200 °F) oven. Small pieces should be baked for 1 day. Larger pieces may require 3 to 4 days of baking.

Check to make sure that the shapes are completely dry by trying to dig a fingernail into the dough. If the dough is still soft, continue baking.

### Advantages

This dough keeps for a long period.
The dough is strong and solid once baked.

### Disadvantages

Long-keeping inert decorating dough is difficult to work. It should be used immediately after kneading because it has the tendency to dry out quickly.

It should not be used for decorated breads because it contains sugar.

### Storage

Once baked, objects shaped from this dough will keep up to 4 years.

Long-keeping inert decorating dough should be used immediately after kneading as it can not be held while raw.

### Uses

Long-keeping inert decorating dough should only be used for rigid objects which need to be kept for long periods such as supports for large presentation pieces.

## Standard inert decorating dough

### Ingredients

*White dough*
1 L. water (34 fl. oz.)
1 kg. sugar (35.5 oz.)
1.8 kg. all purpose white flour (63.5 oz.)

*Brown dough*
As soon as the dough has been kneaded, add coffee extract to obtain the desired color.

### Procedure

Combine the sugar and water and bring the mixture to a boil. As soon as the mixture reaches the boil, add it to the flour and knead the mixture for 5 minutes on slow speed. The finished dough should be fairly stiff and have a perfectly smooth consistency.

### Baking

When the dough has been shaped, allow the objects to dry for 24 hours before baking. This is necessary to ensure that the dough is relaxed and doesn't contract during baking. The dough can be dried at room temperature in the open air or in a proof box.

Objects made of standard inert decorating dough should be baked between 80 and 100 °C (175 to 200 °F) for one day if the objects are small and for up to 4 days if the objects are large. If blisters form on the dough the oven temperature is too high.

Check the doneness of the objects by pressing into the dough with a fingernail. If the dough is still soft, continue the drying.

### Advantages

Standard inert decorating dough is easy to work with and can be used in a large number of preparations.

### Disadvantages

If exposed to air, a skin rapidly forms on its surface. For this reason it should be covered with plastic wrap at all times.

Do not use for decorated breads.

### Storage

Up to 3 years after baking.

After the dough has been kneaded, it can be stored for up to 3 days in the refrigerator before it is shaped.

### Uses

Ribbons, musical instruments, braids, the base for decorated plates and platters, molded objects, and dresses for marquises.

## Inert decorating

### Ingredients

1 L. water (34 fl. oz.)
2 kg. sugar (70.5 oz.)
1.8 to 2 kg. flour (63.5 to 70.5 oz.)
*Coloring*
1 L. water (34 fl. oz.)
1 kg. sugar (35.5 oz.)
Add coffee extract.

### Procedure

Combine the sugar and water and bring the mixture to a simmer. As soon as the mixture comes to the boil, add it to the flour and knead the mixture for 5 minutes on slow speed. The finished dough should have a stiff consistency.

### Baking

When the objects have been cut or shaped, dry them in a 100 °C (200 °F) oven for 3 to 4 days. The dough should be completely dry.

## Salt-based

### Ingredients

800 g. all purpose white flour (28 oz.)
200 g. light pumpernickel rye flour (7 oz.)
1 kg. fine salt (35.5 oz.) Water

### Procedure

Sift the flour and place it on the work surface. Make a well in the center of the flour and place the salt in the middle. This dough can only be made by hand – by working it with the tips of the fingers. Water is added as needed.

### Baking

Once the dough has been shaped into objects, the objects should be dried for 3 days. Bake them in a 80 to 100 °C (175 to 200 °F) oven.

## Rye flour

### Ingredients

500 g. all purpose white flour (17.5 oz.)
500 g. rye flour (17.5 oz.)
500 ml. warm water (17 fl. oz.)

### Procedure

Combine the ingredients and knead in an electric mixer until the dough has a smooth consistency. The finished dough should be quite stiff. Caution! The water must be warm in order to activate the gluten.

### Baking

Rye flour decorating dough is baked in a 200 °C (400 °F) oven. Decorations have a grayish tint after baking.

### Advantages

Dough is easy to work with. The finished decorations retain their shape and detail after baking.

# Different Decorating Doughs

## dough

*Advantages*
Inert decorating dough is easy to work with.
*Disadvantages*
Inert decorating dough cannot be used for decorated breads because it contains sugar.
3 to 4 years once it is baked.

*Storage*
Once the dough is kneaded, it can be kept covered with plastic wrap for 3 to 4 days in the refrigerator. If it is kept any longer, it may ferment.

*Uses*
Inert decorating dough can be used for flowers, decorated plates and platters (sheaves of wheat, grape bunches), and for decorating the tops of flat breads.
Inert decorating dough is usually attached with water.

## Egg white-based decorating dough

*Ingredients*
1.1 kg. all purpose white flour (39 oz.)
500 ml. egg whites (17 fl. oz.)

*Procedure*
Knead the egg whites with the flour in the electric mixer until the dough has a smooth consistency.
Warning! The quantities must be exact.

This dough can only be made just before it is used. If made in advance, it relaxes and becomes too soft.

*Baking*
Egg white-based decorating dough should be baked in a 200 °C (400 °F) oven. Decorations made with egg white-based decorating dough expand slightly during baking.
This dough will brown slightly during baking.

*Advantages*
Can be quickly made and is easy to work with.

*Disadvantages*
Egg white-based decorating dough dries out very quickly when exposed to air. Cover with plastic wrap.

*Storage*
This dough can be stored for up to 3 days in the refrigerator if covered with plastic wrap. It can be kept for long periods once baked.

*Uses*
Egg white-based decorating dough is used exclusively for decorated breads (flowers, bunches of grapes, ears of wheat, etc.). It does not lend itself to other uses.

## decorating dough

*Advantages*
It is easy to work.
*Disadvantages*
Salt-based decorating dough cannot be molded into objects such as scallop shells or bells. It cannot be frozen or it will decompose.

*Storage*
It can be kept in the refrigerator for up to 3 days after kneading. Once baked, it will keep for an extremely long time.

*Uses*
Salt-based decorating dough can be used for modeling figurines and faces. It can also be used for miniature animals and for fruit.

## decorating dough

*Disadvantages*
It can only be used for decorated breads or on decorated plates and platters.

*Storage*
After kneading, it can be kept covered with plastic wrap in the refrigerator for up to 3 days.
Once baked, rye flour decorating dough can be kept for up to 3 years.

*Uses*
Rye flour decorating dough can be used for a variety of flowers (including roses) and sheaves of wheat. Decorations made from this dough can only be used on decorated breads or on decorated plates and platters. It should never be used for other preparations.

## White decorating dough

*Ingredients*
800 g. all purpose white flour (28 oz.)
200 g. light rye flour (7 oz.)
400 ml. warm water (13.5 fl. oz.)

*Procedure*

Combine the ingredients and knead in an electric mixer until the dough has a smooth consistency. The finished dough should be quite stiff. Be sure the water is warm.

*Baking*
Bake in a 180 °C (350 °F) oven.
Decorations can be baked alone and then used to decorate already baked bread or the dough can be shaped and placed raw on the object to be baked.
Decorations made with this dough remain white after they are baked.

*Advantages*
White decorating dough is easy to work with and can be used for detailed decorating work.
*Disadvantages*
It dries out quickly.

*Storage*
When the white decorating dough is finished being kneaded, it can be kept covered with plastic wrap in the refrigerator for up to 3 days. Once baked, it can be kept for up to 3 years.

*Uses*
It can be used for preparing a variety of flowers, for decorating breads, plates, and platters, and also used for braiding. It should not be used for large objects because it is too fragile.

## Special decorating dough for grapes (grape harvester's basket)

*Ingredients* 500 g. all purpose white flour (17.5 oz.)
500 g. dried gluten (17.5 oz.)
600 ml. water (20.5 fl. oz.)

*Procedure*
Combine the flour and cold water in the bowl of the electric mixer. Knead for 5 minutes on slow speed.
Cover the dough with plastic wrap.

*Shaping*
Roll the dough into small balls (5 g./1 tsp. each). Place them on sheet pans (40 by 60 cm./16 in. by 24 in.).

*Baking*
Bake the grapes in a 200 °C (400 °F)

oven. Avoid baking at a higher temperature or they will be misshapen.

*Advantages*
It provides very light grapes.
*Disadvantages*
It is somewhat time consuming to prepare but provides excellent results.

*Storage*
When grapes are baked and assembled, they will last for over 3 years.

*Uses*
It is only used for preparing grapes.

# Miniature Animals

## Introduction

The miniature animals presented here are made out of salt-based decorating dough (see chart of decorating doughs). The designs have been taken from children's books and toy advertisements but any type of animal can be made depending on the baker's imagination. These miniature animals can be sold alone or used on presentation pieces and on decorated breads.

## Equipment

Sheet pans (preferably of heavy blue steel); paring and chef's knives; medium size scissors with pointed tips; pastry brushes; flour brushes.

## Tips for shaping

Each of the animals should be the same size (180 g./6.5 oz.) and have a similar shape. Avoid flouring the decorating dough or it may be difficult to get the pieces to stick together.

Each animal is shaped in stages: the head, the body, and the legs are each made separately.

If the animals are irregular or incorrectly assembled, the dough can be reshaped by rubbing it with a wet finger.

## Drying the animals

When the sections to the animals have been shaped, they should be dried in a proof box at 40 °C (104 °F) without moisture for 24 hours.

## Baking

Bake the animals in a 80 to 100 °C (175 to 200 °F) oven for approximately 3 hours. Do not bake at a higher temperature or their shape will be distorted. Check the texture of the dough after baking to make sure it has completely hardened.

Important! The head is attached to the body with flour paste 'after' baking.

## Staining

The animals should be stained with coffee extract using a pastry brush or sprayer after they are baked and assembled.

## Varnishing

Varnish the animals with commercial clear shellac or gelatin-based sealer.

# Fox

The fox is composed of three sections: the head (22 g./.8 oz.), the tail (22 g./.8 oz.), and the body (72 g./2.5 oz.).

Thin the other end of the pear to form the snout.

The head is attached after baking

## Tail

Carefully roll the dough for the tail so that it is pointed at each end. Make

Each of the parts is attached with water.

### Head

Work the dough into a pear shape.

Cuts small ears out of the thick part of the pear.

## Bear

The bear is composed of 5 sections: the head (20 g./.7 oz.), the body (60 g./2.1 oz.), the front legs (two 8 g./.3

with flour paste.

### Body

Work the dough into a pear shape. Cut into the thick end of the pear to form the front legs.

with water.

For the eyes, make rounds on each side of the snout with the tip of a ball-

stripes on the tail with the back of a paring knife.

Miniature foxes are easy to prepare and can be used alone or as part of a presentation piece.

### Legs

The front and hind legs are prepared in the same way; only their size is differ-

oz.), the hind legs (two 10 g./.4 oz.), and the tail (10 g./.4 oz.). Each of the parts is attached with water.

### Head

Work the dough into a pear shape.

Work the pear so it thins at one end to form the snout.

Make the ears out of two tiny pieces of dough and attach them to the snout

point pen. Attach two pieces of dough with water.

The head will be attached to the body with flour paste after baking.

### Body

Work the dough into a pear shape.

Press lightly on the thin end of the pear so that the head is easier to attach after baking.

ent. Round off one end of each of the legs. Make claws with the tip of a pair of scissors.

### Tail

Roll the dough into a small ball and attach it to the back of the bear.

Miniature bears can be used as part of an assembly such as a zoo or circus scene.

# Miniature Animals

## Sea lion

The sea lion is composed of a single piece of dough (90 g./3.2 oz.) and 2 small pieces for the flippers.

Work the dough into a pear shape with a point at one end for the snout.

Work a small protrusion into the dough with a ballpoint pen to form the eyes. Attach 2 tiny pieces of dough to the protrusions.

Make cuts on each side of the pear to make fins.

The flippers are made with 2 pieces of dough which are later attached to the pear.

Sea lions are easy to shape and can be used to complete a zoo or water scene.

## Elephant

The elephant shown here is sitting down. It is constructed in 5 parts: the head (40 g./1.4 oz.), the body (90 g./3.2 oz.), the front legs (two 12 g./.4 oz.), the hind legs (two 16 g./.6 oz.), and the ears (two 6 g./.2 oz.).

### Head

Work the dough into a pear shape.

Roll one end of the pear to form the trunk.

The ears should be first rounded and then flattened.

Make the eyes in the same way as for bears and sea lions.

### Body

Work the dough into an egg shape.

Press down gently on the thin end of the egg to make it easier to attach the head.

### Legs

The front and hind legs are shaped in the same way.

Flatten one end of each of the legs to form the feet. Elephants can be presented in the bakery window either by themselves or as part of a circus theme to attract the attention of passing children.

# Monkey

The monkey is made up of 7 parts: the head (32 g./1.3 oz.), the eyes (two 2 g./.1 oz.), the body (124 g./4.4 oz.), the feet (two 3 g./.1 oz.), the hand (5 g./.2 oz.), and the tail (6 g./.2 oz.).

The parts are assembled with water.

## Head

Round and flatten two pieces of dough; attach them to each side of the head.

The head is attached to the body after baking with flour paste.

## Body

Work the dough into a pear shape.

Press gently down on the thin side of the pear to make it easier to attach the head.

Shape the hand and attach it to the body.

## Feet

Shape the two feet with half circles of dough and make the toes with a paring knife. Attach the feet to the front of the body.

## Tail

Roll the remaining piece of dough to form the tail. Attach it to the body.

# Squirrel

The squirrel is made up of 3 parts: the head (12 g./.4 oz.), the body (60 g./2.1 oz.), and the tail (24 g./.8 oz.).

All of the parts are assembled with water.

## Head

Roll the section of dough into a hazelnut shape. Roll one end of the ball of dough to form the snout.

The eyes and ears are formed in the same way as the animals described above.

## Body

Work the dough into a pear shape.

Press gently on one side of the dough to make it easier to attach the head.

Cut the top of the pear shaped dough in two to form the two legs.

## Tail

Work the dough into an elongated pear shape.

Make an imprint on the back half of the pear.

Score each side of the tail and attach it to the back of the squirrel.

Squirrels make an attractive decoration especially when accompanied by hazelnuts made of decorating dough.

# Modeling fruits

## Introduction

This method of decoration is little used in baking but once the technique is mastered, it can be carried out quickly.

Fruit is usually modeled with salt-based decorating dough but occasionally rye flour decorating dough is used.

The fruit can be colored or simply baked with a large amount of steam which gives them an appealing sheen.

The fruit can be sprayed with a diversity of colors or simply brushed with a mixture of coffee extract and egg yolks.

The fruit is baked in an oven at a normal temperature (for baking breads). Steam should be used to prevent them from cracking open during baking.

If the fruit is to be used on decorated breads, rye flour decorating dough should be used.

## Ingredients

Salt based-decorating dough
Rye flour decorating dough
Egg yolks
Coffee extract

## Baking

Bake the fruit in a 240 °C (475 °F) oven with a large amount of steam for approximately 15 minutes.

## Types of fruit for modeling

A wide variety of fruit can be prepared with decorating dough. Presented here are:

**Bananas**
**Apricots**
**Pears**
**Apples**
**Pineapples**
**Strawberries**

# Ribbons made with decorating dough

## Ingredients

1 l. water (34 fl. oz.)
1 kg. sugar (35.5 oz.)
1.8 kg. flour (63.5 oz.)

## Procedure

Roll out 4 sheets of brown decorating dough and 4 sheets of white decorating dough each with a thickness of 1 cm. (1/2 in.), a width of 17 cm. (7 in.), and a length of 48 cm. (19 in.).

Lay the sheets over one another in alternating colors.

Trim the edges of the 4-layer sheet of dough with a chef's knife so the rectangle is perfectly even.

Place the layered rectangle in the freezer so that it hardens but doesn't freeze.

Remove the rectangle from the freezer and cut it into 2.5 by 9 cm. (1 by 3.5 in.) strips with a chef's knife.

### Curling the ribbon

Join the two ends of each strip to form a buckle. Place them on their sides on a sheet pan covered with parchment paper.

Dry the sections of ribbon in a dry proof box set to 50 ºC (125 ºF). 24 hours are required for drying the ribbons.

### Mounting the ribbon

The ribbon is mounted on a round of inert decorating dough cut to the correct size with a large cookie cutter.

# Braiding

**Equipment**

Rolling pastry cutter - knife - scissors - cutting board - parchment paper

**Ingredients**

3 kg. flour (6.6 lb.)
1 kg. sugar (35.5 oz.)
1 l. water (34 fl. oz.)

**Procedure**

Sugar syrup-based decorating dough is best for braiding.

Combine the sugar and water. Bring the mixture to a boil and add it to the flour. Knead the dough until it is smooth.

## 1. Straight braiding

This is the classic method used for canvas made from strips of paper or cloth.

Examples of this method are shown under "Decorated plates and platters".

Cover the dough with plastic wrap and let it cool.

Roll out 2 rectangles of dough (each should be a different color). Each rectangle should be the same size and thickness (2 mm./between 1/8 and 1/16 in.).

Depending on the size of the braid being prepared, place one of the rectangles of dough either on a cutting board or on a 40 by 60 cm. (16 by 24 in.) sheet pan covered with parchment paper.

Cut the rectangle into 1 cm. (1/2 in.) wide strips with a rolling pastry cutter.

Repeat this operation with the second rectangle.

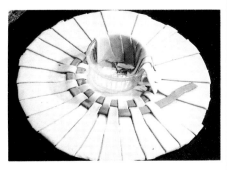

Place the strips of dough in horizontal rows of alternating colors.

*Note:* It is best to start braiding from the center so as to not damage the strips and to minimize movement.

Place a ruler vertically across the center of the strips. Lift up every other strip.

Place a strip taken from the second rectangle on the strips which remain in place.

Return the strips which haven't been covered to their original positions and lift up the others.

Repeat this process until the braiding is complete.

Trim off any strips which protrude out from the rest of the braid.

Make sure that the braid is regular and that the strips are pressed together evenly.

Dry the braids in a 100 °C (200 °F) (maximum) oven.

The braids are dry when it is impossible to make an imprint in the dough with a fingernail.

## 2. Round braiding, (on a flat surface)

This is the method used for the map of France which is described at the end of this volume.

## 3. Round braiding, (three dimensional)

This braiding method works in the same way as the woven basket shown in the chapter on pulled sugar in Volume 3 of the Professional French Pastry Series.

The basket of grapes shown in Chapter 6 illustrates this technique.

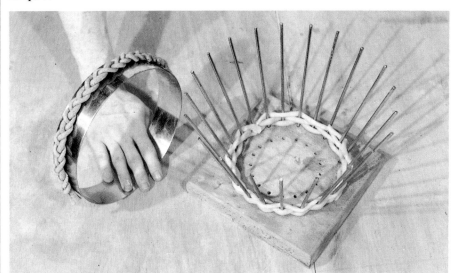

# Making Flowers, Fruits and Leaves

The ideas shown here have been taken from gardening books and directly from nature.

Here we have presented roses, carnations, daisies, dahlias, orchids, gladiolus, bluets, apple blossoms, and tulips.

Remember that flowers which have been fashioned out of inert decorating dough cannot be baked on top of decorated breads or they will burn. (The oven temperature, 200 °C/400 °F, is too hot.) These flowers are best used on top of flat braided surfaces such as plates or platters (baking temperature 100 °C/200 °F). They can be presented with a variety of flowers made from decorating dough to provide contrasting colors.

Roses, carnations, daisies, porcupine dahlias, orchids, gladiolus, and bluets

can be made using recipes number 5, 6, and 7 (see "Comparison of different decorating doughs"). The finished flowers are then placed on the decorated breads.

Apple blossoms, tulips, and pom pom dahlias are prepared using inert decorating dough (recipes 2 and 3) because they are mounted differently.

# Making Flowers, Fruits and Leaves

These flowers can be used to decorate baskets and vases or as part of a flower arrangement used in a presentation piece.

### Recipe for inert decorating dough

1.8 kg. flour (63.5 oz.)
1 l. water (34 fl. oz.)
500 g. sugar (17.5 oz.)

Combine the water and sugar and bring the mixture to a simmer in a saucepan.

Combine the mixture with the flour in the bowl of the electric mixer. Knead the mixture until a stiff, smooth dough is formed (5 minutes on slow speed).

If this dough is overworked, it will become elastic and be difficult to work with.

The recipe given here uses only 500 g. (17.5 oz.) of sugar per liter (34 fl. oz.) of water; inert decorating dough which

contains too high a proportion of sugar tends to dry out very quickly.

The inert decorating dough given above can be used for all the fruits and flowers presented in this chapter.

Caution! The flowers presented here cannot be baked on a loaf of bread because the high temperature (200 °C/400 °F) used for baking will cause them to burn. The fruits and flowers are best baked at 100 to 150 °C (200 to 300 °F).

### Coloring inert decorating dough

To obtain a brown or beige color, add coffee extract near the end of kneading.

### Example No. 1

# Tulips

### Procedure

Roll the decorating dough into a very thin sheet (.5 mm./1/32 in.).

With a number 8 cookie cutter, cut the dough into rounds. Shape each of the rounds into petals 6 cm. (2 1/2 in.) long and 3 cm. (1 in.) wide.

### Assembling the tulips

Four to five petals are needed for each tulip.

Use a small bottle to hold the flowers during assembly.

Place a piece of aluminum foil on the neck of the bottle.

Place a round of dough on the top of the bottle and cut it with a cookie cutter (no. 3).

Attach the petals around the round of dough on the bottle.

### Baking

Bake the tulips for 3 hours in a

100 °C (200 °F) oven. Make sure they are completely dry.

After baking, unmold the tulips and

gently pull away the aluminum foil.

Attach the 3 pistils to the insides of the flowers.

# Making Flowers, Fruits and Leaves

**Example No. 2 (see following pages)**

## Apple blossoms

### Procedure

Roll the decorating dough into a very thin sheet (.5 mm./1/32 in.).

With a number 2 cookie cutter, cut the dough into rounds. Make sure that all the rounds are the same size.

Thin the edges of the petals with a light bulb and a sheet of plastic wrap.

Place the petals on top of a cardboard egg carton.

### Baking

Bake the petals in a 80 to 100 °C (175 to 200 °F) oven for approximately 3 hours.

### Assembling the apple blossoms

Four or five petals are required for each blossom.

Attach the petals in an overlapping pattern with flour paste (in the same way as for a daisy).

When the blossoms are assembled, place them on egg cartons to dry.

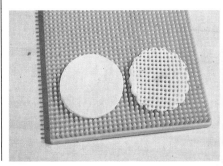

# Making Flowers, Fruits and Leaves

# Decorated Breads

## Introduction

The baker's main job is of course to make wholesome, appetizing bread. Although many bakers leave it at that, a dedicated craftsman can also make his or her breads striking to the eye.

The decorations that bakers make on their loaves help turn the breads into something special in the same way that a pastry chef enhances cakes and pastries with elaborate icings and glazes. The number of themes that can be used for decorating bread is virtually limitless so that a skilled craftsman can quickly adapt to the requests and whims of the clientele.

Decorated breads can be presented in the bake shop window, in a dining room, or even in a living room. The rustic appearance of decorated breads is appropriate in almost any setting.

Decorated breads also make tempting presentations at large buffets where they help show off canapes and other hors d'oeuvres.

These breads can be served not only as food to accompany everyday meals but as objects of beauty which will excite the appetite and the imagination.

## Recipes

### Brié bread

1 kg. flour (35.5 oz.)
20 g. salt (4 tsp.)
3.5 kg. fermented dough (7.7 lb.)
20 g. yeast (4 tsp.)
200 ml. water (14 fl. oz.)
100 g. butter or shortening (3.5 oz.)

### Country-style bread

800 g. white flour (28 oz.)
200 g. light pumpernickel rye flour (14 oz.)
20 g. salt (4 tsp.)
20 g. yeast (4 tsp.)
500 g. fermented dough (17.5 oz.)
550 ml. water (19.5 fl. oz.)

The fermented dough should have fermented for at least 2 hours at room temperature. The use of fermented dough shortens the time required for the first rising hence shortening the overall time needed for making the bread.

## Kneading

The work area temperature should be 22 to 23 °C (72 to 74 °F). Use a base temperature of 65 °C (213 °F). Combine all the ingredients in the bowl of an electric mixer and knead for 10 minutes on slow speed.

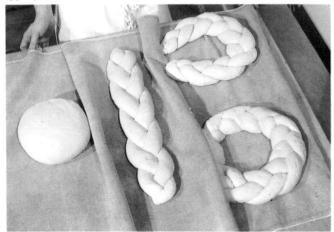

# Large Braided Loaf

# Round Squirrel Loaf

Prepare a stiff bread dough. The dough should be 24 °C (75 °F) at the end of kneading. Do not knead the dough for longer than the recommended time or it will become too elastic. When these loaves are finished baking, the surface should remain smooth and not crack so that it can support relatively heavy decorations.

Keep the dough covered to prevent the formation of a skin.

**First rising:** 30 minutes

**Scaling**

The sections of dough for decorated breads should weigh from 1 to 2 kg. (35.5 to 70.5 oz.). Use 1 kg. (35.5 oz.) sections for round loaves, grape leaves, hearts, and palm trees; 1.2 kg. (42.5 oz.) sections for crown and horseshoe loaves; and 1.5 kg. (53 oz.) sections for large braided loaves.

Weigh the sections without rounding them.

Arrange them on sheet pans according to type.

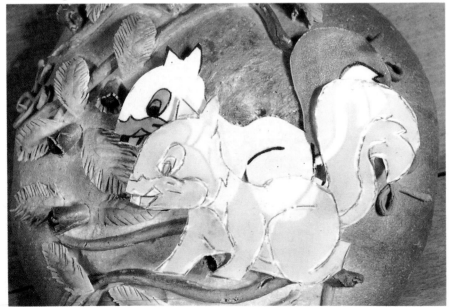

# Sun Loaf (Stencil Method)

Prepare the loaves for shaping:

- round loaf: make sure it is well-rounded.

- crown loaf: cut the sections of dough into 3 equal parts without rounding them.

- grape leaves: make a tight, well-rounded section.

- long braided loaf: cut the sections of dough into 3 equal parts without rounding them.

- hearts: make a tight, well rounded section.

- palm trees: work the section of dough into a pear shape.

- Work the dough over parchment paper to facilitate the shaping.

# Sun Loaf (Solid Decoration)

# Horseshoe

# Palm Tree

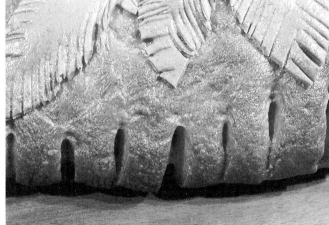

# Crown

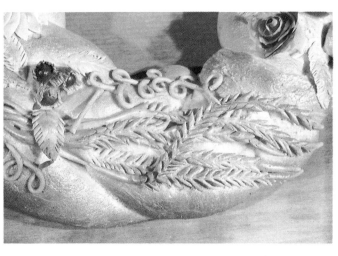

# Heart

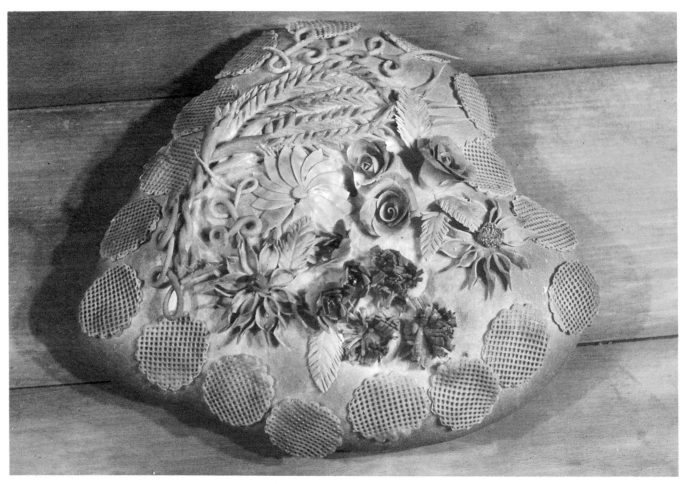

# Grape Leaves

# Decorated Plates and Platters

## Introduction

Decorated plates and platters have much of the same appeal as decorated breads. Because of their flat surface, they lend themselves especially well to detailed work where the decoration is brought into clear relief. They can also be decorated with names and messages and presented on birthdays and special occasions.

These plates and platters can be hung on the wall or held upright with a stand on a table.

They can also be used as a component in larger presentation pieces.

Decorated plates and platters are usually constructed on ordinary plates and platters.

## Procedure

Cover the plate with a sheet of aluminum foil.

Use decorating dough #2 (see chart of decorating doughs).

Roll the dough into a 1 mm. (1/20 in.) thick sheet. Turn the plate over onto the sheet of dough and cut around the edges of the plate with a paring knife.

Carefully turn over the plate and place the circle of dough on the inside.

Smooth the edges of the dough with the thumb.

Brush or spray the plate with coffee extract to give it an appealing natural color. The plates and platters can also be prepared with woven strips of dough (one or two colors).

## Decoration

The plates and platters can be prepared with or without a decorative border.

The decorations are placed on the plates and platters in the same way as decorated breads.

Bake the decorated plates and platters in a 100 to 150 °C (200 to 300 °F) oven for 3 to 4 hours depending on the size and thickness of the decoration. Color the decoration after baking with egg yolk, coffee extract, or India ink.

## Storage

Plates and platters that have been decorated with flowers, ears of wheat, grapes, etc. can be frozen while still raw and baked when needed. Once the decorated plates and platters have been baked, however, they should not be frozen. Once baked, they can be brushed with shellac and should keep for up to 5 years.

# Woven and Decorated Platters

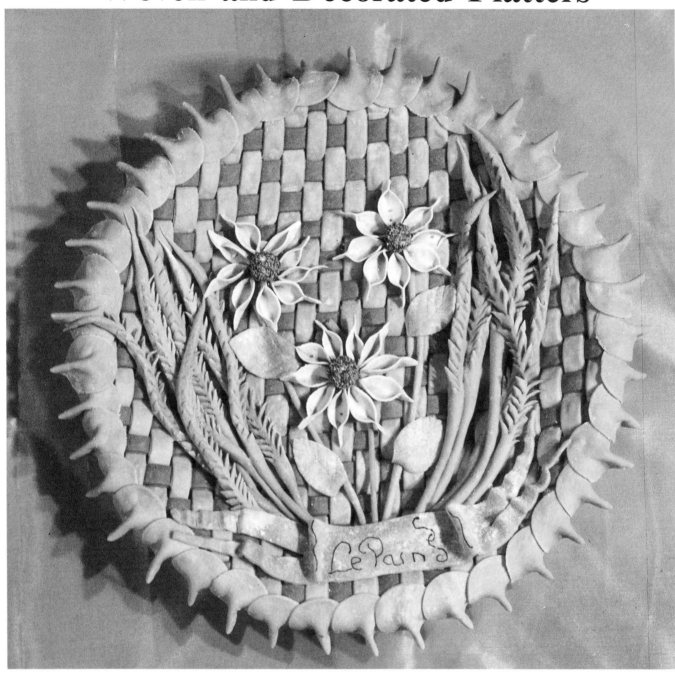

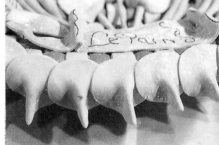

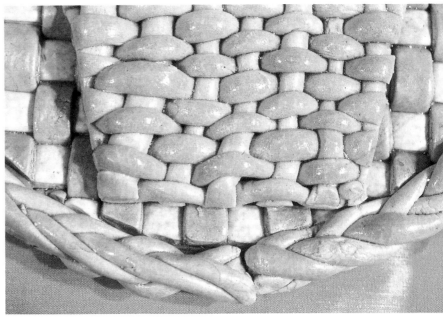

# Woven and Decorated Platter

# Oval Portrait

# Chapter 6

# Decorated Breads and Presentation Pieces

*An unlimited domain for the baker's creativity*

Presentation pieces are increasingly becoming a part of a bakery's everyday sales. A bakery's reputation and the skills of its artisans can be best enhanced by the regular exhibition of these artistic presentations.

Presented in this chapter is a collection of diverse presentation pieces which is designed to offer the reader new areas to explore.

# An Exceptional Selection

## A - Presentation pieces by the Compagnons du Devoir du Tour de France

*Alain Couet and Eric Kayser present a selection of artistic pieces which illustrate a variety of themes and techniques. Each presentation piece contains an explanation and description of special techniques. Certain pieces (scallops, soup terrine, etc.)* *make use of decorating techniques that have been presented in chapter 5. The "French Revolution" was designed by a young member of the Compagnons du Devoir du Tour de France.*

## B - Presentation pieces by Bernard, Isabelle, and Valérie Ganachaud

*The whole Ganachaud family has presented a selection of pieces of varied style and difficulty.*
*Bernard Ganachaud (Meilleur Ouvrier de France) and his two daughters, Isabelle and Valérie (Maîtres en Boulangerie)* *explain the preparation of basic decorating materials as well as illustrate presentation pieces which are a regular offering to their Parisian clientele.*

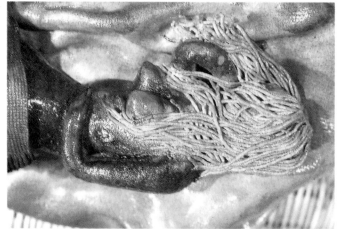

## C - Presentation pieces by Léon Mégard

*Léon Mégard is a highly experienced professional and owner of the famous " Maison du Pain " in Luxueuil-les-Bains in eastern France. It is there that he has streamlined the production of artistic presentation pieces which make use of a variety of inno-* *vative themes: finely sculpted figurines, sculpted logs which double as jewel boxes, and scenes from everyday life animated with miniature life-like reproductions of people.*

# of Presentation Pieces

## D - Presentation pieces by Daniel Hervé

Daniel Hervé contributed to volume 1 of Special and Decorative Breads. In this volume he presents two magnificent presentation pieces "Lyons, gastronomic capitol" and "The breads of Europe" which explore the limits of the baker's skill.

## E - Presentation pieces on the theme of the French revolution

This section includes ten pages of photos taken at a national contest for decorated breads which took place in Lyons for the b i - centennial of the French revolution.

## F - Le Tour de France

The French baker's organization, Compagnons du Devoir du Tour de France, has for centuries contributed to the education of apprentice bakers throughout all the regions of France.

Alain Couet and Eric Kayser present a map of France with a selection of regional breads (see chapter 3 of this volume).

# Presentation Pieces by French Bakers

## Soup terrine

### Introduction

The soup terrine itself is molded around a stainless steel bowl. The lid is shaped over a large stainless steel cutout and the base is shaped over a smaller cutout.

The bowl and the two cutouts are coated with aluminum foil before the dough is molded over.

Roll a sheet of basic decorating dough to a thickness of 1 mm. (1/20-in.).

Cover each of the three sections of the soup terrine with a sheet of the decorating dough.

Trim the edges of the dough with a paring knife.

Lightly brush the parts to the terrine with coffee extract using a pastry brush or a small spray gun.

### Decoration

The cover to the terrine is decorated with flours, bunches of raisins, ears of wheat, and roses which are attached with warm water.

Roll out an extremely thin (.5 mm./ 1/32 in.) sheet of decorating dough. Cut circles out of the dough with a # 4 cookie cutter. Cut each of the circles in half and overlap them around the edge of the lid.

The base for the terrine as well as the bowl can be decorated in the same way.

Bake the sections to the terrine until they are completely dry.

### Varnishing

Brush the terrine with the same colorless shellac used for wooden surfaces.

218

# Sea Scallops

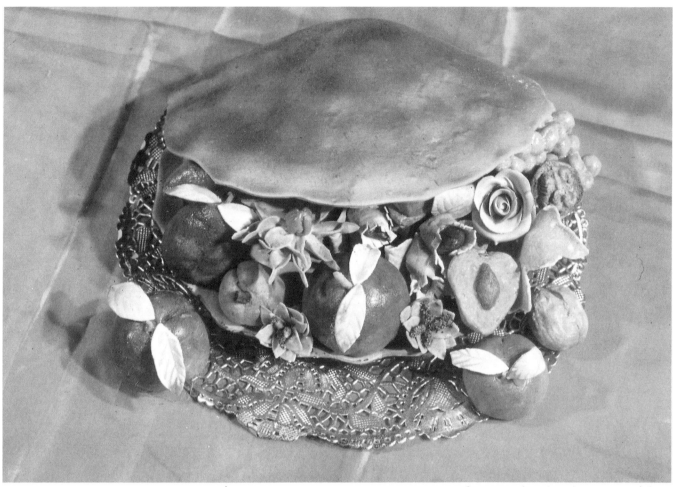

## Introduction

The sea scallops presented here are derived from the more traditional cornucopias and baskets which are always shown overflowing with an assortment of foods and flowers.

## Procedure

The sea scallops are composed of:
a) the shell itself which is molded;
b) the foods and flowers made from decorating dough and used to fill the shells. These are extremely varied.

The two shells shown here were prepared using special plastic molds. If these are unavailable, the molds can be made with plaster.

The decorations for the scallops consist primarily of fruits and flowers.

It is also possible to fill the shells with miniature animals, fish, and crustaceans which have been prepared in advance out of salt-based decorating dough.

The scallops can also be prepared without any decorative filling and used for presenting chocolates on special occasions such as Valentine's day or Easter.

## Finishing the scallops

The scallops are especially attractive when a wide range of color tones are used in the presentation. These varied colors are provided by the fruits and flowers made with the decorating dough.

To help preserve the scallops, varnish the shells and the decorative fillings with colorless shellac.

# Basket of Grapes

## Procedure

Roll a 5 mm. (1/4-in.) thick sheet of decorating dough and cut it into strips with a large knife.

Roll the strips into smooth strands and wrap them around pieces of stiff wire to form the basket.

Make sure the strands are even and firmly stacked all the way to the top edges of the basket.

Dry the basket in a 40 °C (104 °F)

proof box without any moisture for approximately 12 hours.

Bake the basket in an oven preheated to 100 °C (200 °F) for approximately 3 hours. Watch the baskets carefully to make sure they don't become too dark.

When the basket is finished baking, gently pull out the wires with pliers.

## Preparing the handle

Bakers sometimes use a foam material for baking delicate forms such as the handles to these baskets.

Prepare a 3 or 5 strand braid approximately 22 cm. (9 in.) long. Place it on a circle of baking foam, brush it with egg wash and bake it until it is dry.

Attach the handle to the basket base with flour paste; this is very exacting and must be done carefully.

Place a decorative strip of dough over the joint where the handle is attached.

# Parrot

The parrot presented here is attached to a grapevine on a woven mat. Each of the components in the presentation is made with decorating dough.

The dough has been colored with a mixture of coffee extract and egg yolks that have been applied with a spray gun.

## Equipment

Rolling pin; 2 sheet pans; 2 cardboard egg cartons; pastry bag tip (1 cm./1/2 in. diameter); pair of scissors; chef's knife.

## Ingredients

600 g. salt-based decorating dough (21 oz.)
200 g. sugar syrup-based decorating dough (7 oz.)
Coffee extract

## Procedure

Mold 400 g. (14 oz.) of the salt-based decorating dough and mold it into a pear shape.

Continue to work the thin end of the pear shaped dough to form the parrot's tail. Gently set the dough on an egg carton and bake it in a 100 °C (200 °F) oven to harden it.

Roll the sugar syrup-based decorating dough into a thin sheet with a rolling pin or dough sheeter. Cut miniature ovals out of the dough with the tip of a pastry bag. Attach them immediately with flour paste.

## Wings

Cut 2 wings out of a 2 mm. (1/16 in.) sheet of sugar syrup-based decorating dough.

Place the wings on cardboard egg cartons to help give them a natural, rounded shape and bake them in a 100 °C (200 °F) oven until they are dry. When the wings have hardened, attach them to the body of the parrot with flour paste.

# Marquises

## Equipment

Rolling pin - set of cookie cutters - sheet pan - plastic figurine as a mold for the marquise.

## Ingredients

700 g. modeling dough (24.5 oz.)
300 g. salt-based decorating dough (10.5 oz.)
500 g. sugar syrup-based decorating dough (17.5 oz.)
Coffee extract

## Preparing the mold

Prepare a 3 cm. (1 1/2 in.) thick sheet of modeling dough. Cut the dough in 2 and place the 2 sections over each side of the plastic figurine. Make sure the figurine is well floured so the dough can be easily removed. Place the dough-coated figurine in the freezer.

Roll out a 150 g. (5.5 oz.) section of salt-based decorating dough. Remove the 2 frozen sides of modeling dough from the plastic figurine and line the insides with the salt-based decorating dough.

Work quickly so the modeling dough doesn't thaw. Trim the edges with a serrated knife.

Unmold the 2 molded sides of dough and dry them in a 100 °C (200 °F) oven for approximately 10 hours. Attach them together with flour paste. Smooth the seam where the sides join with salt-based decorating dough which has been softened with water.

## Preparing the dress

Roll out a thin sheet of sugar syrup-based decorating dough. Cut the dough into 2 cm. (1 in.) wide strips. They should be long enough to wrap completely around the figurine.

Thin one edge of the strips with a light bulb.

## Constructing the dress

Start at the bottom by spreading on a layer of flour paste and placing over a strip of dough, thick side down. Be sure and give it natural looking folds. Continue attaching additional strips of dough with flour paste until the dress reaches the middle of the figurine.

Use a pastry brush to decorate the marquises with coffee extract or food coloring.

# Clowns

## Ingredients

800 g. white flour (28 oz.)
200 g. light pumpernickel rye flour (7 oz.)
1 kg. salt (35.5 oz.)
400 ml. warm water (13.5 fl. oz.)

## Kneading

Sift together the white and rye flours.

Combine the ingredients in the bowl of an electric mixer or kneading machine. Knead on slow speed.

Continue kneading to obtain a stiff dough.

Cover the dough with plastic wrap to prevent a skin from forming.

Salt-based decorating dough should never be frozen but can be kept in the refrigerator (5 °C/41 °F) for up to 3 days.

## Procedure

Carefully shape the head, torso, legs, arms, and the support for the figures.

Roll out a 1 mm. (1/20 in.) thick sheet of salt-based decorating dough. Use a razor blade to cut strips out of the dough to form pants which should be attached to the figures with water.

Gently cover up the seams on the figures by rubbing them with water using a finger or pastry brush.

Continue in the same way to make the jacket.

## Drying

Dry the clowns in a 40 °C (104 °F) proof box without moisture for 24 hours.

## Coloring the clowns

Color the clowns with a mixture of coffee extract and egg yolks using a pastry brush or a sprayer.

Attach the head to the body using a glue gun.

## Varnishing

When the clowns are hard and dry, they should be varnished with shellac or a gelatin-based sealer.

# The Bill of Rights

## The house

This presentation piece is constructed with sugar syrup-based decorating dough.

Before beginning to construct the house, draw a scale model and prepare cardboard cutouts for each wall with spaces left for doors, windows, etc.

Cut the 6 major sections of the house out of a sheet of dough using the cardboard cutouts.

Prepare bricks and tiles ahead of time with decorating dough. Make sure they have been well dried out in the oven before attaching them to the house.

## The panels

The panels presented here are inscribed with the French bill of rights and are flanked on each side by paintings of Robespierre and Danton drawn with coffee extract.

This project was completed by an 18 year old apprentice.

Preparation time: Approximately 200 hours.

# Bernard, Isabelle, Valérie GANACHAUD: "Master Bakers"

## A family of bakers

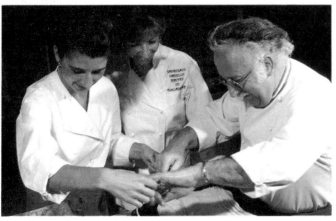

The Ganachaud bakery, located in the Belleville section of Paris, is one of France's most respected and best known food establishments. The Ganachaud name has become synonymous with quality, reliability, and innovation.

The reputation of the Ganachaud family bakery is the result of the dedication of Bernard Ganachaud (Meilleur Ouvrier de France) and his two daughters, Isabelle and Valérie who offer a continuously changing variety of traditional, regional, and specially decorated breads.

# Some facts about the Ganachaud family

## Bernard Ganachaud

Born in 1930, Bernard started out at eight years old helping his father in their bakery in Clisson, near Nantes on France's Atlantic coast.

He passed both the C.A.P. in baking and pastry with honors. (The C.A.P. is the degree given by the French government for artisans and craftsman in various fields.)

After receiving his C.A.P., Monsieur Ganachaud went on to obtain diplomas and win awards including a diploma from L'Ecole des Grands Moulins in Paris and a degree recognizing his mastery in the field of baking from the French ministry of education.

He established his own bakery in the city of Tours in the Loire valley where he remained for 5 years before establishing himself in 1960 at his present location in the Belleville section of Paris.

In 1979, Bernard Ganachaud was designated Meilleur Ouvrier de France, the highest award a craftsman can obtain. He went on to be accepted into the Confrérie des Chevaliers du Bon Pain – a prestigious French baking organization, was awarded a diploma as a master baker from the Club Prosper Montagné, and won first prize for baking in a contest sponsored by Gault et Millau. He has also been awarded first prize by the Coq d'Or des Gourmets Associés.

M. Ganachaud's bakery is not only well known in France but is starting to be recognized internationally. There are already 15 locations where products bearing the Ganachaud name can be found in Japan.

Bernard Ganachaud dedicates much of his free time to the education of apprentice bakers. He has taught at professional baking schools in Nantes as well as served on juries for the C.A.P. and Meilleur Ouvrier de France. Perhaps most importantly, Monsieur Ganachaud has trained 32 apprentices, 31 of whom have successfully passed their C.A.P.

## Isabelle Ganachaud

Ms. Ganachaud studied a wide variety of subjects before deciding to follow in her father's footsteps and become a professional baker. After completion of her high school degree, she studied to become a medical secretary and then went on to become a nurse. After four years as a nurse, Isabelle entered the Ecole des Grands Moulins, one of Paris's best baking schools where she obtained her baking diploma. Soon after, she passed her government baking exams and obtained her C.A.P. She continued to take advanced courses in baking at the Institut National de la Boulangerie in Rouen where she obtained her diploma. After graduation from the advanced baking school in Rouen, she continued to obtain advanced degrees in the baking profession.

In 1989, Isabelle Ganachaud opened her own bakery, called "La Flûte GANA" on Paris's rue des Pyrénées.

When asked what made her give up nursing to become a baker, Isabelle Ganachaud said that the decision was based on her need for independence as well as her desire to carry on a tradition which has been in her family for generations.

## Valérie Ganachaud

Like her older sister, Valérie Ganachaud graduated from high school and studied to become an executive secretary before making the decision to become a professional baker.

She obtained her degree in baking from the Ecole de Boulangerie in Paris and went on to obtain her French government degree, the C.A.P..

She went on to study further in baking at the Institute National de Boulangerie in Rouen where she obtained a diploma.

Valérie has become a partner with her sister Isabelle in the family bakery, "la Flûte GANA".

# A word from Bernard Ganachaud:
# The Ganachaud philosophy

Its a well-known fact that for several decades or even several generations (if we start back at the time of the farm at Clisson), that I have a very personal approach to baking and that I have had the opportunity to share my ideas with other bakers.

The essence of being a baker, and I'm not talking here about industrial baking, is that the work be kept to a human scale. If we enlarge beyond this scale, quality and freshness will be compromised; the quality of bread depends first and foremost on its freshness, regardless of the type of loaves.

At the Ganachaud bakery, we work with natural starters. This is not something that can be done in a large, industrial establishment. Natural starters are almost never the same so it takes an accomplished craftsman with good intuition to know how to work with them.

Even though first and foremost we are bakers and craftsman, we also have to be businessmen and keep our clientele returning to the shop. My natural reaction as a businessman has been to keep the range of breads I offer as wide and appealing as possible. This is particularly true with decorated breads that always catch the customer's eye and give him or her a sense that we're doing something special and beyond the norm. Most modern bakeries have neglected this area of decorated breads because they require too much attention and care and are not adaptable to mass production.

From the time I first settled in Paris in 1960, I knew that I was going to keep the bakery small and move in the direction of a skilled craftsman. Until two of my daughters, Isabelle and Valérie joined me during the last few years, I worked almost entirely alone. I've been fortunate, for they have contributed their own imagination and creativity to the work. And to my mind, creativity is the essence of craft without which we could no longer call ourselves artisans.

I also must add that genuine creativity for a craftsman like myself would not be possible without the cooperation of the entire family, and I'll take the opportunity now to thank my wife for the 30 years of help and support she has given which has made the Ganachaud bakery what it is today.

In the following pages are examples of decorated breads that the Ganachaud family has developed and contributed as part of the advancement of the baking profession.

*A selection of*

*Ganachaud breads*

We have made a selection from the long list of Ganachaud creations which ranges from a quick and easy decorated loaf, to more complicated assembled pieces which not only require mastery of certain baking techniques but a developed artistic sense as well.

We have presented these creations in the following order:

### Valentine bread
*(Isabelle Ganachaud)*
Decorated bread

### Money pouch
*(Didier Lemaire, head baker at Ganachaud bakeries)*
Easily prepared, small loaf

### The signs of the zodiac
*(Isabelle Ganachaud)*
Decorated breads which can be sold throughout the year

### Crocodile loaf
*(Bernard Ganachaud)*
Presentation piece which can be quickly prepared

### Sheaves of wheat
*(Bernard Ganachaud)*
Presentation piece which can be quickly prepared

### Grape Basket
*(Bernard Ganachaud)*
Presentation piece

### Traditional grape harvester's basket
*(Bernard Ganachaud)*
Complicated presentation piece

### Christmas manger
*(Valerie Ganachaud)*
Complicated presentation piece with modeled clay figurines

227

# Valentine bread

## Uses

The month of February seems relatively calm after the activity of the Christmas season and is a good time for bakers to work on decorated breads and presentation pieces.

Valentine bread can be prepared by decorating a round loaf with a prebaked design made from decorating dough or by simply using the design as a decoration in itself. Either of these makes an appealing decoration for a table or window display. A round loaf, decorated with a heart loaf is an appropriate and appealing for Valentine's day. If a country loaf is used as the support, the bread itself can be served.

## Equipment

Piece of cardboard - pencil - pair of scissors - knife - decorating dough - rolling pin.

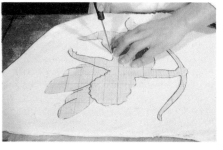

### Cutting a design in cardboard

Draw the heart and the cherubim on the sheet of cardboard. Cut around the drawing with the scissors to make cutouts.

Roll the decorating dough into a 1 cm. (1/2 in.) thick sheet. Place the sheet of dough in the freezer. Remove it from the freezer before it has completely hardened.

This preliminary half-freezing of the dough makes it easier to cut.

### Cutting the dough

Place the cardboard cutouts over the dough and cut around the edges with a sharp knife. Cut the heart and cherubim out as separate pieces.

### Preparing the braid

Roll the decorating dough into strands and make a braid to wrap around the heart.

### Attaching the braid

Dust the heart with flour and wet the bottom of the braid with water before attaching the braid to the heart.

# Valentine bread (continued)

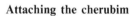

## Baking

Bake the heart and cherubim assembly on a piece of parchment paper in a low oven to prevent it from coloring too rapidly.

As soon as the heart comes out of the oven, brush the edges of the cherubim with coffee extract using a pastry brush. Allow to dry.

Varnish the decor with regular wood varnish. An apricot glaze can also be used.

## Attaching the cherubim

Attach the cherubim by first wetting the heart. Place the cherubim carefully on the heart; it's important to get it perfectly centered on the first try.

To make the cherubim easier to work with, it can be partially frozen before attaching it to the heart.

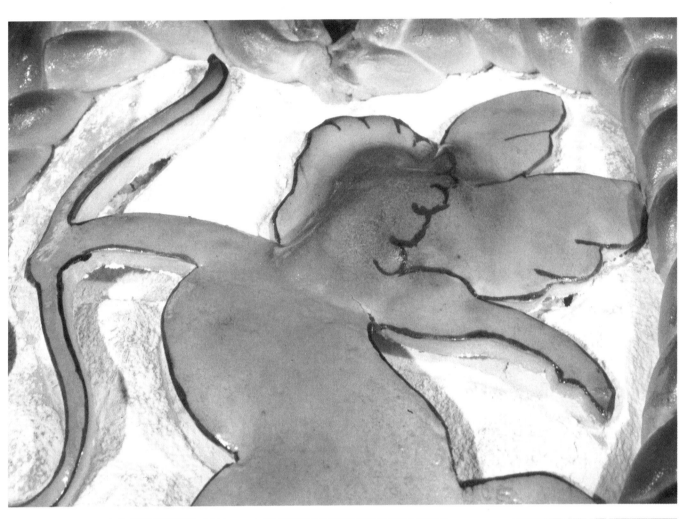

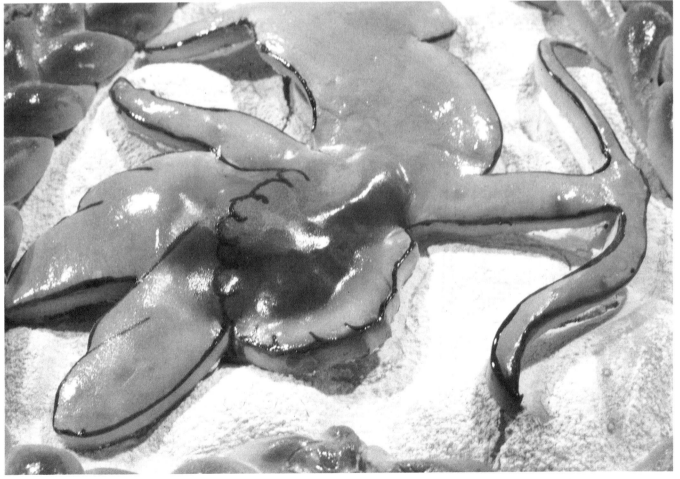

# Variations on the Valentine's day theme

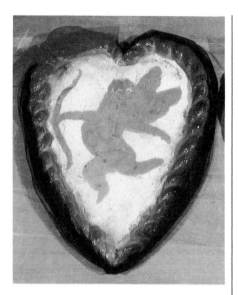
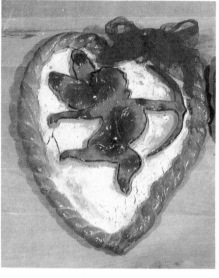

### Using a stencil

The cherubim can be applied to a large, round loaf such as country bread using a stencil plate or cardboard.

### Round Valentine breads

Use a section of rounded dough which has finished proofing. It is important that the base loaf be thoroughly proofed so that it doesn't expand too much in the oven and cause the decoration to break apart.

Make a thick rope with soft textured decorating dough and wrap it around the top sides of the rounded dough. Cut into the edges of the rope of dough with scissors (see page 234, " The signs of the zodiac ").

Bake the loaf until it is half done, remove it from the oven and attach the heart and cherubim assembly by brushing the underside of the heart with water. Put the loaf with the heart back in the oven.

When the loaves are finished baking, decorate the edges by brushing with coffee extract. Brush the loaves with apricot glaze.

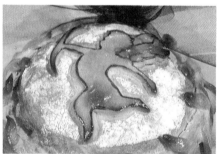

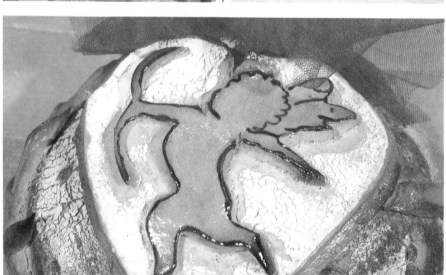

# Money pouch

### Uses

This decorative money pouch is simple to prepare and makes an attractive decoration for a feast day table. It can also be used as a vase and filled with dried flours or even be used as a jar for pens and pencils.

### Equipment

Decorating dough containing rye flour (see Volume 1, Recipe 2, page 180) + 30° syrup to make the pouch look like canvas and make it more solid - knife - aluminum foil - coffee beans

### Procedure

Roll out the decorating dough into a sheet the same size as a baking sheet (60 by 40 cm/24 by 16 in.) and .5 cm. (1/4 in.) thick.

Cut the dough into 3 strips approximately 15 by 35 cm. (6 by 14 in.)

Make a support in the shape of a large garlic clove by wrapping coffee beans in a sheet of aluminum foil. Wrap a strip of dough around the support.

Fold and seal the edges of the dough to form the flat bottom of the pouch.

Cut a thin strip of decorating dough and roll it to form a cord which will be used to tie the pouch. Tie the cord around the pouch and tie a knot.

Gently pinch and bend the top rims of the pouch to give it a natural appearance.

### Baking

Bake the pouches for 30 minutes in a low oven.

When the pouches have finished baking but are still warm, cut off the top of the aluminum foil protruding out of the pouches and pour out the coffee beans. Gently pull out any aluminum foil adhering to the inside of the pouches.

The pouches can sold as they are, or they can be varnished to increase their shelf life.

# The signs of the zodiac

## Uses and appeal

These original breads are a pleasure to the eye and palate alike and have the advantage of being appropriate at any time of year. They are also an original idea for birthdays.

These attractive breads can be used as centerpieces for special occasion dinners and have the advantage of being both decorative and edible.

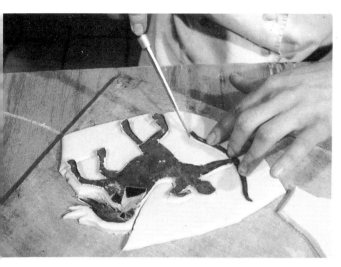

## Preparing the templates

Make stylized drawings of all 12 signs of the zodiac on sheets of cardboard. Don't use too much detail around the edges or they will be too fragile.

Cut around the designs with scissors to make cutouts which will be used as templates to cut the designs in the dough.

## Procedure

Roll out a sheet of decorating dough 1 cm. (1/2 in.) thick. Put the sheet of dough in the freezer to harden it, but do not let it freeze completely.

Place the cardboard template over the dough and cut around it with a sharp knife.

Put the zodiac cutouts of dough back in the freezer.

## Note

A stack of dough cutouts appropriate for the current month can be prepared, frozen and used as needed. Be careful when storing the dough cutouts to wrap them tightly in plastic wrap to prevent frost from collecting or a crust from forming.

# The signs of the zodiac (continued)

### Preparation

To prepare these loaves, use a round of dough the same shape and size used for making large country loaves. The loaves should be fully proofed before any decoration is applied otherwise they will expand too much in the oven and cause the decoration to split or crack.

Prepare a rope of dough and attach it around the edges of the tops of the loaves by first brushing its underside with a pastry brush.

Cut into the sides of the rope of dough with scissors to form ears of wheat.

Dust the top of the loaves, but not the rope of dough, with flour.

## Baking

The loaves are baked in two stages; during the first stage the loaves are baked alone, during the second they are baked with the zodiac cutouts:

a) Bake the loaves for 20 minutes with steam.

b) Remove the partially baked loaves from the oven and place a frozen zodiac dough cutout on the center of each. Wet the bottom of the cutouts so they adhere to the loaves.

c) Place the loaves back in the oven and finish baking.

If the decorative cutouts begin to color too quickly, they can be covered with a sheet of parchment paper.

*Note*

Some of the zodiac cutouts (e.g. libra), are extremely fragile, so work quickly and carefully.

237

# The signs of the zodiac (continued)

**Aries**
Courageous and sometimes violent, Aries is a fire sign and an intense one at that. Those born under the sign of Aries are often initiators and are quick to jump into challenging situations.

**Taurus**
Hard working, persistent, and organized, a Taurus will not give up before finishing what he or she has set out to do.

**Gemini**
Always eager to be with people and make new friends, and especially interested in partnerships, a Gemini's greatest fear is growing old and death itself, especially dying alone.

**Cancer**
Secretive and profound, Cancers don't like superficiality and are interested in deep relationships with people. These sensitive souls sometimes tend toward melancholy.

**Leo**
Often domineering and willful, Leos know how to make themselves heard and heeded. More gifted in justice than in love, Leos often find themselves alone.

**Virgo**
Virgo is the sign of the family and of devotion. Virgos are usually confident of their destiny and often adapt happily to family life.

**Libra**
Pleasant and courteous, Libras are often mistakenly judged superficial, but they have a profound side to them which makes them appreciate solitude.

**Scorpio**
Scorpios are tireless in both love and work. Jealous and passionate, they are relentless in their search for truth and in their tormented need for seduction.

**Sagittarius**
Peaceful, yet forceful, a Sagittarius will always prefer offense to defense. Although stubborn at times, Sagittarians are good decision makers. Their romantic side may hide a violent streak.

**Capricorn**
Never extravagant with either money or emotions, Capricorns are cautious and economical. Deep and quiet, they like to be alone and do not like superficiality.

**Aquarius**
Willful and sometimes domineering, Aquarians are easily angered but can also be generous and loving. They will always share what they have and protect a friend in need.

**Pisces**
Mystical and vulnerable to change, Pisces are driven by their thirst for liberty and stability. Sometimes jealous, Pisces are sometimes fatalist and impulsive.

### Finishing the decor

When the loaves are finished baking, bring out the relief of the designs by brushing the contours with coffee extract using a small pastry brush.

Let the surface dry.

Brush the zodiac design and the ear of wheat wrapping around the loaves with apricot glaze to give them extra sheen.

The contrast between the colored decorations and the white flour on the top of the loaves creates a striking effect.

## Offering zodiac breads to your customers

Zodiac breads will often sell themselves. All that you need to do is ask the customer " What is your sign? " and show him or her the appropriate loaf. Also suggest the loaves as surprises for relatives or to offer the hostess of a dinner party.

# The signs of the zodiac

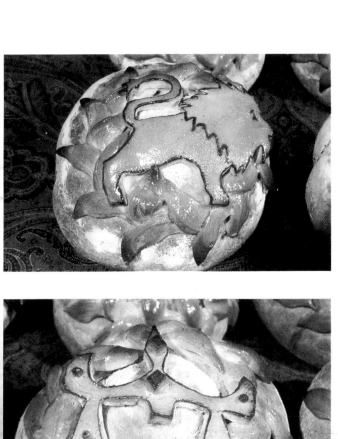

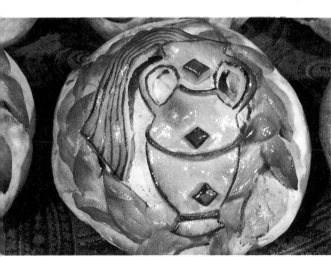

# Crocodile loaf

## Introduction

A large crocodile loaf is so striking that it can be presented by itself in the bakery's display window.

These large loaves are also excellent for buffets.

## Preparation

To make large crocodile loaves, weld together two 60 by 40 cm. (24 by 16 in.) sheet pans.

10 kg. (22 lb.) of dough is required to make one large crocodile.

Experienced bakers should count on 1 1/2 hours of work to complete the shaping of one crocodile.

The shaping of the crocodile is greatly facilitated by working with a straight, long piece of dough.

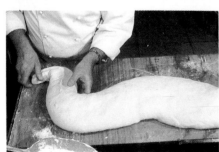

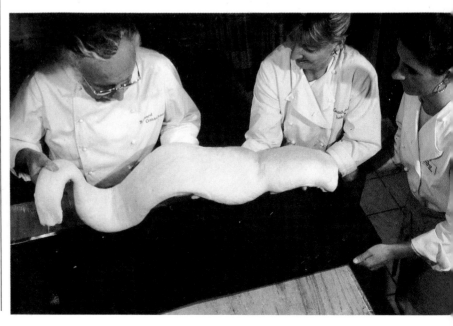

## Shaping

Most of the time shaping the crocodile is spent making decorative cuts over the surface of the dough with a pair of scissors.

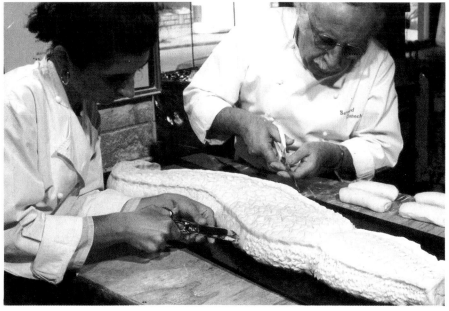

Do not try to make the cuts too even or the crocodile won't look natural.

While making the cuts in the dough with the scissors, gently shape the crocodile to give it a natural look.

It is advisable to use a fairly firm dough and to work quickly while decorating and shaping the crocodiles. If the dough waits too long before being baked, the decorative cuts are liable to sink into the dough and the effect will be lost.

The surface design on the crocodile can be accentuated by quickly pinching the cuts in the dough between the thumb and forefinger before baking the loaves in a 230 °C (450 °F) oven.

### Choosing the best size for the crocodile loaves

Crocodile loaves are the most dramatic when they almost life size.

The loaf shown here which is 1.2 m. (4 ft.) long is almost the actual size of a real baby crocodile.

Remember to adjust baking temperatures according to the size of the crocodile loaves.

# Crocodile loaf

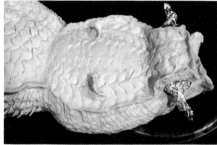

### Claws

The claws for the crocodile loaf should be shaped separately and attached to the main loaf just before baking.

### Face and mouth

The crocodile loaves can be shaped to portray an open or closed mouth crocodile depending on the whim and imagination of the baker.

The crocodile shown here has its mouth open, holding one of the Ganachaud bakery's famous "flute" loaves.

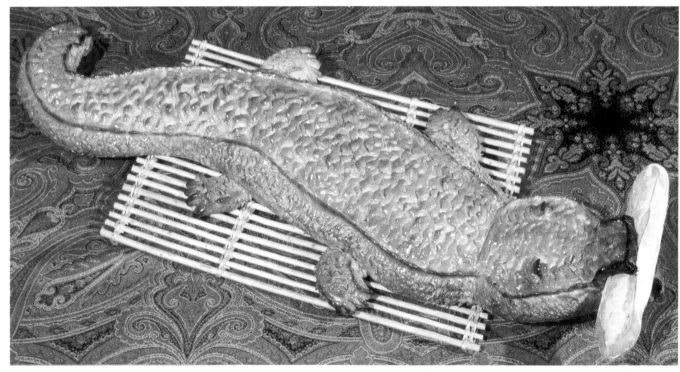

# Sheaves of wheat

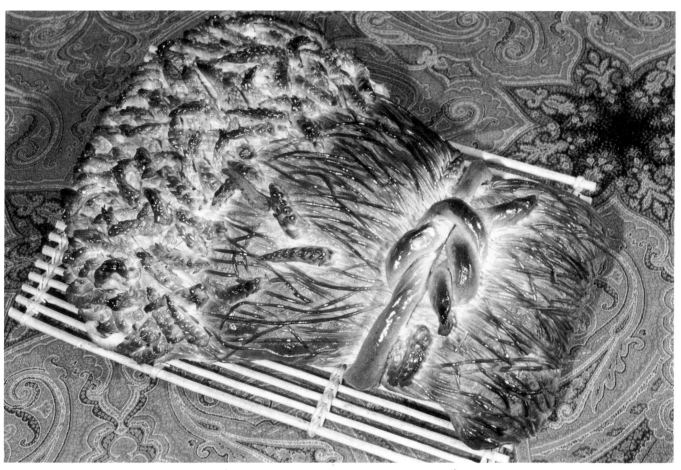

### Introduction

These attractive loaves are simple to prepare and are appropriate for a bakery that uses traditional bread making techniques.

The loaves should be prepared from natural bread dough and then decorated with sheaves of wheat fashioned out of decorating dough.

Count on approximately 2 hours to prepare the loaves provided the dough itself has already been made.

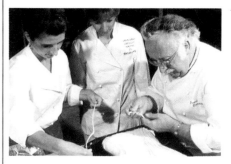

# Sheaves of wheat

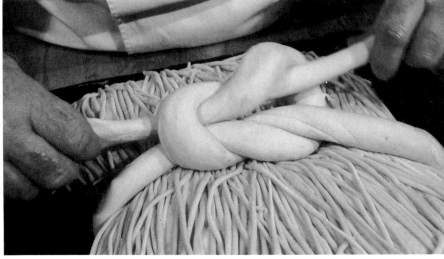

## Procedure

Prepare 8 kg. (17.6 lb.) of country bread dough. Let the dough rest in the refrigerator or cold fermentation chamber.

It is best to prepare the individual ears of wheat with decorating dough during lulls in the day's schedule and then freeze them until enough have been collected to assemble finished loaves. Prepare 100 branches and 200 ears.

## Shaping

Once the loaves of natural bread dough have been shaped and proofed, lay the wheat branches over the loaves.

Do not try to arrange them in even rows, but rather toss them on the loaves so they have a spontaneous, natural look.

Sprinkle the ears of wheat over the branches by starting at one end of the

loaves and working your way down toward the bottom of the branches.

The arrangement of the ears depends on the style and whim of the baker.

## Wheat strap

Prepare a rope shaped section of dough with decorating dough. Cut the rope in half.

Tuck one end of each of the halves under the sides of the loaf and tie the two ends together on the top of the loaf to form a decorative knot as shown in the photo.

## Baking

Bake the loaves in a 230 °C (450 °F) oven with a small amount of steam injected near the beginning of baking.

Watch the loaves carefully to make sure they don't color too quickly. Cover the decor with parchment paper if necessary to protect it.

## Glazing or varnishing

As soon as the loaves come out of the oven, brush them with a small amount of water. After they have cooled, brush them with apricot glaze.

If the loaves are being used in a window display, they can be brushed with varnish.

If the loaves are being delivered to someone's home, it is better to let customers varnish the loaves themselves so they don't confuse an inedible varnish with edible glaze.

# Grape Basket

## Introduction

This beautiful presentation piece is moderately difficult to prepare; several steps in particular require special attention.

The basket can be presented alone or filled with short loaves and rolls.

## A. Basket base

### Shaping

Use a wooden crate with the same dimensions needed for the basket.

Wrap the crate tightly with aluminum foil and brush the foil with butter to make it easier to remove the bread after baking.

Roll a thick sheet (2 to 3 cm./1 to 1 1/4 in.) of decorating dough. Spread the sheet of dough over the bottom of the crate.

Take the added precaution of reinforcing the corners with an extra square of dough.

## Preparing the base for baking

Brush the dough with egg wash and poke it lightly with a skewer or the tip of a knife.

Don't worry if the dough blisters slightly; an irregular surface can help give a natural look to the basket.

## Baking

Brush the dough a second time with egg wash and then bake it for approximately 40 minutes in a 230 °C (450 °F) oven.

### Shaping

Before preparing the lid, the grapes and grape leaves should be prepared in advance and kept frozen until needed.

Roll out a 2 to 3 cm. (1 to 1 1/4 in.) thick sheet of decorating dough.

Carefully measure the exact size of the top of the basket base and add 2 cm. (1 in.) in both directions to compensate for shrinkage.

# B. Basket lid

Carefully shape the basket lid to fit the basket base. The lid can be shaped in a variety of ways. If a rounded lid is wanted, use inverted aluminum plates for molding the dough.

Be sure and reinforce curved or angled sections of the dough with extra squares of decorating dough so the lid doesn't collapse during baking.

Caution: When attaching the handle, be sure and anticipate the size of the oven to make sure the basket isn't built too high.

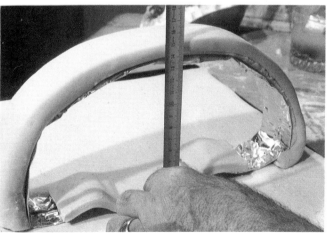

# Grape Basket

### Decoration

The basket cover is decorated with grapes and grape leaves of varying sizes.

Attaching the handle is particularly delicate. Construct a handle first with aluminum foil. This serves as a support for the handle made of decorating dough which is set over it.

Make sure the dough is cut from 2 to 3 cm. (1 to 1 1/4 in.) thick; any thicker and it may cause the aluminum support to collapse.

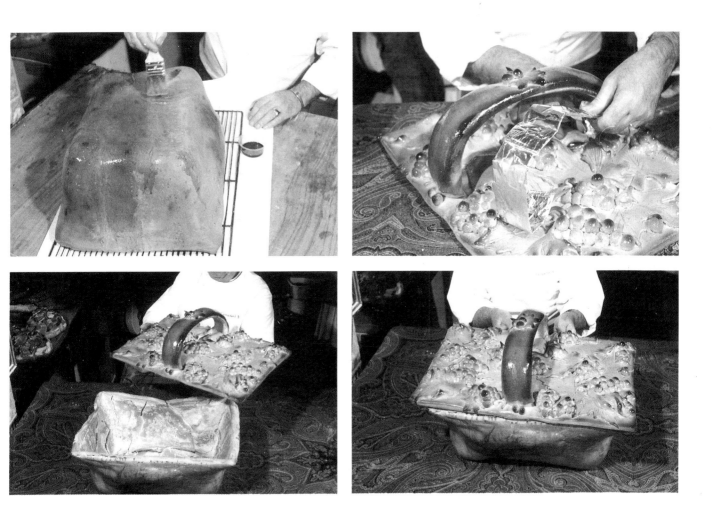

## Baking

Brush the lid with egg wash and very carefully slide it into the oven using a piece of the handle of a peel or a metal bar.

Be careful handling the peel itself.

## Final presentation

Once the sections of the basket have finished baking and have cooled, carefully remove the aluminum foil. Brush them with apricot glaze or varnish.

# Traditional grape harvester's basket

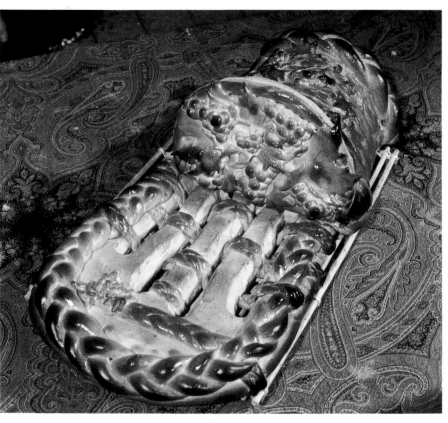

## Introduction

Despite its difficulty, this is Bernard Ganachaud's favorite presentation piece.

## Preparation

To prepare this presentation piece, a wooden or plastic tub such as the type used for sour cream or mayonnaise should be used as a mold.

Cut 1/3 of the tub off one of the sides. Tightly cover it with aluminum foil and brush the foil with butter.

Make a cardboard cutout by tracing around the outside of the top of the tub. This will be used later to form the lid to the basket.

## Shaping

Roll a sheet of decorating dough to a thickness of 2 cm. (1 in.) to form the back of the basket. The sheet should be wide enough so there are 6 to 8 cm. (2 1/2 to 3 in.) excess dough on each side of the tub.

Wrap the tub with braids of dough (3 strands for each braid) which should be prepared in advance. Use two double thick braids for the top and bottom rims of the tub.

After positioning the braids, put the basket in the refrigerator while preparing the slats for the back frame.

**Finishing the back**

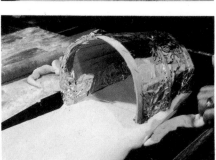

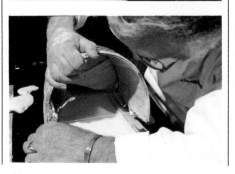

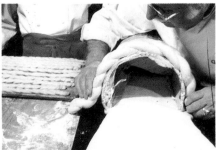

To bake the basket, use two baking sheets (60 by 40 cm./24 by 16 in.) which have been welded together (the same setup used for the crocodile loaf).

Use 8 kg. (18 lb.) of decorating dough to form the back of the basket which should be approximately 80 cm. (32 in.) high and 35 cm. (14 in.) wide.

Put the dough in a cold refrigerator or freezer before beginning the shaping. Cut strips out of the dough with a sharp knife so that decorative slats stand out in relief. Decorate the slats with thin braids of dough. Finish decorating the back by wrapping the edge with a braid having the same thickness as those used for the top and bottom rims of the tub.

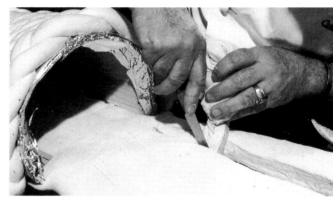

### Decorating the basket

Decorate the tub with miniature grapes and grape leaves.

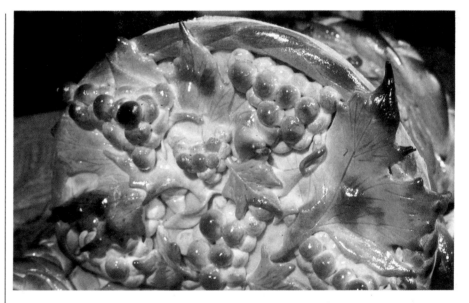

### Baking

Brush the finished basket with egg wash before baking. Remember to limit the size of the basket so that it will fit in the oven.

Prepare the lid to the tub with decorating dough using the cutout prepared at the beginning. Decorate the cover with grapes and grape leaves in the same style as the sides of the tub.

### Final presentation

Present the grape harvester's basket on a plywood sheet. The basket looks most impressive when presented upright at an angle.

# Christmas manger

**Introduction**

This traditional presentation piece makes a perfect window display during the Christmas season. It is prepared in 2 distinct stages:

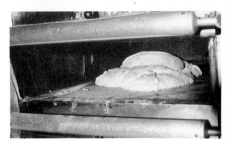

a) The base of rocks for the Christmas scene is made with country bread dough which gives the scene a rugged, natural look.

b) The figurines are modeled on supports with decorating dough. Their design depends on the whims and talent of the baker.

**Preparing the base for the manger**

Dust the peel with flour and cover it with a large mass of country bread dough. Toss the mass on the floor of the oven.

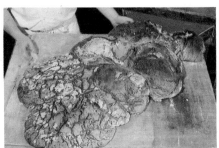

Repeat with a second mass of dough. The finished dimensions of the manger will of course depend on where it is being displayed and on the size of the oven.

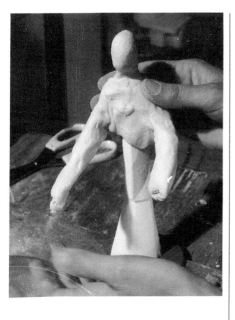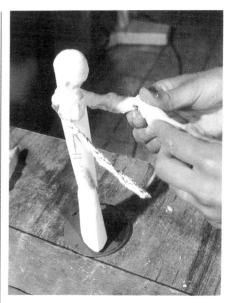

### Organizing the workload

The rocks for the manger scene can be easily prepared by baking some dough taken from a batch of country bread; little extra time or preparation is needed.

The figurines, on the other hand, are time consuming to prepare. Each one must be completed all at once because the dough dries very quickly.

Count on 2 to 3 hours for the preparation of each figurine. This includes preparation of the various colored doughs, assembling the support, and the sculpting itself.

### Bread figurines

The sculpting of the figurines is delicate and requires considerable talent and dexterity. The results are personal and different for every baker.

### Method

The bread figurines are made by superimposing layers of different colored decorating dough. The supports for the figurines can be made from various materials including cardboard, iron, aluminum, etc.

The figurines shown here were constructed on supports made from cardboard paper towel rolls and aluminum foil rolled into balls for the heads and into stiff rods for the arms. The entire structure is supported with a paper spike.

### Baking or drying

Baking helps dry the figurines quickly and also gives them a warmer color than simply letting them dry. The only advantage to drying is that the size of the figurines is not limited by the size of the oven.

Do not varnish the figurines until several days after baking or until they are well dried. This ensures that no moisture is trapped under the varnish.

### Final decoration

Arrange the rocks made from country bread dough so they serve as a natural looking backdrop for the manger scene. They can be hollowed in places to expose the crumb if this adds to the effect.
Arrange the figurines in the scene.
When the manger scene is in place, brush the entire surface with varnish.

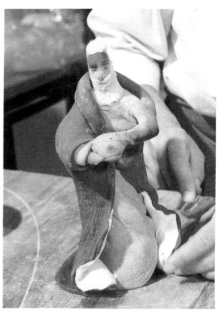

# Christmas manger

# Presentation Pieces by Léon Mégard

# A Master Baker in Love with his Art

Léon Mégard grew up in a family of bakers from the Ain region in eastern France. Several years ago, he opened his own bakery, "Maison du Pain", in Luxeuil-les-Bains.

In his well-equipped spacious bakery, Léon Mégard prepares over 30 varieties of special breads in a custom designed wood burning oven which he has placed within the customers' view.

More than one out of five of his customers regularly buys his special breads and the number continues to grow every day.

Beyond his role as an innovative local baker, Léon Mégard invests his extra time filling his shop window with a variety of constantly changing decorated breads. The window has become a local attraction and the frequent object of many a Sunday stroll.

Besides the increasing popularity of Léon Mégard's special breads there is a growing local interest in his custommade presentation pieces. Sometimes these personalized presentation pieces are the result of special requests by customers who for sentimental reasons may wish to have a postcard or photo reproduced in bread dough.

The example shown here is modeled after a photo of the bridge at Saint-Astier in France's Dordogne region.

M. Mégard's interest in decorated breads began only several years ago when he saw the first volume of "Special and Decorative Breads". From that point on, he has worked eagerly to expand the variety of decorated breads that he makes available to his clientele.

Because Léon Mégard has the full responsibility of running his own bakery, he has little time left over to devote to elaborate decoration. It is only through careful organization that he has been able to make use of gaps in the work schedule which can be devoted to decoration.

With experience comes speed. At one point the bird bath shown here was baked in too hot an oven and had to be redone; Léon Mégard shaped 18 birds in 20 minutes!

Despite M. Mégard's duties as the owner of a large bakery, he has also devoted much of his time to teaching future bakers.

*We have included the creations of Léon Mégard in this volume for several reasons:*

*1. the quality of the workmanship;*

*2. the diversity of themes and techniques that are used;*

*3. the exactness of the renderings shown by the facial expressions, proportions, and stances of the figures.*

*The presentation piece "Construction Site", was first conceived as an animated piece. It was presented in Léon Mégard's shop window and each week the construction was advanced further like an authentic construction site.*

For more information, write directly to Léon Mégard at
**La Maison du Pain -
Rue des Ecoles -
70300 Luxeuil-les-Bains**

## Technical details

# A Moment of Relaxation

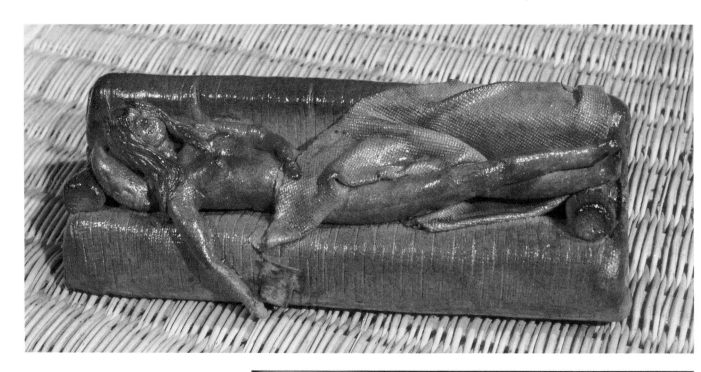

**An art all its own**

The female nude has long been an inspiration for the painter and sculptor.

Before the works of Léon Mégard, bakers had never attempted to portray the female nude.

As can be seen in the photos presented here, he has succeeded with remarkable finesse and artistry.

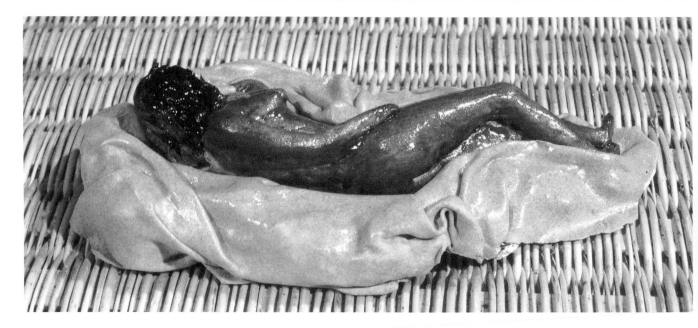

# Seduction

# Wooden Clogs - " Luxeuil " Heart

**Wooden clogs**

These clogs are prepared with salt-based decorating dough. Pegs have been inserted on the bottom of the clogs so they can be hung on a wall.

**" Luxeuil " heart**

This heart is prepared with decorating dough and is left hollow so it can be used as a box.

# Our Daily Bread - The Grape Harvest

### Our daily bread

This hollow presentation piece is designed so it can be hung on a wall. The base is prepared with salt-based decorating dough.

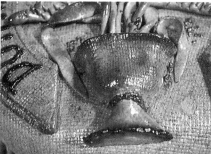

### The grape harvest

This is a composition of some of the favorite themes of French bakers-bunches of grapes, sheaves of wheat, etc.

The decoration is prepared with sugar syrup-based decorating dough. The decoration is applied onto the surface of a stale round loaf.

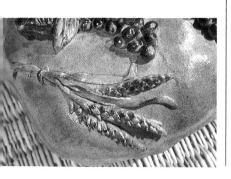

# Angelus - Wine Drinker - Lovers

## Angelus

The background is prepared in advance with salt-based decorating dough so that it is completely dried out before the decoration is applied.

Decorating time: 1 hour

## The wine drinker and the lovers

Same procedure as the angelus.

# Bird Bath

The bird bath makes an original presentation for candy and chocolate.
The birds on the edge can be presented in varied poses.

Below, *the jewelry box decorated with sheaves of wheat* is surrounded by a strand of braided decorating dough.

# Bakery - Bridge

# Decorated Logs

These attractive boxes can be used to present a variety of gifts such as candies, chocolates and even foie gras!

The base can be washed with water after each use.

# A Game of Pétanque

# Card Players

# Construction Site

# BELFORT's Lion

# "LYONS" and "EUROPE"
## *A master's presentation pieces*

Daniel Hervé, the principal author of the decorated breads section in Volume I of "Special and Decorative Breads" has contributed the two masterpieces shown on the following pages.

Both of these masterpieces, constructed in two contrasting innovative styles, are presented here as examples of the degree of artistry and mastery that can be achieved with hard work and long experience. When constructing pieces as elaborate as these, it is not only essential to have completely mastered the techniques of working with decorating dough but to also be familiar with principles of architecture and mathematics. Beyond this technical mastery lies the unlimited domain of artistry.

### " Lyons, gastronomic capital "

This presentation piece was specially constructed for the meeting of the SIRHA (Salon des Métiers de Bouche), a prestigious group of food professionals, held every two years in Lyons.

In the descriptions that follow, technical points are emphasized as construction of this presentation piece was particularly delicate.

### " The breads of Europe "

This elaborate presentation piece was constructed for the biennial meeting of the Salon Europain in Paris where bakers gather from around the world.

The construction of this piece required not only technical mastery but extensive research to ensure the authenticity of the coats of arms.

# " Lyons, Gastronomic Capital "

This presentation piece is constructed in five parts:

*1. The back* which is decorated with a lion dressed in a baker's uniform positioned amidst grape vines.

*2. The sphere* which is constructed with interwoven grape vines, leaves, and grapes.

*3. The scrolls* which list the principle growths of Beaujolais.

*4. Lighting* inside the sphere.

*5. The glass showcase* which consists of the pedestal, the molding, and the panes of glass.

## Construction procedure

This presentation pieces was constructed in 18 steps which required 295 hours of work.

1. Prepare a drawing of the lion used on the back.

2. Prepare the lion itself.

3. Prepare the grapes.

4. Assemble the grapes in bunches.

5. Prepare the leaves.

6. Prepare the scrolls and write in the inscriptions.

7. Construct the supports for the scrolls.

8. Prepare the grape vines.

9. Construct the sphere with its stand.

10. Prepare the " canvas " for the backing.

11. Baking

12. Coloring and lightening

13. Prepare the pedestal, the molding, and the brackets.

14. Prepare the cloth backing (satin or felt) as well as the braids.

15. Varnish the individual pieces; arrange the pieces and attach them in place.

16. Install the lighting in the globe.

17. Install the glass pains on the pedestal.

18. Attach the panes with scotch tape.

It is recommended to first construct the most difficult parts of the presentation piece so the other elements can be constructed around them. Most every step requires patience, skill, and a delicate touch but the lion is particularly difficult to make look realistic.

The assembly of the sphere is straightforward except for the assembly of the two halves which is delicate.

# " Lyons, Gastronomic Capital " (cont.)

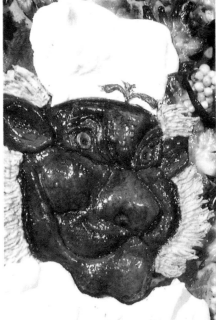

## The logo

### Equipment

Paper, pencil, eraser, cardboard, glue, cutter.

### Procedure

The easiest method is to first draw the lion to the exact size needed for the construction. When the drawing is complete, glue it to a sheet of cardboard and cut out each of the sections – the chefs hat, the ears, the eyes, the snout, the chin, the mane, the jaws, the knot, the arms and the jacket – so they make a jigsaw puzzle.

Each of these individual pieces is then used as a template for cutting the dough.

## Assembling the lion

### Equipment

Decorating dough, rolling pin, sheet pan, knife, aluminum foil, water.

### Procedure

The sections of the lion are first constructed with aluminum foil which is shaped accordingly. Once the sections of aluminum foil have been shaped, they are each covered with a thin sheet (4 mm./1/8 in.) of decorating dough.

When each of the sections of decorating dough has been shaped around the pieces of aluminum foil, they are then attached with water. The seams are then rubbed with a wet finger until they sink into the background.

Allow the constructed lion to dry for 24 hours before baking it in a 180 °C (350 °F) oven.

When the lion is finished baking, carefully remove the pieces of aluminum foil.

***Note:*** The lions mane is cut out of a 2 mm. (1/16 in.) thick sheet of decorating dough which is then hatched with a paring knife.

## Individual grapes

### Equipment

Decorating dough, sheet pan.

## Procedure

Preparing individual grapes is a straightforward process of rolling balls of decorating dough in the palms of the hands.

Use irregular size sections of decorating dough so the grapes have a natural appearance when assembled in clusters.

After rolling the dough in the palms of the hands, make sure each of the grapes is perfectly smooth and let them dry for 24 to 48 hours before baking them in a 170 °C (350 °F) oven. Keep them in a dry place until needed.

# Grape bunches

## Equipment

Flour paste, cardboard egg cartons.

## Procedure

See assembly directions on page 199 of " Special and Decorative Breads ", Volume I.

# Scrolls and inscriptions

## Equipment

Rolling pin, paring knife, mixing bowl, sheet pan (or sheet pan for baguettes), plastic wrap, flour.

## Procedure

See assembly directions in " Special and Decorative Breads ", Volume I.

# Supports for scrolls

## Equipment

Decorating dough, paring knife, scissors.

## Procedure

Construct a cone with 50 g. (1.8 oz.) of decorating dough. Cut miniature branches with a pair of scissors and place on a sheet pan.

Bake at 180 °C (350 °F).

Each scroll can be held with a single support.

# " Lyons, Gastronomic Capital " (cont.)

## Pedestal for the sphere

### Equipment

Decorating dough, sheet pan.

### Procedure

Use 1 kg. (35 oz.) of decorating dough to construct the pedestal. The pedestal is straightforward to construct; it is made from a single sheet of dough which is curved in the middle.

Let the pedestal dry for 48 hours before baking in a 180 °C (350 °F) oven for 1/2 hours.

## Half-spheres

### *1. Preparing the mixing bowl*

### Equipment

Round-bottomed mixing bowl, decorating dough, chef's knife, sheet pan.

### Procedure

Turn the round-bottomed mixing bowl face down on the marble.

Cover the bottom of the bowl with a sheet of wet parchment paper. Make sure the paper comes beyond the rim of the bowl on the marble so it can be folded onto the inside of the bowl. Transfer the paper-coated mixing bowl to a sheet pan.

Leave a 5 cm. (2 in.) border on each side of the half-sphere. The decorating dough is placed on the outside of the wet paper.

### *2. Decorating the half-spheres*

### Equipment

Decorating dough, chef's knife, water.

### Procedure

*A. Rim*
Roll a section of dough into a long cord which will reach around the circumference of the half-spheres. Press the cord around the rim so that the cord is against both the wet paper and the sheet pan.

*B. Grape vines*
Work with a section of decorating dough. The weight can vary from 150 to 600 g. (5.5 to 21 oz.) depending on the size of the sphere.

Shape the dough into a cone and then divide it into two, then four branches.

Attach the first grape vine on the rim by moistening the base with water then arrange the branches on the surface of the half-sphere.

From 4 to 8 grape vines can be used for a single half-sphere, depending on its size. Arrange the grape vines carefully to obtain an attractive effect.

Repeat the construction and arrangement of the grape vines on the second half-sphere.

Allow the decorated half-spheres to dry on a rack for 24 to 48 hours.

Bake the half-spheres in a 170 to 180 °C (350 to 375 °F) oven for 1 to 2 hours depending on their size and thickness. Keep the oven vents open during baking.

Let the half-spheres dry in the open air for 1 hour after baking.

*Note:* No egg wash or glaze is used.

### *3. Removing the half-spheres from the molds*

### Equipment

2 chef's knives, sheet pans.

### Procedure

This is a delicate operation and requires careful attention.
a) Carefully slide the half-sphere off the sheet pan onto the marble.
b) Pull the half-spheres to the edge of the marble and remove the excess paper from the edges of the bowls with a chef's knife. This makes it easier to remove the half-spheres from the bowls because the rim is no longer held on with the paper. Continue trimming off the paper by rotating the bowl over the edge of the marble.
c) Removing the mixing bowl: Place an inverted sheet pan on the marble. Slide the half-sphere to a convenient place on the marble. Spread your hands over each side of the half-sphere and on to the rim.
Gently rotate the half-sphere of dough to make sure that it isn't adhering to the bowl.
Carefully lift the half-sphere off the bowl which should remain in place. Place the half-sphere on the inverted sheet pan.
d) Removing the parchment paper: Use a paring knife (both the tip and handle) to push the paper into the inside of the sphere. The paper should easily peel off the inside of the grape vines. Be careful and attentive especially around the more detailed parts of the grape vines, or they may chip.
e) Gently lift up the half-spheres and remove the pieces of parchment paper from underneath.
f) Store the half-spheres in a dry place.

## " Canvas " base

### Equipment

12 kg. (26.5 lb.) decorating dough, dough sheeter, rolling pin, sheet pan (extra large), stiff board.

### Procedure

This part of the presentation piece consists of a large sheet of dough rolled out 1.5 cm. (1/2 in.) thick and measuring 1 m. by .9 m. (40 in. by 36 in.). It is best to start rolling the dough with a dough sheeter and then finish rolling by hand; the final hand rolling is necessary to ensure a perfectly even sheet. The sheet of dough is then rolled up onto a broom handle (a rolling pin isn't long enough) and placed on an extra large sheet pan for baking.

Bake the sheet of dough for 2 hours in a 170 °C (350 °F) oven. Halfway through the baking, place several layers of sheet pans on top of the dough to keep bubbles from forming.

When the sheet of dough is finished baking, remove the sheet pans and let the dough cool before transferring to a rigid board.

Store the base in a dry place until needed.

## Baking

Baking the parts of the presentation piece is an important stage and must be carefully controlled.

Depending on the size of the parts, the baking temperature may need to be adjusted considerably.

For the larger parts of the presentation piece, such as the " canvas " base, the grape vines, the half-spheres, the pedestal, and the lion, the baking temperature should never by higher than 170 to 180 °C (350 to 375 °F) so that the parts cook all the way through without becoming too dark during baking.

On the other hand, thinner parts of the presentation piece such as leaves and scrolls, should be baked in a 280 °C (525 °F) oven for no more than 2 minutes so they take on a deep, natural color.

### *Watch the baking continuously*

The edges of the scrolls and grape leaves should be dark brown while the inside area should be beige.

## Staining

### Equipment

Coffee extract, pastry brush, cooling rack, high sided sheet, or hotel pan (candissoire).

### Procedure

Coffee extract is indispensable for staining the parts to the presentation piece. Two methods can be used:

a) The grape vines, pedestals, lion and "canvas" base can be brushed completely with coffee extract when they come out of the oven and are still hot.

b) If the parts have already cooled or are being stored, they can be reheated in the oven and coated in the same way as above.

Whatever method is used, place the parts on a cooling rack to drain after being coated with the coffee extract.

*Note:* The grape bunches, grape leaves, and scrolls should not be coated in this way.

# Lightening the stain

To give a natural look to the stained parts of the presentation piece, place them on a hotel pan and brush them with gelatin sealer which has been heated to 70 °C (150 °F). This removes excess coffee extract. After the gelatin sealer has been applied, the parts should have the look of natural wood.
Allow the pieces to drain.

# Pedestal

### Equipment

Small handsaw, files, pencil, yardstick, wood glue, hammer, nails, scissors, upholstery glue.

### Procedure

Be sure that the pedestal is large enough so that there is plenty of room to arrange the various parts of the presentation.
Cut the pedestal out of a (1 cm./1/2 in.) sheet of fiberboard or plywood.
Two supports should be placed under the pedestal to elevate and reinforce the finished presentation piece.
Buy commercially available ready-made molding.
Choose a warm colored felt such as burgundy, red, or chestnut as a covering for the pedestal. Cut the felt with scissors and attach it to the pedestal with upholstery glue.

### Important

Finish the pedestal in the following order:

a) Attach the supports to the bottom of the pedestal.

b) Brush the top surface of the pedestal with glue.

c) Cover the surface with felt.

d) Cut the molding to size and attach it to the sides of the pedestal. Make sure the ends meet squarely.

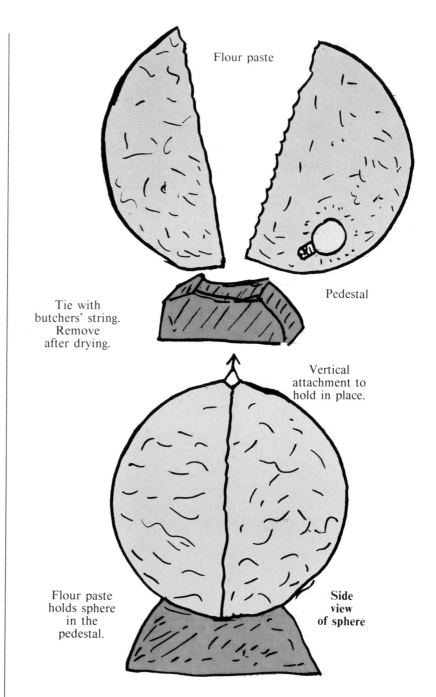

Flour paste

Tie with butchers' string. Remove after drying.

Pedestal

Vertical attachment to hold in place.

Flour paste holds sphere in the pedestal.

Side view of sphere

Make sure that the size of the supports is appropriate for the size of the presentation piece.

# Gluing together the two half-spheres

This stage is best accomplished with two people.

Use a metal spatula to coat the rim of the half-spheres as well as the concave part of the pedestal.

Position the first half-sphere on the pedestal and then attach the second half-sphere to the first.

*Important:* At this point, the completed sphere can be held up with butcher's string.

*Attention:* Place a light bulb in the two half-spheres before gluing them together. Once the sphere is completed, it will be very difficult to insert a light bulb through the grape vine design.

The sphere should be tied together and suspended with string.

Allow the sphere to dry for 2 to 3 days before removing the string.

# " Lyons, Gastronomic Capital " (cont.)

## Final assembly

### Equipment

Scissors, aluminum foil, upholstery glue, thumb tacks, staple gun and staples, felt, felt with adhesive backing, satin, decorative strip of cloth for base.

### Procedure

The final assembly of this presentation piece is important for bringing the various elements in relief. The colors of the fabrics used for the piece should be carefully chosen to best show off the different elements of the presentation. Warm colors such as burgundy or deep green help lend a peaceful harmony to the finished piece.

### *A note on fabric*

Felt with adhesive backing is easy to work with. Simply follow the instructions on the package.

Plain felt is somewhat more difficult to use because it needs to be glued or stapled to the surface.

Plain or adhesive-backed felt is excellent for covering both the top of the pedestal and those supports which remain visible.

Satin is used for those parts of the presentation which puff out. It is supported with pieces of crumpled aluminum foil and then held in place with staples or thumb tacks. The decorative strip of cloth is used around the edges of the base.

### Varnishing

Each part of the presentation piece, including those areas which are not visible, must be completely coated with varnish. Varnish not only improves the appearance of the presentation piece but also acts as a preservative so that the piece can be kept for several years.

### Procedure

Use a colorless varnish or lacquer spray.

Prepare a work area by laying out newspaper to protect the floor and table. Be sure and work in a well ventilated area to avoid breathing fumes from the spray.

Place the different parts to the presentation piece on the work area and give them a first coating of lacquer or varnish. Let them dry completely before giving them a second coating of spray. Each piece should be sprayed twice on all surfaces.

Once both coatings of varnish or lacquer have completely dried, the various elements can be attached with flour paste.

### *Advantages*

Lacquer or varnish protects the dough from oxygen and will preserve it for several years.

The varnish or lacquer will give the pieces a brilliant sheen which will last for a minimum of a year.

## Lighting

Lighting the presentation piece is optional but when used, will improve its appearance and give the final assembly a professional look.

### Equipment

Section of stiff sheath, 1 yard of wire, light socket, light bulb (preferably red), plug (for wall outlet), extension cord.

### Procedure

a) Make a hole in the presentation case for the light socket.

b) Cut the sheath to the desired length; it should exactly fit the light socket.

c) The lighting fixture should be as discrete as possible, preferably invisible. If necessary, coat the edges with flour paste and stain it with coffee extract.

*Important:* Make sure that the flour paste has dried all the way through before turning on the electricity.

d) Attach the wiring to the light socket and make all necessary connections.

e) Screw in the light bulb.

*Important:* Place the light bulb inside the two half-spheres before attaching them. This is especially necessary when using a large light bulb which would make it impossible to install it in the fixture.

## Assembling the show case

Carefully measure the inside dimensions of the base to within 1 mm. (1/16 in.). Use 4 mm. (1/4 in.) glass panes; be sure to anticipate this added thickness when making the calculations.

Two people are needed to position the glass planes around the assembly.

Carefully position the panes around the assembly so the corners join.

Example: for a base measuring 1 meter (39.4 in.) on each side, use:

4 panes measuring .96 m. (37.8 in.). The exact height is optional.

1 pane measuring 1 m. (39.4 in.) on each side placed on the top edge of the other panes.

*Note:* for smaller assemblies, 3 mm. (1/8 in) thick panes can be used. Be sure and take this into consideration when calculating the dimensions of each pane.

## Attaching the panes

1. As each pane is held in position, attach the corners with 2 or 3, 6 cm. (2 1/2 in.) strips of scotch tape. These strips will hold the panes in place during the rest of the assembly.

2. Finish attaching the glass with scotch tape cut to the same dimensions as the panes. Leave the temporary strips of scotch tape during this step.

3. Trim off pieces of excess tape, including the ends of the temporary strips.

# " The Breads of Europe "

## An assembly of European breads

This presentation piece includes breads from 18 Western European countries. Each bread has been prepared differently depending on its country of origin. This piece serves as a reminder that for hundreds of years, bread has been the staple food of all of Europe.

| | |
|---|---|
| France (Paris) | Ireland |
| West Germany | Italy |
| Austria | Luxembourg |
| Belgium | Norway |
| Denmark | Portugal |
| Spain | Holland |
| Finland | Sweden |
| Great Britain | Switzerland |
| Greece | Turkey |

# The Breads of Europe (cont.)

## Ingredients and preparations

**Decorating dough**
25 kg. bread flour (55 lb.)
12.5 kg. granulated sugar (27.5 lb.)
6.25 kg. glucose (13.5 lb.) + water

**Flour paste**
1 kg. flour (2.2 lb.)
400 ml. water (13.5 fl. oz.)
90 gelatin sheets
500 ml. coffee extract (17 fl. oz.)

## Equipment

**Wood**
1 sheet 1.6 x .9 m. (63 x 35.4 in.)
1 sheet 1.6 x .95 m. (63 x 37.4 in.)
1 strip 1.6 x .2 m. (63 x 7.8 in.)
4 strips .7 x .08 m. (27.5 x 3.1 in.)
1 disk with diameter of .63 m. (24.8 in.)
1 disk (with hole), diameter .65 m (25.6 in.)
8 sections .18 x .16 m. (7 x 6.3 in.)
8 strips .2 x .04 m. (7.9 x 1.6 in.)
3 2 meter (79 in.) strips of molding

**Fabric**
Sheet of adhesive-backed felt measuring: 6 x .9 m. (20 ft. x 35.5 in.)
Satin type fabric: 6 x .9 m. (20 ft. x 35.5 in.)
Decorative strip: 3.5 m x .05 m. (11.5 ft. x 2 in.)
Upholstery glue

**Glass**
4 panes 4 mm. (1/4 in.) thick:
2 panes measuring 957 x 860 mm. (37.7 x 33.9 in.)
1 pane measuring 1558 x 975 mm. (61.4 x 38.4 in.)
1 pane measuring 1558 x 877 mm. (61.4 x 30.9 in.)

**Electrical equipment**
1.5 m. of cord + socket + bulb + plug

**Varnish**
5 cans of colorless spray varnish

| Chronological progression | Time |
|---|---|
| **1. Contacting the embassies** | |
| Phone calls (10 min.) + deliveries ........................ | 5 hours |
| **2. European coats of arms** | |
| Photocopies, sizing, preparing molds, cutting, transferring to cardboard, gluing ......................................... | 72 hours |
| Preparing with decorating dough ......................... | 90 hours |
| Baking, finishing ......................................... | 4 hours |
| **3. Kneading the decorating dough** | |
| 6 times 4 kg. (8.8 lb.) flour (over several days) ............ | 2 hours |
| **4. Paris coats of arms** | |
| Molds, cutting, transfer to cardboard, gluing .............. | 3 hours |
| Preparing with decorating dough ......................... | 7 hours |
| Baking, finishing ......................................... | 1 hour |
| **5. Baking emblem** | |
| Molds, cutting, transfer to cardboard, gluing .............. | 3 hours |
| Preparing with decorating dough ......................... | 2 hours |
| Baking, finishing ......................................... | 2 hours |
| **6. Ear of wheat** ....................................... | 3 hours |
| **7. Oven peels** ......................................... | 1 hour |
| **8. Plaques (26)** | |
| Preparing the plaques .................................... | 1 hour |
| Preparing the letters..................................... | 64 hours |
| Preparing roses and leaves ............................... | 6 hours |
| Baking, gluing, finishing ................................. | 4 hours |
| **9. Two half-spheres** | |
| Composition: 1,160 ears, 32,500 grains .................... | 51 hours |
| **10. Frames and supports (18)** | |
| Preparation .............................................. | 8 hours |
| Baking .................................................. | 1 hour |
| Sanding ................................................. | 15 hours |
| Finishing (gluing) ....................................... | 2 hours |
| **11. Assembling the display** | |
| Pedestal and base, molding, presentation of coats of arms, support for half-sphere ..................................... | 7 hours |
| Panes of glass, moving the assembly, installation ........... | 5 hours |
| Attaching fabric, arranging elements of the display, presentation, electrical installation ............................... | 10 hours |
| Varnishing............................................... | 3 hours |
| **Total (approximately)** .......................... | **372 hours** |

# The half-spheres of the world

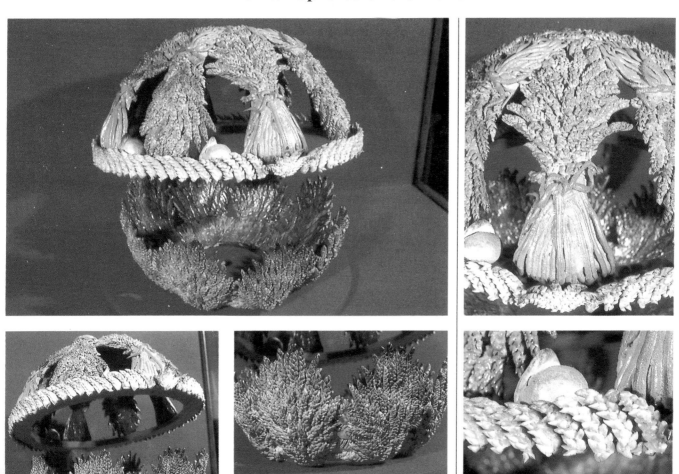

# Coats of arms, frames, and supports

# " The Breads of Europe " (cont.)

Belgique België

Danmack

Deutschland

Éire

España

Hellas ΕΛΛΑΣ

Island

Italia

Luxembourg

Nederland

Norge

Österreich

Portugal

Suisse

Suomi

Sverige

Türkiye

United Kingdom

# " The Breads of Europe " (cont.)

España

## "The Breads of Europe" (cont.)

# Competition Presentation Pieces

### French National Decorated Bread Contest -SIRHA Lyons 1989

# Competition Presentation Pieces (cont.)

Vitrine réalisée en Pain
Par la Commission Des
Boulangers
Du Département de l'Ain
thème Prise de la Bastille

Que notre Alsace est belle
Avec ses frais vallons
L'été mûrit chez elle
Blés, vignes et houblon
ju-hé!
Sa plaine et ses montagnes
Un beau ciel radieux
L'aspect de ses campagnes
Tout réjouit les yeux
ju-hé!

Le pain
nourriture des
gourmets
Pagnol

Strasbourg. 1792
chant de guerre
Allons enfants de la
Patrie le jour de
Gloire est arrivé.
Rouget de l'Isle

# Competition Presentation Pieces (cont.)

# Competition Presentation Pieces (cont.)

Peryeu lo gastronomie
coumenço oici dim mo cousino
Quercynolo. Nouy regolalem
dé l'odour rustique del pa
del cambarou qué pindolie
din lo chomineyo...
dé lo soupo qué bulliot
din l'oules et las.
Salcisses quépindolia-
bou sur lo bartou
dé boué

4

# Competition Presentation Pieces (end)

# "Le Tour de France"

## The France of Baking

For the members of "Les Compagnons du Tour de France", what could be more natural than making a presentation piece on the theme of France itself?

Alain Couet and Eric Kayser have presented here a map of France made in a "basket-weaving" style and illustrated with miniature regional breads.

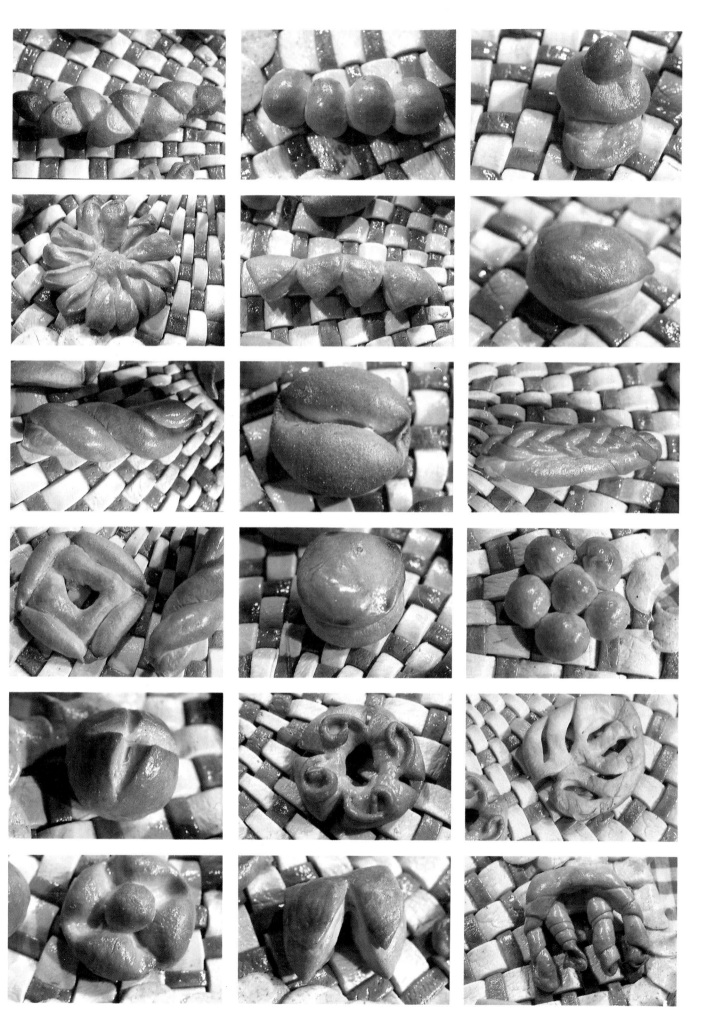

# "Le Tour de France"

## Methods and Techniques

**Wicker rosette**

Prepare a syrup-based decorating dough.

The syrup can be prepared using one of two methods:

a) with boiling sugar syrup which breaks up the gluten,

b) with cold sugar syrup which helps prevent a crust from forming on the surface of the dough (it is important to keep the kneading time to a minimum.)

To braid the rosette, it is best to use two doughs with distinctly different colors. (e.g. one white, the other dyed brown with coffee extract or by adding rye flour.)

After preparing the dough, roll it out to a thickness of between 2 and 3 mm. (about 1/8 in.).

Cut the dough into two rounds of the exact same size: one is used for the base, the other for the rosette itself.

Place the rosette on the base and then place the whole assembly on a wooden board.

Find the center of the circle. Use a compass to trace a 2 cm. (3/4 in.) diameter circle.

Cut the circle in 4, 8, and 16 until you obtain an odd number of strips about 5 mm. (1/4 in.).

A more delicate rosette will be obtained using thin bands; it will also be more fragile.

Caution! Never cut the center circle.

Adjust the strips so there is an equal distance between each one. Lift every other strip while working toward the center.

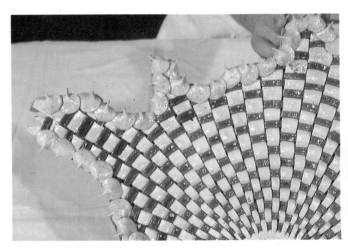

## Map of France

Find a map slightly smaller than the dough sheeter. If a map this size is unavailable, roll the dough with a rolling pin.

Trace the shape of the map on a wooden board or sheet of stiff cardboard. This can then be cut to the proper shape and used as the base.

Place the map on the sheet of dough.

Prepare a rosette which goes around the edges of the cutout shape.

When the braiding is completed, decorate around the outer edges of the map with rounds of pinched dough.

Overlap the rounds of dough by moistening them with water and placing them around the map.

Place the pinched edges toward the outside.

Dry the finished map of France in a 100 °C (200 °F) oven for approximately 12 hours depending on the thickness of the dough.

Prepare miniature regional breads with leavened dough (1 kg./35.5 oz. flour + 20 g./4 tsp. salt + 5 g./1 tsp. yeast + 100 ml./3.5 fl. oz. oil + 400 ml./14 fl. oz. water).

Shape and bake the miniature breads.

When the breads have cooled, attach them to the presentation with flour paste.

Braid the strips working from the center toward the outer edges.

Place the strips (alternating colors) on the parts which haven't been lifted up.

Reverse the strips.

When the braiding is complete, trim off any excess pieces of dough. Bake the rosette in a 100 °C (200 °F) oven to dry it out.

## The "Tour de France"

### Alain Couet (in blue)

1. Gien
2. Bordeaux
3. Nîmes
4. Nantes
5. Strasbourg
6. Lyons
7. Bordeaux

### Eric Kayser (in red)

1. Lure
2. Paris
3. Cherbourg
4. Tours
5. Marseille
6. Lyons
7. Bordeaux
8. Nîmes
9. Paris

# A Union of Serious Professionals

## Eric KAYSER

Born in 1964, Eric Kayser apprenticed as a baker in Fréjus in the south of France. In 1984 he joined "Les Compagnons du Devoir", an important French baking organization and set out to work in different regions of France.

After his experiences in French bakeries, M. KAYSER settled in Paris where he now teaches and devotes much time to "Les Compagnons du Devoir" which he organizes on a national level. He also contributes his teaching expertise to "L'Institut National de la Boulangerie", a prestigious baking organization in Rouen. His educational activities take place at all levels – from simple apprenticeship to the highest professional levels.

Eric Kayser has won several important baking prizes including first prize at Romorantin and Sète.

M. Kayser also spends time working in bakeries around France to stay in touch with the everyday realities of the professional baker and to continually increase his own knowledge and experience.

## Alain COUET

Alain Couet was born in 1961 in Gien, a small city in the Loire Valley. When he began his French military service, he had no idea he would eventually become a baker until a baker apprentice friend invited him to join his own baker's organization. Soon after, he set about apprenticing himself all over France. He started in Bordeaux where he learned about Viennese pastries and decorated breads. Travelling to the south and east, he learned to make the traditional and regional breads of Nîmes and Strasbourg.

It wasn't long before Alain Couet began to take special interest in presentation pieces and win prizes in national contests.

Since 1989, M. Couet has been head baker in a large bakery in the Vendée region of France.

## Jean CHAZALON

Jean Chazalon comes from a family of bakers and has worked in the profession for 36 years. In addition to his duties as a professional baker, M. Chazalon's free time has been devoted to his work in professional and baking organizations such as the Syndicat Professionnel, for the past 30 years.

## Pierre MICHALET

Pierre Michalet received his formal education in economics. He has since specialized in communications and educational media and is currently the director of the respected educational publishing firm Editions St-Honoré. He is responsible for the editorial and pictorial organization of Special and Decorative Breads, volumes 1 and 2, as well as for numerous other publications in France and around the world.

## Yves SAUNIER

Yves Saunier is a master baker and instructor of professional baking in Vesseaux, near Aubenas. In the following pages, Yves Saunier has recreated a selection of traditional breads from his native Ardeche: 4 varieties on the theme of chestnut breads including several personal creations (pages 36 to 39).

## Bernard, Isabelle and Valérie GANACHAUD

Bernard Ganachaud (Meilleur Ouvrier de France) is known throughout the world for his contribution to the baking profession. His daughters, Isabelle and Valérie are also recognized as masters in their field (Maîtrise en Boulangerie). Both Bernard and each of his daughters have presented a selection of presentation pieces.

## Léon MÉGARD

Léon Mégard is a professional baker in Luxeuil-les-Bains in eastern France. M. Mégard has developed innovative presentation pieces which attest to his deep, artistic sensibility (pages 257 to 272).

## Daniel HERVÉ

Daniel Hervé is the principle author of the chapter on decorative breads in volume 1 of "Special and Decorative Breads". Daniel Hervé has contributed 2 presentation pieces. These masterpieces are shown here on pages 273 to 288.

Library of Congress Cataloging-in-Publication Data
(Revised for vol. 2)

Pains Spéciaux et Décorés. English.
Special and Decorative Breads.
Translation of: Pains Spéciaux et Décorés

Vol. 2 has imprint: New York, N.Y.: Van Nostrand Reinhold
Includes index.

Contents: V. 1 (without special title)

V. 2: Traditional and Regional Breads, Special and Foreign Breads,
Fancy Breads, Viennoiseries, Examples of presentation pieces,
Models of presentation pieces / by Alain Couet.

1. Bread. I. Bilheux, Roland, 1944
II. Chazalon, Jean. III. Michalet Pierre. IV. Decorative Breads.
V. Title.

TX769.P2313 1989 641.8'15 89-8999
ISBN 0-442-31954-1 (v. 1)
ISBN 0-442-00144-4 (v. 2)

First published as Pains Spéciaux et Décorés by Éditions St-Honoré,
Paris, France: copyright © 1989.
English translation copyright © 1990 by Van Nostrand Reinhold for
the United States and Canada; by CICEM (Compagnie Internationale de Consultation Éducation et Media) for the rest of the
world.

© CICEM ISBN 2-86871-013-6
Dépôt légal 4ᵉ trimestre 1989
Imprimé en Italie par l'Imprimerie VINCENZO BONA

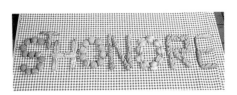